Summer 2015

To Jean and Skip,
Fellow travelers on the same path as me. May God bless you greatly!
Hugs,
Jody

# THE PATH

***a Journal, a Memoir, a Walk Through the Gospels***

JODY WEIGEL

WESTBOW
PRESS
A DIVISION OF THOMAS NELSON

*WestBow Press books may be ordered through booksellers or by contacting:*

*WestBow Press*
*A Division of Thomas Nelson*
*1663 Liberty Drive*
*Bloomington, IN 47403*
*www.westbowpress.com*
*1-(866) 928-1240*



*ISBN: 978-1-4497-5299-6 (hc)*
*ISBN: 978-1-4497-5297-2 (sc)*
*ISBN: 978-1-4497-5298-9 (e)*

*Library of Congress Control Number: 2012909053*

*Printed in the United States of America*

*WestBow Press rev. date: 4/25/2013*

# CONTENTS


Acknowledgments ........ vii

PART I: MATTHEW

CHAPTER 1 Matthew One - Three ........ 3
CHAPTER 2 Matthew Four - Six ........ 11
CHAPTER 3 Matthew Seven - Nine ........ 15
CHAPTER 4 Matthew Ten - Twelve ........ 21
CHAPTER 5 Matthew Thirteen - Fifteen ........ 25
CHAPTER 6 Matthew Sixteen - Eighteen ........ 28
CHAPTER 7 Personal ........ 34
CHAPTER 8 Matthew Nineteen - Twenty-One ........ 40
CHAPTER 9 Matthew Twenty-Two ........ 43
CHAPTER 10 Matthew Twenty-Three - Twenty-Five ........ 48
CHAPTER 11 Matthew Twenty-Six - Twenty-Eight ........ 56

PART II: MARK

CHAPTER 12 Mark One - Three ........ 61
CHAPTER 13 Mark Four - Six ........ 68
CHAPTER 14 Mark Seven - Nine ........ 73
CHAPTER 15 Personal ........ 78
CHAPTER 16 Personal ........ 84
CHAPTER 17 Mark Ten - Twelve ........ 89
CHAPTER 18 Mark Thirteen - Fourteen ........ 96
CHAPTER 19 Mark Fifteen - Sixteen ........ 101
CHAPTER 20 Personal ........ 107
CHAPTER 21 Personal ........ 112

## PART III: LUKE

CHAPTER 22 Luke One - Four ........ 117
CHAPTER 23 Purely Personal ........ 122
CHAPTER 24 Luke Five - Eight ........ 126
CHAPTER 25 Luke Nine - Twelve ........ 131
CHAPTER 26 Luke Thirteen - Sixteen ........ 141
CHAPTER 27 Luke Seventeen - Twenty ........ 147
CHAPTER 28 Luke Twenty-One - Twenty-Four ........ 154

## PART IV: JOHN

CHAPTER 29 John One ........ 163
CHAPTER 30 John Two - Four ........ 172
CHAPTER 31 John Five - Seven ........ 182
CHAPTER 32 John Eight - Ten ........ 189
CHAPTER 33 John Eleven - Thirteen ........ 197
CHAPTER 34 John Fourteen ........ 208
CHAPTER 35 John Fifteen - Seventeen ........ 216
CHAPTER 36 John Eighteen - Nineteen ........ 223
CHAPTER 37 John Twenty - Twenty-One ........ 233

# ACKNOWLEDGMENTS

"O God, do not forsake me until I declare Your strength to this generation, Your power to everyone who is to come."

Psalm 71:18b

A dedication to and for the most precious grandchildren anyone could ever have:

Marisa Marsh
Kipper Marsh
Joshua Weigel
Jared Weigel

Thank you to my husband, Bob, for his encouragement, patience, and computer skills, which enabled me to put this in readable form.

Thank you to my dear sister, Nancy Gavaghan, for her proofreading, constant encouragement, and prayers.

Thank you to my round-robin letter friends of fifteen plus years, and especially my friend, Jean Beyer, who has always encouraged me to write a book.

There are several others to thank before we begin. I am grateful to three friends who prayed for me during a crucial time of illness, which ultimately led me to a life of following Jesus. They are Kathy Peterson Owen, a good friend for over 50 years, Ann Morse, a friend from PTO who became my first Bible teacher, and Judy Wikle Gibson, my childhood friend who loved me enough to not leave me in my (then) state of self-satisfaction, illness and misery. I am living proof of the positive results of prayer!

I am so fortunate (blessed) to have three excellent churches with pastors who believe with all their heart that the Bible is the living and powerful word of God, sharper than any two-edged sword, piercing even to the division of soul and spirit, and of joints and marrow, and is a discerner of the thoughts and intents of the heart. (Heb.4:12) They are Pastor Bryan Clark, senior pastor of the Lincoln Berean Church, Lincoln, Nebraska, Pastor Mark Cedar, senior pastor of Desert Springs Church, Palm Desert, California, and Pastor Bruce Miles, senior pastor of Rocky Mountain Bible Church in Frisco, Colorado. These three pastors have never failed to teach and encourage me in my walk with the Lord.

Dear Friends,

Before you begin this book, an explanation is in order. First of all, thank you for reading it, but it is not the kind of book to just pick up and read for your information. It is meant to be read with your own personal Bible on your lap, to read several specified chapters, and this book secondly . . . and hopefully with a pen and notebook nearby, so you can make your own observations about the chapters you are reading. I hope to stimulate your thinking with some of my own stories and encourage you in your daily walk with God.

The title comes from Proverbs 4:18, where I have this note in my bible: "The path of the righteous is like the first gleam of dawn, shining ever brighter till the full light of day." NIV A path is something that we walk on, something we move along. It suggests motion, change, development. Well, I'm saved, here I am, I'm righteous. All I need to do now is sit in church and sing hymns until the Lord calls me home. That's a mistake. Any static condition in which you do not change, progress and develop is not the righteousness of the Bible. The righteousness of the Bible is a path. And we enter into that path through an encounter with the Son of Righteousness, the Lord Jesus Christ. And when He shines into our lives, that's like the first gleam of dawn. It's the beginning of light. And then, as we move on in the path of righteousness, the words are beautiful: "The light shines ever brighter till the full light of day." If you are walking in the path of righteousness, today's light is brighter than yesterday's and tomorrow will be brighter than today's. So do not settle down and say, "I've arrived", because that's a mistake, that's a deception. The path of righteousness leads us always on until we come into the full light of the noonday sun and to the full and final revelation of God in eternity. So if you are on that path, keep moving on, and if you haven't yet found the path, you need to meet the Son of Righteousness, the Lord Jesus Christ." Derek Prince ( a deceased international Bible teacher and author.)

Lastly, welcome to my personal world, and God bless you as we walk The Path together.

Agape,
Jody

Come and hear, all you who fear God,
And I will declare what He has done for my soul.
I cried to Him with my mouth,
And He was extolled with my tongue.
If I regard iniquity in my heart,
The Lord will not hear.
But certainly God has heard me.
He has attended to the voice of my prayer.

Psalm 66:16-19

# PART 1

# MATTHEW

# CHAPTER 1

# MATTHEW ONE - THREE

Among my favorite things in the world is coming home again after time spent somewhere else. (It doesn't matter which home; my heart is wherever I am.) This morning it is one of my favorites: back home in Nebraska, where spring has sprung in all her glory! Every flowering tree and bush is in full bloom—the forsythia is brilliantly yellow, the lilacs gorgeous purple, the spirea in full splendor, and the peonies promising a blossom in a few weeks. It is one of those days when it just feels good to be alive! The new, light green leaves of the deciduous trees against the darker green of the pines paint a beautiful picture of spring on the prairie.

This past winter was one filled with blessings almost too numerous to recall. The Wednesday morning women's Bible study (Sister Chicks), which I taught with my dear friend Monica Tauber and where I got to know and love another small group of ladies in my church in Palm Desert, California, was definitely a pleasure and a stretching, learning, growing time for me. I carry all these memories with me as I look ahead to what's next. "What's next?" should be my mantra. I'm always looking ahead.

Sitting in my quiet-time chair with Bible, journal, pens, and pencils on the hassock in front of me, I realize I have a decision to make this day. We will be home in Lincoln for about six weeks this time. What Bible passages will I choose? The study we did over the winter took us all over the Bible, but for now, for right now, I have a hunger and thirst for the Gospels. In the past, I have chosen for a devotional *God Calling, by A.J.Russell, Jesus Calling, by Sarah Young,* and *My Utmost for*

*His Highest* by Oswald Chambers. It has been five years since I have read the latter, so I believe I will snatch that out of my library and do that as well as the Psalms as I start my morning. I was very cross with myself for not bringing back with me the new devotional by my tennis friend here in Lincoln, Sandy Hilsabeck, titled "Drop Shot". The biggest problem with moving around for long periods of time is not knowing what to do with my precious books. How many can I ship UPS so I don't have to schlep them on the planes? My friend's new devotional got left behind, which makes me very sad but gives me something special to look forward to in about six months.

I invite you to come with me through the Gospels and see if some of your favorite passages are the same as mine. I don't intend for this to be a commentary (I am not qualified for that), as I will be taking large chunks of passages at a time and share a journal entry, hoping it will encourage you to do the same. I am again strolling through the Psalms because I am still getting through a new Bible my son, Andy, and daughter-in-law, Sandy, gave me three years ago. It is John MacArthur's *The MacArthur Study Bible,* New King James Version (NKJV,1997, and I am enjoying it very much. I still have some areas of the Old Testament to conquer yet. I always try to start my quiet time with a familiar Bible passage, which often turns into a prayer time. I hope you will find some of your favorites here also.

Please grab your own Bibles and read the first three chapters of Matthew. Then come along with me on a personal journey, hopefully one of insight and growth.

"May the word of my mouth and the meditation of my heart be acceptable in your sight, O Lord, my strength and my redeemer" (Ps. 19:14). Amen.

## *Chapters 1-3*

The first thing I notice in chapter 1 of Matthew is the genealogy of Jesus going back to Abraham. Matthew, whose Hebrew name is Levi, was writing to the Jews in the language and custom that all Jews would understand. Matthew was one of the two apostles chosen to talk with Jesus who wrote a gospel about their time together. The other apostle, of course, was John, who wrote much later than Matthew (and Mark and Luke). The first thing any good Jew would do was establish a genealogy to provide the character and background of the subject he or she was writing about. Matthew's genealogy was highly controversial in the first century, because it contained the names of five women, a practice never done until this gospel. And to make matters even more suspect, four of the five women were Gentiles, not Hebrew—heathen—not from the "proper" flock. Oh my! God was already mixing the blood of Gentiles into the lineage of His people. The four Gentiles' names are Tamar, Rahab, Ruth, and Bathsheba (the wife of Uriah). The fifth female, naturally, is Mary, the mother of Jesus. When you have time, I urge you to go back to the Old Testament and read the stories of these four women. They are all fascinating. I think Tamar is my favorite, because I love the book of Genesis so much, and I love that she was spitefully used and yet found a way to righteousness in God's plan. You'll find her story in chapter 38 of Genesis. Plus, I like knowing there were four Gentiles in Jesus' lineage. Somehow it makes me "fit" a little better. For a long time, I was a Gentile, too. Which reminds me:

> Dear Lord, in starting Your Gospels again, help me not to miss something, because the words have become so familiar to me that I don't anticipate a new revelation or at least one new to me. Open my spiritual heart and mind to Your Word. Thank You. Amen.

It seems a little confusing in Matthew that Mary is called "Joseph's wife," and Joseph is called "her husband" right away. This was simply the custom of the day. When a couple became engaged, which usually lasted about a year, they were betrothed to each other and considered married in the eyes of the community, even if the "coming together" didn't happen until after the very long ceremony at the end of the year of betrothal. Whew! Poor little Mary, who was probably only about fourteen years old at this time (doesn't that just blow your mind?), found herself in a whole lot of hot water with the local gossips. Can you imagine her confusion? If it hadn't been for the angel Gabriel coming to her (Luke 1:26) and explaining God's initial plan, I don't know how she could have survived that surprise pregnancy. Matthew doesn't tell us about Gabriel, but he does tell us an angel of the Lord came to Joseph in a dream to reassure him. (What do you want to bet that angel's name is Gabriel?) Fortunately, in those days, people believed in prophetic dreams, and God's plan went on without a hitch.

Fortunately too, in this present age, people in Middle East Muslim countries are receiving messages in their dreams and visions about Jesus being the Messiah, the Son of God. As a result of their dreams, they are being saved through supernatural means. Any book of Ravi Zacharias, an Indian-born evangelist, will report hundreds if not thousands of people in third world countries finding Jesus in dreams and visions. Incredible! Praise the Lord, indeed.

Speaking of supernatural phenomena, just yesterday I got an e-mail that a CBS station in Egypt ran a story of a Muslim wife and mother whose husband came home to find her reading a Bible at her kitchen table. He was so incensed that he killed her and buried her with their infant daughter and eight-year-old daughter. Weeks later, there was another killing in their family, and when they dug in the sand to bury the dead uncle in the family plot, they found the murdered wife with her two daughters—who were both alive! The eight-year-old was interviewed on a live Egyptian TV station, and when asked how she was able to stay alive for so long, she described a very kind man dressed all in shiny white, whose hands were bleeding, who came to them every day. He fed the eight-year-old and touched the mother so she could continue to nurse the baby and keep her alive. The husband was tried for murder. I don't know about you, but I love stories like this! No, I didn't check with snopes.com to verify this story. I preferred to simply be blessed by it. So it didn't surprise me that Joseph was given the gift of faith and believed the angel that Mary was pregnant by God's Holy Spirit. After all, he was "chosen" too. And who among us would ever doubt the words of an angel?

The interesting story in chapter 2 is the visit from the wise men (plural, but we're not told how many), who came to Jerusalem and then went on to Bethlehem. I had always been taught these magi were Gentiles, astrologers who had "seen the star in the East and have come to worship Him", Matt. 2:2. Amazing the insight God gave these men, who presumably did not know ancient prophecies yet came to worship because of what they had perceived in the heavens. Much to my surprise, John MacArthur believes these men were possibly Zoroastrians from Persia, whose knowledge of Hebrew scriptures could be traced back to the time of Daniel (Dan. 5:11). Awesome! Of course, "Herod was troubled" (Matt. 2:3). He didn't want his authority challenged in any way, so he inquired where the prophecy predicted the Messiah's birth would be. Little Bethlehem was the answer. If Herod had known his scriptures, he would have known this from Micah 5:2. The star led the magi to "where the young Child was." We can only assume that after the census was finished, the village of Bethlehem had lost most of the taxpayers who had come to sign the census, and allowed Mary, Joseph, and Baby Jesus a house to live in while they caught their breath. The supernatural star led the astrologers directly to the house where the Holy Family was living. Scripture tells us these wise men "fell down and worshiped Him." They also gave Jesus gifts suitable for a king: gold, frankincense, and myrrh. Because the scriptures tell us there were three gifts, Matthew may have assumed three men. Not necessarily so. Remember, Matthew wasn't there. These wise men were called "magi"—stargazers, astrologers—not kings. The manger story depicted at Christmastime is totally fictionalized. The wise men found the baby, not wrapped in swaddling clothes lying in a manger, but probably two years old and living in a house with His mom and earthly dad.

Luke tells us the only people who saw Jesus lying in a manger were shepherds who had been in the fields when the "Shakina Glory" of the Lord shown about them, and an angel announced the arrival of the Christ Child in Bethlehem. What really interests me about this story is that shepherds did not abide in the fields, watching over their flocks in the winter months at night. There was nothing for the sheep to eat in the winter. Only in the spring and summer was there enough grass to feed flocks of sheep. Does it matter that we really don't know the real date of Christ's birth? Of course not! (The only really important Jewish holiday in the spring that I can recall is Pentecost, except of course for Passover. Pentecost would have been a lovely time for Christ's birth. It is a date important to both Christians and Jews.) This is simply a "Jody-ism." Just thinking. The important thing is we know all the circumstances and the relevant facts. Another fact about the shepherds is they were the lowest class of people in that culture. In fact, they were so despised they were outcasts of respectable society. Their honesty and integrity were so questionable that they were not allowed to testify in a court of law.

This reminds me of growing up in Omaha in the forties (that would be the 1940s). My mother would not allow me to be outside when the garbage truck came down our street. With some fear, I would run inside and watch the "suspicious" men walk into our backyard. I imagine that was how shepherds were regarded. What do you want to bet those shepherds' lives were changed forever? No one comes in contact with the Living Christ and leaves the same person. No one!

Last year I purchased a new nativity set for my front hall table in California. It has three lovely, carved, wooden kings in the set, which I'm sure will look better than a bunch of shabbily dressed shepherds, which would have been more "biblically correct." I know I will chuckle every time I see those gorgeous, regal kings and remember they should have been shepherds . . . and not kings at all.

Now back to Matthew and the gifts the wise men brought. The gold was appropriate for a king; the frankincense was holy and meant for the use of a priest for worship. Myrrh was a costly oil or perfume used for burial and/or anointing. Perhaps it was the nature of the gifts that gave Matthew the idea they may have been kings. This story is only in the gospel of Matthew, by the way.

When the wise men departed, they were warned in a dream not to return to Herod, as he had requested, but to return home another way. We become new creatures in Christ when we encounter Him. The old has gone. The new has come. We simply don't go "back" the same way (2 Co. 5:17). Praise the Lord indeed!

The remainder of the chapter tells about the sad circumstances of why Joseph had to take his family to Egypt, when it was safe to return to Israel, and why they went to Nazareth. Remember, that was Mary and Joseph's home when they were betrothed. They only traveled to Bethlehem to fulfill the prophecy of Micah. And for the census. God's perfect plan! I love that all this information was communicated to Joseph in dreams. Do you pay attention to your dreams? Apparently we should. I believe we are so bombarded electronically by phone, radio,

TV, e-mails, texts, and other methods of communication I don't even know about that our sleep is not as deep and relaxed as it could be. Just watching the 10 o'clock news at night is sometimes so disturbing it is difficult to tune out all the bad news and replace it with pleasant, restful thoughts. I know I have gone to bed with a problem or a concern that I have given to the Lord and awakened in the morning with a solution and a feeling of well-being. I can't explain that. I only know that is how God sometimes works in my life. I am not aware of a dream . . . only of a solution. And it wasn't mine.

The remarkable thing about chapter 3 is reported right after Jesus came out of the Jordan River. The heavens opened, the Spirit descended like a dove, and God the Father's voice came from heaven, saying, "This is My Beloved Son in whom I am well pleased." The Trinity is not mentioned often in the same sentences or paragraphs, and when I find these instances, I always mark them with a triangle in the margin. I don't know why these details are important to me, but they are. The word "Trinity" is not found in the Bible at all, but I love seeing these triangles in my margins. I often mark healings with an "H" in the margin, and the Holy Spirit ministering with a silly looking bird that is supposed to be a dove. Two inverted u's will do the trick. Usually only I can tell what it's supposed to be. If a passage has special significance to me, I highlight it with a yellow highlighter and put a star in the margin as well. Often I turn to the concordance. I have been known to pick up the phone and call Andy, our son, to find a passage I just can't find. He always knows and, in fact, has taught me how to use a computer to find a reference. If everything else fails, I ask the Holy Spirit. He always leads me in the right direction. Why is it that human nature waits until the last option to ask God for help? I must be a slow learner!

At the end of my Bible reading for the day, which we have now come to, I turn to the Lord in prayer. At this point, the words of Scripture have prepared my heart for worship, praise, and prayer. Five years ago, I took a class called Radical Intimacy, written by my friend Catherine Martin. She had a great acrostic for prayer, which is: *P*repare your heart, *R*ead and study God's word, *A*dore God in prayer, *Y*ield yourself to God, *E*njoy His presence, and *R*est in His love. For many years, we have all heard ACTS: adoration, confession, thanksgiving, and supplication (really serious prayer). I loved Catherine's study so much that I brought it to my neighbors in Colorado several years ago, where we spend many summers. By then the name of the class had been changed to Six Secrets to a Powerful Quiet Time. I could never understand why anyone would take a wonderfully descriptive title and commercialize it so much, but regardless of its name, it's a wonderful study that I highly recommend. In a class or alone. It's the kind of study you will want to review every few years just to encourage yourself in the Word. Through trial and error, I think we all find a formula that works best for us. A short devotional followed by consecutive Bible reading works best for me, because that way, I know I have the Word of God in my mind before I am interrupted. It's surprising how many chapters you can read in just twenty minutes. This can include a Psalm or two, which I always like to do because the psalmist has a way of praising God that far exceeds my ability. I will write about prayer in a future section. Right now, just like Nike, I need to "just do it"!

# CHAPTER 2

# MATTHEW FOUR - SIX

Good morning, Lord. Another lovely spring day and a date to play bridge this afternoon with three dear friends. What fun! Such a nice welcome back home. I can't wait to hear news from their winter. They all had extended trips also, so we will have lots to catch up on.

My devotion this morning is also my prayer. When I pray God's word back to Him, I know I have it right!

> Teach me, O Lord, to follow Your decrees: then I will follow them to the end. Give me understanding and I will keep Your law and obey it with all my heart. Direct me in the path of Your commands, for there I find delight. Turn my heart toward Your statutes and not toward selfish gain. Turn my eyes away from worthless things; preserve my life according to Your Word. (Ps. 119:33-37) Amen

## *Chapters 4-6*

Chapter 4 begins with a rather detailed account of Jesus in the wilderness, being tempted by Satan. What I learned from this is that Satan knows Scriptures very well. That's enough to put us on notice! At the end of the temptation, Jesus told Satan something we should all know, memorize, and use:

> "Away with you, Satan! For it is written, 'You should worship the Lord your God and Him only you shall serve.'" (Mt. 4:10)

That wouldn't be quite so hard for us if Satan always presented himself in a red suit with horns and a tail. Then we could easily recognize him and avoid him at all costs. The epistle of James says absolutely to, "Resist the devil and he will flee from you" (Jas. 4:7). It is both a command and a promise.

This is where we must pray for discernment, because Satan knows how to disguise himself as almost anyone. He will often not try a head-on approach but back you into a corner into which you had no intention of going. Wisdom and discernment. We must pray for both.

Jesus begins His ministry by choosing His apostles. Note that Jesus had, and still has, many disciples, but there were only twelve who could call themselves apostles. Actually, at one point, Paul calls himself an apostle, and I believe he had every right to do so. The one "requirement" they all had in common was that they all walked with Jesus during His earthly ministry. Paul only met with Jesus after His crucifixion and resurrection, but this was a powerful story and witness. His story was so powerful it is retold three times in the book of Acts.

In Matthew, Simon Peter and Andrew were the first apostles called. They had originally been disciples of John the Baptist and as such, had most probably met Jesus previously, possibly at His baptism. (This is my conjecture only.) They had no problem dropping their fishing gear to follow Him. Nor did the next two, who happened to be the brothers James and John. Their names are always mentioned together, and James had the distinction of becoming the first apostle to be martyred by Herod Agrippa. Jesus' preaching and healing ministry really starts in this chapter.

The fifth chapter contains Jesus' first great discourse, which continues through chapter 7. It is called the Sermon on the Mount and contains the Beatitudes, some of the most beautiful promises ever written. When I was a child, I was often taken to my mother's hometown of Albion, Nebraska, a tiny town on the edge of the sand hills in Nebraska, to visit my grandmother (Grammie Mansfield), several aunts and uncles, and eleven cousins. For some reason, a small framed picture of Jesus with the caption "Sermon on the Mount" always captured my attention in Grammie's bedroom. It showed Jesus, sitting on a hill all by Himself, and was very dark in colors, mostly blues, like it was evening or night. It didn't even look like what I expect Jesus to look like, but when my Grammie died, Mother and my aunts asked me if there was anything of Grammie's I would like to have. I was only ten years old at the time, and not a child with biblical knowledge or insight, unlike all four of my grandchildren. I asked for two things: the picture of Christ on the Mount and Grammie's plain gold wedding band. I was granted both objects, and they are still very precious to me. I wore the gold band with my wedding rings for many years, and the framed picture is in a bookcase in our home in Lincoln. I think of all my maternal relatives and the fun times in Albion every time I see that picture, and I always thank God for giving me such a godly, loving grandmother.

Matthew's discourse begins with Jesus, sitting on a mountain and teaching His disciples. This would mean any who follow after Him. I'm one. Are you? The implication of Jesus sitting to teach has to do with the normal position of rabbis when they taught. So Jesus is taking on the persona of a rabbi. A teacher. He said:

> "You are the salt of the earth." (Mt. 5:13)

Salt was used to improve flavor and preserve food. We can all use our attitudes to be the salt of the earth. Do people want to be around you? Think about it. How can you become "saltier"? Also, we can use our salvation knowledge to be a light of the world. Jesus also said:

> "Let your light so shine before men that they may see your good works and glorify your Father in heaven." (Mt. 5:16)

This incredible chapter covers Jesus' views on murder, adultery, divorce, oaths, retaliation, and love. *Don't* do the first five. *Do* wholeheartedly the last one. Is there anything at all more heartwarming than to hear the words, "I love you" from the heart?

How can I not say something about the most beautiful prayer in the entire Bible? Here it is in Matthew 6:9 (and also in Luke). One of the churches we belonged to for many years said the Lord's Prayer every week, and sometimes it can be so repetitive we really don't think deeply about the meaning. If you are not in the habit of saying this prayer, and even if you are, do it now, to the Lord, and think about each phrase. Jesus, Himself, taught it. It doesn't get any better than that! I have to admit I don't say it regularly. I miss it, and when I think about it and use it, it is very meaningful to me. I also love the musical version of this prayer. I have a disk in my car by the Gaithers that contains the "Lord's Prayer," and I look forward to singing right along with them each time it is played. It doesn't matter what I sound like. The Lord hears it in perfect pitch. That's my story, and I'm sticking to it!

Another special verse for me is the following:

> Therefore, do not worry, saying, "What shall we eat, or what shall we wear?" For after all these things the gentiles seek, for your heavenly Father knows that you have a need of all these things. But seek first the Kingdom of God and His righteousness and all these things will be added to you. Therefore, do not worry about tomorrow, for tomorrow will worry about its own things. Sufficient for the day is its own trouble. (Mt. 6:31-34)

Did I tell you I tend to be a worrier? An anxious person? I give problems to God so fast I can hardly keep track and then I "forget" and snatch them right back again. Sheesh! I know better, and when I catch myself doing that, I stop and apologize. Confess. Worrying about anything at all simply means I am not trusting God with whatever it is. Forgive me, Lord. Help me to learn to trust You more. Every day. I am better than I was, but not as "better" as I want to be. Sigh.

> Dear Lord, I get the message to get my priorities right. When I have the first, everything else just falls in place. Thank you, Lord. I hope and pray I always have You first. You are the Alpha and the Omega, the beginning and the end (Rev.1:8). Amen.

# CHAPTER 3

# MATTHEW SEVEN - NINE

Thank you, Lord, for such a nice afternoon with my friends yesterday. Bless them, Lord, and watch over their families. We are invited to our daughter, Kim, and son-in-law, Mike's for swimming this afternoon and dinner tonight. We have not seen our grandchildren, Marisa and Kipper, yet. They are still in school for another week and are so busy with end-of-school activities, including final exams and year-end parties. We are so anxious to see them! My "swimming" consists of sitting in the shade with a cool iced tea or glass of wine in my hand and listening to family conversation. Is there anything better than family getting together and just enjoying each other? I don't think so.

> Create in me a pure heart, O God, and renew a steadfast spirit within me. Do not cast me from Your presence, or take Your Holy Spirit from me. Restore to me the joy of Your salvation and grant me a willing spirit to sustain me. (Ps. 51:10-12) Amen.

Lord, I do thank you for that beautiful prayer from Psalm 51. It makes me feel good every time I pray it!

Now on with Matthew. The first verse to grab my attention is:

> Do not give what is Holy to the dogs, nor cast your pearls before swine, lest they trample them under their feet and tear you to pieces. (Mt. 7:6)

This verse has often stopped me in my tracks and causes me to be very cautious in my witness for the Lord. I don't believe it contradicts Matthew 5:44, which says:

> Love your enemies and bless those who curse you; do good to those who hate you and pray for those who spitefully use you and persecute you.

What we give to others which is holy, is our witness . . . our testimony—what and Who we believe. If your contacts, acquaintances, or friends are the kind of people who could be called "dogs" or "pigs," I caution you to be very circumspect in your speech, and look very carefully for new friends! In this life we are going to run into people who simply don't like us. I do believe these are the people God put in our lives so we can pray for them. Darkness doesn't want anything to do with light, and we are the light of the world. The more our light shines forth, the more darkness will hate us. I think that's why it's so comfortable to make such good friends within the community of believers. We can talk so freely and heart to heart with so few misunderstandings. This has to be tempered with Peter's statement to:

> Be prepared to give a reason for the hope that is within you. (Peter 3:15)

And make it very short, sweet, and to the point! Sheesh! I can't even get out my name and make it short and sweet! Our pastor in Palm Desert gave such a good message recently on how to give a short testimony, and he modeled it for us by giving his own story in about two minutes. I loved that message and him for his willingness to let us see into his heart, but I am still trying to figure out how to tell people Jesus came into my bedroom and saved me in two minutes or less without being carted off to the loony bin! We walk a balancing act as sons and daughters of the Lord. We are so comfortable with fellow believers, yet we are called to go out into the world. That can be a scary place to go if we are not prayed up, confessed up, and praised up to the Lord. We can be wonderful witnesses without using words, which never ceases to amaze me! I feel truly blessed that I have such a love for both tennis and playing bridge because both activities take me out of my comfort zone. (Which is one reason not to leave the house without being prayed up every day.) If in my "flesh" I can get "testy" in my attitude toward a nasty store clerk, what's going to happen to me when I meet a mean tennis player on the court (yep . . . they're out there) or a duplicate bridge player who only plays for blood? Sheesh! The only thing that holds my tongue from retaliation is the Holy Spirit, and believe me, He has had a real number to do in changing me. I have always had a quick tongue; I could think of a sarcastic response in nothing flat! And I used to think it was funny. It's a real wonder I had any friends at all before 1975!

When I had two strokes in 1998, several things happened to me to slow me down, which reminds me of this wonderful prayer supposedly written by an unnamed southern pastor, and certainly each word resonates with me. I wish I could give credit to the author, but it has been in my "Precious Keepsakes" file for so long, I just don't have a name. Here it is:

> Slow me down, Lord! Ease the pounding of my heart by the quieting of my mind. Steady my hurried pace with a vision of the eternal reach of time. Give me, amidst the confusion of my day, the calmness of the everlasting hills. Break the tension of my nerves and muscles with the soothing music of the singing streams that live in my memory. Help me know the restorative power of sleep. Teach me the art of taking minute vacations . . . of slowing down to look at a flower, to chat with a friend, to pet a dog, to read a few lines from a good book.
>
> Remind me each day of the fable of the tortoise and the hare, that I might know that the race is not always to the swift; that there is more to life than increasing speed. Let me look upward into the branches of the towering trees, and know that they grow tall because they grow slowly and well.

> Slow me down, Lord, and inspire me to send my roots deep into the soil of life's enduring values that I may grow toward the stars of my greater destiny. Amen

Back to when I had strokes: my left hand was so weakened I could no longer play the piano. I had to relearn the keyboard to use a computer. My ear for music was all but gone. I could no longer sing a note, and I grew up in a family who sang all the time. I was the alto in our high school quartet, and I used to joke that I could harmonize with a duck. Now I sound just like one! I also "forgot" how to serve a ball in tennis, but thanks to my husband's tenacity and patience, hitting with me for hours at a time, it slowly came back. Kind of. But the thing that brings me back to the subject of speech is my speech was affected by the strokes. I had great difficulty getting words out of my mouth, especially if they had vowels in them. (Believe me, there are lots of words with multiple vowels!) This very effectively stopped my "quick quips."

No more sarcasm! I couldn't get the words out of my mouth until after the moment passed. Do you think that was God's pruning? I do. And I'm grateful. Really. It's truly all God's doing that I am able to teach in front of a class of Sister Chicks and be understood. The other great verse in chapter 7 is:

> Ask and it will be given you. Seek and you will find. Knock and the door will be opened to you. For everyone who asks, receives, and he who seeks, finds, and to him who knocks the door will be opened. (Mt. 7:7)

Is this not one of the greatest verses to put on your prayer sheet and to believe? Of course this comes with a few caveats, depending on where your heart is. For instance, "You do not have because you do not ask God. When you ask, you do not receive because you ask with wrong motives, that you may spend what you get on your pleasures" (Jas.4:2b-3).

Chapter 8 of Matthew finds Jesus healing again, beginning with the leper, who we assume was a Jew. But the next healing was for a

Centurion's (Roman) servant. When Jesus saw the great faith the Centurion had, he "marveled," and the servant was healed "that hour." The Gentiles are slowly making their way into the holy ministry.

The story in Matthew 8:21 of the disciple who asked if he could "go and bury his father first," always had me confused. If the father was dead, wouldn't Jesus allow this duty to the son? But what we are *not* told is this phrase is often used to mean, "Wait until I inherit what I have coming." What a world of difference in our understanding! The man may have been afraid he would miss out on his inheritance if he left. We don't know the details of stories like this one. We can only surmise and pray for understanding. Or what if his father had been very ill, and there was no one else to put him in a burial chamber, where he would stay for a full year while his family officially grieved his loss. And when his body had turned into bones, it would be transferred into a burial box, called an ossuary, before it was buried. This entire process would take more than a year to accomplish. The point is many of these stories can only be understood by the customs of that day that we neither know nor understand.

The story of Jesus casting demons into the swine is also told in this chapter . . . except Matthew remembers two demon-possessed men, while Mark and Luke only mention one. I have a theory about these insignificant differences in Scripture, and here it is: Matthew was probably with Jesus when this incident occurred. Mark and Luke were both recording what they had been told. I'll leave it for you to decide which is the accurate version. I choose not to nitpick over anything of this nature. The important thing is that a very serious healing took place, and many demons and a whole herd of pigs were destroyed. And the townspeople were unnerved, because their financial investment just went down the drain. Obviously they were not Jews, or they would not have been the owners. Jesus probably saved a lot of people from trichinosis!

In Matthew 9:16, Jesus said:

> "No one puts a piece of un-shrunk cloth on an old garment, for the patch pulls away from the garment and the tear is made worse. Nor do they put new wine in old skins or else the wineskins break, the wine spills and the wineskins ruined."

Jesus used this teaching to illustrate old practices of the Pharisees and devout Jews would not fit into the "new wine" of the New Covenant. The old teaching had gone and the new begun.

Dear God, in my senior years, please keep me pliable and with an open mind for all you would have me know. I truly don't want to be a "crusty old lady," bent on my own limited expectations of how things should be done, especially in church, or how songs should be sung, or what order should be observed. I can see how easily this could happen to me when I don't allow the Holy Spirit to reign in my life and attitude. Now that we are back in our "home" church, we are experiencing steel guitars and very loud drums playing songs I have never heard before, and it is very difficult for Bob and me to enjoy this kind of music or to prepare our hearts for corporate worship. I keep repeating the phrase, "Make a joyful noise unto the Lord," but I'm not sure that it is any more enjoyable to Him than to us. Our pastor here in Lincoln says the present-day church is compromising its values and original mission statement by trying to fit into the culture of the day. O Lord, I believe him. Now help me conform where I need to. Amen.

## CHAPTER 4

# MATTHEW TEN - TWELVE

Oh Lord, what fun to see our grandchildren yesterday, although just overnight they have both grown up! Marisa is almost sixteen years old and just finishing her sophomore year in high school, and she has become such a gracious, self-confident, lovely young lady. It shocks me when she is dressed up she could easily pass for twenty. And Kipper. Wow! He is thirteen years old and going into his last year of junior high. His voice has already changed—he sounds like his dad on the phone—and he is already taller than me. I've never seen children grow so fast! Where have all the years gone? What fun to be with them. Thank You, Lord, that we feel so welcome and comfortable in both our children's homes. We are blessed beyond words!

My devotional this morning is something I need to write down and think about. It's from Oswald Chambers's *My Utmost for His Highest:*

> If you will remain true to God, he will lead you directly through every barrier and right into the inner chamber of the knowledge of Himself. But you must be willing to come to the point of giving up your own convictions and traditional beliefs.

Oh my. This is such good news, and so convicting for me. Lord, does this mean my traditional beliefs about music need to change? Thank You, Lord. I find faulty thinking and poor theology in the world all around me, but I am blind to my own faults and wrong theology. I want with all my heart to give up any traditional convictions that would hinder my relationship with You. Keep me close. Keep teaching me, Lord. I seek Your face, I search for your hand, I listen for Your voice.

## *Chapters 10-12*

Chapter 10 is the second great discourse of Matthew. Jesus is sending His twelve apostles on a mission, healing, and teaching trip. Interesting that He sent the first and foremost to the "lost sheep of Israel." It wasn't until after His crucifixion and resurrection that He commanded His message to go to all the nations.

Here is His teaching to the apostles:

> But when they deliver you, don't worry about what you should speak, for it will be given you in that hour what you should speak, for it is not you who speaks but the Spirit of your Father who speaks in you. (Mt. 10:19-20)

Jesus is preparing His apostles for their immediate ministry and for what is to come when they are persecuted for His sake. Since the Holy Spirit had not yet been given except in special circumstances, they probably didn't understand fully what He meant. But the point is, we now have the Holy Spirit, and when push comes to shove, we can always speak words from the Lord's Spirit, not ours. What a comforting thought! Surprisingly wonderful when that happens.

Let's go to:

> "Therefore whoever acknowledges me before men, him I will acknowledge before my Father who is in Heaven. But whoever disowns Me before men, I will disown before My Father." (Mt. 10:32-33)

I agree it's important to acknowledge Jesus, and almost every crusade or tent meeting makes a point of doing this. But I also think it's important to let friends know what you believe. There is not much point in being a secret believer. After all, we need to make ourselves available to friends who may be experiencing trauma, may have questions about Christianity, or just need someone to pray with them. Remember, you don't need to be afraid of what to say, because the Holy Spirit will take over for you. I can hear many of you saying, "But I don't know how to pray well. I wouldn't know what to say." That reminds me of the story of the elderly man talking to his friend on a park bench. The man confessed he didn't know how to pray to Jesus and was told to "Imagine Jesus sitting on a chair in front of you, and talk to Him, just like you talk to me." Soon afterward, the elderly man was taken ill and went to live with his daughter. The daughter was concerned about her father and didn't know whether he was really a believer. She asked her pastor to call on her father. When the pastor arrived, he found a chair pulled alongside the bed and assumed in expectation of his visit. When he inquired about the man's spiritual beliefs, the man asked the pastor to shut the door. Then he told him the chair was for Jesus, and every day they had the most wonderful private conversations. Weeks later, the elderly man died. The pastor inquired of the daughter about her father's death and was told it was very peaceful, but the strangest thing had happened. When she discovered her father had died in the night, his head was bent over, resting on the chair by his bed. Oh yes, he knew the power and privilege of prayer. Just talking toYou, Best Friend.

In the eleventh chapter of Matthew, Jesus taught that John the Baptist was the messenger who came before Him to prepare the way. Now we Christians know this, but for centuries, the Jewish people were taught when their Messiah comes, Elijah would come first to prepare the way. The Jews could not see that John the Baptist was the very messenger who came in the spirit, power, and function of Elijah. You may recall the interesting story of Elijah and Elisha, the prophet who replaced him. While the two were walking and talking, Elijah was taken up to Heaven in a whirlwind. He didn't die. He was taken up. Great story, isn't it? You can find it in the second chapter of Second Kings in the Old Testament.

This eleventh chapter of Matthew also contains such a beautiful invitation from Jesus:

> "Come to Me all you who labor and are heavy-laden and I will give you rest. Take my yoke upon you and learn from Me, for I am gentle

> and lowly in heart, and you will find rest for your souls. For My yoke is easy and My burden is light." (Mt. 11:28-30)

Have you ever read such beautiful promises? How could anyone resist that offer? Maybe because they haven't heard it. Do you think that strange? I don't. I attended a mainline denomination church for nearly thirty-nine years and never heard the message of salvation, or that we could have a personal relationship with Jesus. I am not blaming those churches, but I am saying my spiritual ears were closed until a friend very clearly laid out the non-denominational facts to me. It changed my life. Chapter 12 of Matthew gives us sobering words to consider in verses 36 and 37:

> "But I say to you that for every idle word men may speak, they will give an account of it on the Day of Judgment. For by your words you will be justified and by your words you will be condemned."

> Lord, thank you that my words no longer slip out quite so easily, because I am still so capable of slips I would not want You or others to hear. I pray fervently I will not bang my finger with a hammer or other calamity in front of them or You. James says, "We all stumble in many ways. If anyone is never at fault in what he says, he is a perfect man (person) able to keep his whole body in check" (Jas. 3:2).

> Lord, please keep working on me! Perfection is something I will never achieve in this lifetime. Only forgiveness is possible, and I am grateful beyond words for that.

# CHAPTER 5

# MATTHEW THIRTEEN - FIFTEEN

Thank You, Lord, for a dark, gloomy, rainy day in Nebraska. It is a perfect morning to curl up with a good book and watch the lightening and listen for the thunder. I look forward to an afternoon with three good friends, playing bridge at a local coffee shop. How much fun is that?

Chapter 13, all by itself, is the third great discourse around which Matthew writes. At this point, Matthew has written four parables, and from chapter 13 onward, he will write sixteen! No, that's not the most of the Gospels. Luke has the record with a whopping twenty-seven. The Gospel of John has no parables. It is the easiest of the four to understand. No guessing as to what the parables might mean. It was predicted in Psalm 78:2 that Jesus would "open His mouth in parables and utter things secret from the foundation of the world." In chapter 13 alone, there are seven parables. "The Sower" is my favorite parable, because I can vividly see it work. The story starts in Matthew 13:3 and is fully explained in Matthew 13:18-23: Please read it in your own version. Pretty cool, huh? How the Word gets snatched away, or planted and grows.

The one thing I know for sure about the parables is the more we read them and ask for Holy Spirit guidance and understanding, the more we receive. Maybe because I am not a baker, it took me a long time to figure out the Parable of the Leaven:

> The Kingdom of heaven is like leaven which a woman took and hid in three measures of meal till it was leavened. (Mt. 13:33)

I've read several explanation of this parable, but the one I like the best is that the Kingdom of Heaven had an insignificant beginning (you could hardly tell it was there), but it will have a magnificent ending. The Kingdom will penetrate and influence the world! Can't get much better than that, and yes, we can do our part to help! Pray about what your role is, and if you need help, you might pray the prayer of Jabez. Be prepared, as you are in for the ride of your life if you do!

> And Jabez called on the God of Israel saying, "Oh that You would bless me indeed and enlarge my territory, that Your hand would be with me, and that You would keep me from evil, that I may not cause pain." (1 Chron. 4:10)

Chapter 4 recounts the heartbreaking beheading of John the Baptist and three more miracles. The miracle of the feeding of the five thousand is in all four of the Gospels. These writers do not want us to miss this one! Most leading commentaries say if the figure is five thousand men—women and children were not counted—think of doubling or tripling this number. Wow! This was some picnic!

The verse that is very special to me is 14:36, which says, "As many as touched the hem of His garment were made perfectly well." The reason this is so special to me is that I did touch the hem of His garment thirty-five years ago. I not only touched it, I cried buckets all over it, and I was not only saved, I was healed as well. Thank You, Lord, and I didn't see this passage until this reading today! Sometimes I feel absolutely spiritually stupid! It's incredible to me that after reading Scriptures for thirty-five years (I don't know how many times all the way through), I can still find something I never saw before. It really proves that "The word of God is living and powerful and sharper than any two-edged sword, piercing even to the division of joints and morrow, and is a discerner of the thoughts and intents of the heart" (Heb. 4:12).

Chapter 15 has a verse I have on my prayer card for friends who go to liturgical churches and feel they need an intercessor. The Word says it better than I:

> "These people draw near to Me with their mouth, and honor Me with their lips, but their heart is far from Me, and in vain they worship Me, teaching as doctrines the commandments of men." (Mt. 15:8-9)

I probably have a dozen names on this list, including a niece and her family, and am not comforted when Jesus goes on to say:

> "Every plant which My heavenly Father has not planted will be uprooted. Let them alone! They are blind leaders of the blind and if the blind leads the blind, they will both fall in a ditch." (Mt. 15:13-14)

My responsibility is simply to continue to lift these names up to the Lord and to ask His wisdom to penetrate their hearts and minds, so they might worship in truth and beauty by the grace and mercy of the Lord Jesus.

CHAPTER 6

# MATTHEW SIXTEEN - EIGHTEEN

Thank You for the reading of Your Word this day. It is such a beautiful early morning, with sun streaming through the French doors on the east and the sound of morning doves cooing outside. It will be in the seventies today and a lovely Nebraska spring day. Be with us this day, Lord. Protect us from fiery darts that fly out of darkness. Allow me to serve You in any way possible to glorify Your name. Thank you for precious time alone with You this morning . . . time to read, meditate, journal, and bring names to you for your healing touch. O Lord, so many health problems among my dear friends: heart, strokes, Parkinson's, foot surgery, eye problems, knee problems, gout, Alzheimer's, cancer. Lord, You know them all. I bring these names to You for your healing touch, mercy, and grace. Please touch each name on my healing card who is surrounded by these verses. Please add your own names to these:

The Lord bless and keep you, the Lord make His face to shine upon you, and be gracious toward you and give you peace. (Nu. 6:24-26)

Blessed is he who considers the poor (or sick), the Lord will deliver him in time of trouble. The Lord will preserve him and keep him alive. The Lord will strengthen him on his bed of illness: You will sustain him on his sickbed. (Ps. 41:1-3)

The Lord will guide you continually, and satisfy your soul in drought, and strengthen your bones: You shall be like a well-water garden, like a spring of water whose waters do not fail. (Is. 58:11)

Then Jesus told them a parable to show them that they should always pray and not give up. (Lk. 18:1)

Draw near to God and He will draw near to you. (Jas.4:8)

Be still and know that I am God. (Ps. 46:10)

## *Chapters 16-18*

> Show me Your ways, O Lord, teach me Your paths; guide me in Your truth and teach me, for you are God my Savior and my hope is in You all day long." (Ps. 25:4) Amen

Then Jesus said to them, "'Take heed and beware of the leaven of the Pharisees and the Sadducees'" (Mt. 16:6). Let's think about this for a while. First of all, the word "leaven" here and almost everywhere else in the Scriptures refers to evil. This seems very confusing when, just three chapters back, the Parable of the Leaven means almost the opposite: a good, heavenly ingredient that starts small and expands beyond our wildest dreams. In this case, the Pharisees and the Sadducees were so inflexible and so negative to any opinions or ideas other than what they had been taught from childhood, they were incapable of hearing or seeing the Truth, even when He was right in their faces! The Pharisees were the elite ruling class of the Jews, holding great political clout, and composed the majority of the Sanhedrin. The Sadducees were known as the "free thinkers" and did not believe in life after death. The Essenes were the third class and comparable to the Puritan sect. They were not interested in political clout and had little influence on the culture of their day. I would imagine many of them would have welcomed Jesus' message quickly. Throughout Scripture, Jesus denounced the doctrines of the Pharisees and Sadducees, who lived by the mantra, "Do as I say and not as I do." They put heavy loads on people they themselves could not carry. Not much has changed, has it?

Let's take our lead verse and see what we can learn from it. I have always been very grateful so many people of different denominations had such an influence on my spiritual journey. Perhaps insignificant at the time, but all were steps leading to my finding the Way, the Truth, and the Life (Jn. 14:6). When I was a teenager, I often stayed at my girlfriend's house when my parents were away. Her family always accepted me just like another daughter, and around the dinner table, they always held hands and prayed before their meals. This wasn't lost on me. It was something precious that was tucked into my heart. I think in some ways, Jill's parents had more influence on me than my own during those years. I could see their faith, which they lived out daily, and they were fun people. As a result of being exposed to many denominations and having very little knowledge or faith in my own, after coming to Christ, I found it was extremely easy to worship with most Christian denominations. But as a twenty-one-year member of a Presbyterian church (which is where I was when I became saved) when they ordained a known abortionist as elder and came very close to accepting homosexuals as clergy (still an ongoing debate), we had to "take heed of the leaven" within our own church and move on. You can place your own experiences in this verse and grow from them. Yes, there are a few churches I would insert for the name "Pharisee," as I would not be comfortable attending either a Mormon church or Jehovah's Witness church. It is my personal belief that their doctrines do not coincide with the teachings of Christ. "And if some of you think differently, that too, God will make clear to you" (Phil. 3:35b). Lord, please give us the gift of Discretion that we might recognize the "leaven" when we come in contact with it.

In chapter 16 of Matthew, Jesus begins to teach about His coming death. Simon Peter cannot understand or accept what he is hearing and tries to stop Jesus. This is where we hear (read) the words, "'Get behind me, Satan. You are an offense to Me and you are not mindful of the things of God, but the things of men'" (Mt. 16:23).

Oh how often do we see this in our society today! This story is such a warning to me. Simon Peter, the "lead" apostle who had walked with Jesus for nearly three years by now, is letting his own opinions, culture, and experiences influence his thinking. Dear God, if St. Peter can get confused after walking, talking, listening, and praying with Jesus for three years, what hope do I have? My own culture and peers have always been very important to me. I have concluded Jesus stopped Peter and set him straight, and He will do the same for me. And you. And now we, too, have the indwelling Holy Spirit, which was not yet given at the time of this story. The Holy Spirit leads and directs us to all Truth. Thank You, God.

Chapter 17 describes the transfiguration, which includes the inner circle of apostles: Peter, James, and John. Certainly by now it is apparent Peter has been forgiven, and the Lord's chastisement of him straightened out his thinking. How very extraordinary and amazing that the apostles recognized both Moses and Elijah! How do you suppose this was possible? Both men lived hundreds of years before this event, and they each had something very special about their deaths. In Moses' case, when he died, God actually "buried him in Moab," and no one knows where the grave is; only that he died in Moab. You can read about this in Deuteronomy 34:5. Jude 9 makes reference to Moses' death and tells us the angel Michael was involved somehow. (I couldn't even guess about what this means.) We have already discussed Elijah being carried to heaven on a whirlwind. Both deaths have supernatural aspects to them. Maybe "they" can't find Moses' grave because there isn't one. And maybe God doesn't want us going to a gravesite to grieve, because the grave is never the end. The wonderful thing about this story is these Old Testament saints were immediately known and identified, were alive, and were obviously conversing with Jesus to encourage Him about what He was about to experience. Isn't that enough to give even the most stubborn nonbelievers hope for the future? I mean, of course, concerning the future of Heaven itself. And by the way, speaking of Heaven, if you haven't already read the book by that name written by Randy Alcorn, a pastor and author, may I suggest you do so in the near future? It is quite wonderful! Really a textbook on the subject.

The book of Matthew is composed of five major discourses, around which the entire book is written. The author makes no attempt to place events in any kind of chronological order but deals with themes and broad concepts that would be familiar to Jewish readers. The Sermon on the Mount, chapters 5 through 7, is the first discourse.

The commissioning of the apostles, chapter 10, is the second. The Parables about the Kingdom is the third discourse, found in chapter 13. A discourse about the childlikeness of the believer in chapter 18 is the fourth, and the fifth discourse is in chapters 24 and 25, still ahead of us, is about His second coming.

Now, in chapter 18, we have come to the fourth discourse, which instructs us on humility, childlikeness, openness, and vulnerability. One of the great paragraphs in this chapter is in verses 10 and 11, which tell us our "little ones" have angels in heaven watching over them. I don't know about you, but I wish I had known this when my children were young. It would have given me great comfort, and maybe I would not have been quite so protective. It does give me peace, though, thinking about my own grandchildren. This doesn't excuse us from praying for their guidance and protection. Thinking about my grandchildren reminds me to always pray for their parents, Kim and Mike, and Andy and Sandy, for their wisdom and parenting skills in raising these precious kids.

In the same paragraph, Jesus tells us why He came to earth: "For the Son of Man has come to save that which was lost" (Mt. 18:11).

I also love the paragraph on prayer that states:

> "Again I say to you that if two of you on earth agree concerning anything that they ask, it will be done for them by My Father in Heaven. For where two or three are gathered in My name, I am there in the midst of them." (Mt. 18:19-20)

What a reason for Bible study groups to get to know each other and pray for needs we wouldn't ordinarily know over coffee or bridge. In my small groups, I always imagine Jesus sitting right in the midst of us and listening to all our conversation . . . not just prayers, but every word and thought. His Presence is often palpable! It is always God's timing and His will that these prayers are answered. Three of us have been praying for nearly twenty years for a friend's husband to know the Lord, without a hint of his acceptance. Does that mean we give up? Of course not! This is God's timing, not ours. The same with grown children who choose not to walk with the Lord. We simply offer these dear ones up to the Lord and wait for His timing. Nearly thirty-five years ago, after I became saved and tried to tell my family what had happened to me, my husband became so exasperated with me, he would not listen to a word. I was not the same person he had married, and he didn't know if he wanted any part of me or my stories. Actually, that too was part of God's plan, because while Bob didn't want to listen, I found fertile ground in my children, Kim and Andy. I needed very much to learn the lesson that I can't be anyone else's Holy Spirit. The Trinity doesn't need a fourth member! Years later, Bob came to the Lord without any help from me through the influence of a dear pastor named Curt Lehman, who has now gone home to be with the Lord. He is one of God's "saints" we can't wait to see again!

I found the advantage of having the local junior high school too far away to walk, so my children and I had at least fifteen minutes of uninterrupted conversation twice a day. Often at the end of the day, I would have a story about answered prayer that I could share with them. As a result, each child accepted the Lord when they were fifteen years old and in high school. What good timing! They each have their own stories to tell and are both active in their churches and various ministries. In fact, Andy has gone to seminary, part-time now, to get a master's degree in apologetics. Sure my buttons are popping! While they were still teenagers, I started praying for their future spouses. I didn't tell them what I was praying for; they were having too much fun being teenagers to think that far ahead. They both have great stories and great spouses. I'd like to interrupt this study of Matthew for a few pages just to tell their stories. Don't forget now, the subject is prayer.

## CHAPTER 7

# PERSONAL

Our daughter, Kim, stayed in Lincoln and graduated from the University of Nebraska with a degree in business. She had a successful career managing commercial real estate when she was engaged the first time. We grew to like her fiancé, but something just wasn't "right," and the engagement was ended. We never knew what it was and didn't question Kim's judgment. She was walking with the Lord and had very high standards. A few years later, and one boyfriend in between, she was engaged the second time, and this time I grew very concerned. With all apologies to my Democratic and Catholic friends out there, he was both, plus divorced with a child and an ex-wife who phoned frequently. This just didn't seem like a good fit to Bob and me, so one holiday when Kim was visiting us in Rancho Mirage, she agreed to a counseling session with our pastor. The session was for 4 o'clock in the afternoon, and she didn't return home until after 6:30. When she came in, she had removed the engagement ring and was totally peaceful about her decision to break the engagement. I will forever pray for that pastor, who took the time and concern to counsel our daughter.

Kim was nearly twenty-eight years old at the time, almost all her friends were married, and she was a little discouraged but still waiting for her Prince Charming. She did something I really don't recommend: she made a deal with God. Now God says not to test Him, but He doesn't say not to make a deal with Him. Kim's deal was she would not date any man unless the Lord gave her a "sign." I know, I know; the Lord says the only sign this perverse generation will get is the sign of Jonah. But nevertheless . . . I knew about that prayer and continued to pray for the right one to come along. It only took a few months. Kim came for dinner one Sunday afternoon (she had her own apartment at this point) and I said to her, "I was at the Racquet Club a few days ago and noticed that Mike Marsh is back in town from California and temporarily working at the club as a tennis pro."

Kim's reply absolutely stunned me! She said, "Yes, Mom, I saw him too. He had three Persian kittens in his hands, and I just went up to him and grabbed one!"

I started laughing. "Kim, what do you love more than almost anything in the world that is waiting home for you right now?"

She thought awhile and said, "Cats? Do you think that's a sign?"

My reply was, "Let's just leave that one up to the Lord." I was still grinning from the inside out. It was just as if God was tapping me on the shoulder and telling me to pay attention. Oh, I was!

Monday evening Kim went to the Racquet Club for her tennis league that was just starting that fall, and she greeted Mike and welcomed him back to Nebraska. (God has written this script, believe me.) Mike asked if it was true she was no longer engaged, and when that was understood, he asked her out for coffee after her league. The rest is history.

Mike's story is just as good. He was raised in Orange County, California, by a single mother, learned how to play tennis in Iran as an "ex-pat," excelled at the sport, and accepted a full scholarship to Nebraska for tennis. He was a pro at a local country club during the summers, which is how we knew him in the first place. They were both engaged to others during that time. When Mike graduated from the university, he moved back to Orange County and got an excellent job appraising demolitions for a construction company. But one day, after working several months, he stopped the car, looked up at the sky, and for absolutely no reason, decided to quit his job and move back to Nebraska. That's where we pick up the story at the Racquet Club, where Mike was working as a pro until he knew what he wanted to do as a career. Kim and Mike hit it off right away, until Kim discovered Mike was not a Christian. She explained to him why she couldn't continue to date him with serious intentions because they would be "unequally yoked". "Do not be yoked together with unbelievers, for what do righteousness and wickedness have in common?"(2 Cor. 16:14)

They sat up until wee hours one night, talking. Kim explained to him the whole story of why Jesus died on the cross for us and why it was important for her to marry a committed Christian. As late as it was, Mike went home and called Kim the next morning at 6:30 to tell her he had asked Jesus to come into his heart, and could they now continue to date? Thank You, Lord, for a wonderful story! There were engaged on New Year's Eve in San Francisco, where Kim met Mike's mother for the first time, and planned a wedding for the following September. Bob and I both loved Mike and were so pleased with this news.

No, that's not the end of the story. I was so excited about our first wedding coming up and wanted to fly home to Nebraska ASAP to help Kim find a gown and plan. She absolutely would not let me come home! She said we would be there in March, which would give us plenty of time. You've got to be kidding! But I relented, and when Kim picked us up at the airport in March and took us home, she put us in our living room with a glass of wine and told us to stay put until she returned from her old bedroom upstairs. When she returned, she was wearing my wedding gown from our 1959 wedding. It had been hanging in a cedar-lined closet on the third floor for many years. It fit her perfectly; it only needed the sleeves modified and more seed pearls added. Of course I cried. Kim told me later she had tried on the dress twice before, and it didn't fit. Oh Lord, You are so good!

And there's more. Kim and Mike had already changed churches and were attending a much smaller church in the suburbs. Bob and I knew we eventually wanted to join them, because it was important to us to be on the same page spiritually with our daughter, but it was very hard to leave a whole church family we had grown to love so much over the years. It was ultimately easier to leave than to try to change from within (remember the story of the leaven.) Kim and Mike's wedding was everything beautiful we had dreamed of. The staff of their church took a special interest in this stunningly good-looking young couple, who obviously loved the Lord, and asked them after their honeymoon if they would please come and take over their junior high Sunday school class of eight boys and girls. (I told you it was a small church.) They had never done anything like this before, and Mike was a brand-new Christian, so they prayed about it and accepted the challenge. They started with eight children, but then there were twelve and then sixteen. Kids were bringing their friends, because the class was interesting with fun, young leaders who were also eager to learn. The kids asked questions, and Kim and Mike taught them how to look up biblical answers by subject in a concordance. Of course, you might expect with this age group the subject of sexuality and homosexuality came up. Kim and Mike explained the latter was a sin, just like stealing or murder. Hate the sin, love the sinner. While the class looked up some passages on homosexuality, several kids asked, "Do our parents know this is in the Bible?" Kim replied, "Ask them."

The following week, Kim got a phone call from the assistant minister, telling her they didn't need to return to the junior high classroom. The elders had found another couple to take over the teaching responsibility. That was the straw that broke the camel's back. By now, Bob and I had joined them in this little suburb church and were trying to get used to it. Bob had been a member of this denomination all his life, and neither of us wanted to sever ties unless it was absolutely necessary. It was. We started our search for an evangelical church that believed in and taught from the Bible. We had found the "leaven" and left it behind.

Our son, Andy, also has a wonderful story. He got all the way through Pepperdine with lots of dear friends but no "girlfriend," and was working in Palm Desert after his graduation. Andy was teaching the college-career group at our evangelical church in the desert one winter. Kim was visiting us, and Andy came for Monday night dinner. He asked me if I would come with him that evening and speak to his group. Gulp! Nothing like giving me a little notice! "What do you want me to talk about and how long?"

"Oh," Andy said, "just tell your story."

My story. I had just finished a session of radiation therapy for breast cancer and felt the Lord leading me through difficult decisions that went against my Nebraska physician's advice. I felt my body was "fearfully and wonderfully made in the image of God" (Ps. 139:14) and needed a chance to heal in a more natural way than what my surgeon had in mind. So after lots of prayer and trips with Andy and Bob to check out several different options, I had checked out my X-rays and slides that contained level 4 cancer cells and found the exact doctor I needed. He was associated with Eisenhower Hospital in Rancho Mirage at the Peter Lake Center, right around the corner from our home. This doctor was a Jewish oncologist on a spiritual journey. How much better can you get than that? After hearing my theories why my immune system had plummeted so badly (that's another story entirely) and examining all the slides and X-rays I had brought with me, he recommended a course of radiation treatment for nine weeks, which I was relieved to accept. It seemed much easier than the mastectomy recommended in Lincoln.

I grabbed Kim and told her she was coming with us to Andy's meeting. I really have no idea what I said to those thirty or so young people that evening, but I do remember I had a wonderful time and loved being with them. Afterward, a darling, little, honey-blond girl introduced herself to me and told me she had grown up in a small town in central Nebraska and moved to the desert with her parents two years before. It turned out this was the Sandy I had prayed for all along; I just didn't know it yet. Andy and Sandy started dating shortly after that, and it didn't take long for them to fall in love. It didn't take long for all of us to fall in love with Sandy, either! We had just moved into a larger home in Rancho Mirage and planned a "new house" party. Kim flew in from Nebraska, and many of Andy's Pepperdine friends came also. Andy proudly escorted Sandy, and when everyone arrived, we discovered Kim and Sandy had selected the exact same shade of blue cocktail dress to wear that evening. One of my good friends said during the evening, "I can't tell which one is your daughter."

"Yes," I replied, "Isn't it wonderful? They are both so special." And they are. As it turned out, Andy and Sandy were married first, in June, and we had the honor of having the rehearsal dinner at our home with Sandy's parents co-hosting. It was a perfect year for us.

Kim, Sandy, and I have so much fun together doing girl stuff . . . shopping, talking, laughing, crying. It doesn't matter what we are doing. We just have fun enjoying each other's company. When the three of us go shopping together, I get such a kick out of trailing behind and watching people watch "my" two girls. They are both so attractive that heads turn wherever they go, and a clerk will often ask me which one is my daughter, and I am proud to reply, "Both." Marisa will be joining us soon, I'm sure. And I haven't even started on our other grandchildren yet! Oh dear. I don't know how I get so side-tracked except this whole family was put together with the Lord's hand and in answer to frequent, fervent prayer. You already know about Kim's two teenagers, and now I will tell you about Andy and Sandy's two adorable, towheaded boys, ten and eleven and a half years old. Joshua is the older one, and what a little "hug-a-bear" he is! He is so quick with hugs and kisses to greet us when we arrive for a visit, it just leaves us breathless and with a deep joy hard to explain but so easy to thank God for. As he grows older, I hope he will not lose that joyful spontaneity that just fills us up and warms our hearts. His brother, Jared, is equally hospitable and joyful but in a quieter way. He has dimples when he grins that endears him to us immediately. They are only eighteen months apart in age and are now showing their separate strengths and interests. They are both absolute joys to be around! Just writing this makes me homesick for them. They live in Southern California, about ninety minutes from our door in the desert to theirs. Please excuse me for presenting my blessings in such a blatant manner!

Now, let's get back to Matthew.

# CHAPTER 8

# MATTHEW NINETEEN - TWENTY-ONE

This morning I read in Oswald Chamber's *My Utmost for His Highest,* "Certainty is the mark of the commonsense life . . . Gracious uncertainly is the mark of the spiritual life . . . Full of breathless expectation . . . Joy."

Yes! Exhilaration for "what's next!" Joy in knowing whatever it is, it's coming from God, and we're going to do it together. Yes! Oh what fun to walk with Jesus . . . just to know He's at my side!

> Thank You, Lord, for Your very Presence with me this morning. Knowing we have time together is such a gift to me. Right now, right this minute, all's well with my world. My family is healthy, my sister Nancy is coming with her friend and neighbor in three weeks, and in two weeks, we will be in Laguna for a weekend with all four adult children to celebrate and bless Kim and Mike's new "villa." I don't believe anyone else has been so blessed as me, and I can never think of enough words to express my gratitude. I know the world is a total mess politically, morally, culturally, spiritually, and economically, but right now, in my quiet time chair, I feel the peace and joy of Your Presence down to my toes! I have not even opened my Bible yet; I've only read a devotional and said good morning to You. It is enough. It is more than enough. With my whole heart I desire to serve You any way I am able. Amen.

*Chapters 19-21*

Chapter 19 has a story of the rich young man who wanted to know what he must do to have eternal life. By his question and lack of humility, he shows his first loves were his possessions. If he had true faith, he would have surrendered his all to Christ's bidding. The Lord is not saying rich people cannot enter into the Kingdom of Heaven; what He is saying is we'd better have our priorities in order.

> So the last will be first and the first last. For many are called but few are chosen. (Mt. 20:16)

I always think of this verse in connection with my dad, who didn't find Jesus until he was nearly ninety years old. Thank you, Lord! Oh he went to the Methodist church with my family whenever we went, but his true "church" was the Masonic Lodge: the Royal Order of Masons, the Scottish Rite, and Jesters. I've never seen a person so loyal to an organization as Dad was to that one. It was almost like a "cult" to him. When he got too old to drive, and so were his friends, he sat at home and watched TV. Billy Graham "got him" one night, and he gave his heart to Jesus. He never entered a church after that, except to attend my mother's funeral, where he could do nothing but cry. But my dad is with You now, Lord, and I can't wait to see the transformation in him. Oh so much to look forward to! It brings me so much happiness to think about future reunions! I don't think my work on earth is done yet, but Lord help me to number my days. I don't want to waste any. My dad would have been 105 today. It's his earthly birthday. Please hug him for me, Lord.

I got excited about our reading for today and forgot to put our Bible verse prayer in before we started. It's not too late:

> Therefore, my beloved (friends), be steadfast, immoveable, always abounding in the Lord, knowing that your labor is not in vain in the Lord. (1 Cor. 15:58)

Verse 21 of Matthew 20 takes us to Palm Sunday, beginning Jesus' last week before the cross. Jesus tells two parables in this chapter, both condemning Israel of their lack of foresight in recognizing Him. He points out the wicked will be destroyed (the Jewish leaders), and the vineyard will be leased to other vinedressers, who will render to Him the fruits in their season. Clearly, Jesus is referring to Gentiles, and the original Jewish believes, who would become followers of "the Way", and finally the church. This is repeated twice in this chapter so that the chief priests and Pharisees could not misinterpret it. They didn't.

> Lord, today is Saturday, and I bring my prayer card for the week to you: our country, our president, his family, and cabinet. Lord, I know no one is placed in authority without Your hand on them, but I don't understand what is happening to our wonderful country. Nevertheless, I bring these leaders to You for Your blessing, Your influence on them, and with a plea that they might know You. I often wonder if this is some kind of test of our collective integrity. Sigh. I am on my knees, Lord. Please bless and watch over the ministries I care so much for: Focus on the Family, Rovi Zacharius, S. R. G., Young Life, Campus Crusade for Christ, my three churches, and their pastors and families. Give them wisdom and guidance as they lead their flocks, with their hearts firmly planted and led by You. I give You my previous two pastors, whose authority I also taught under and who, for long periods of time, were important mentors to me and my family. Forgive me, Lord, that I only bring these folks and institutions to you sporadically. Amen.

# CHAPTER 9

# MATTHEW TWENTY-TWO

Today in *My Utmost for His Highest:* "Our reach must exceed our grasp. It is a bad thing to be spiritually satisfied."

I personally don't believe it is ever possible to be spiritually satisfied. There is always such a need for more: a deeper relationship with You, a better grasp of doctrine, a greater interpretive understanding of Daniel and Revelation, the next biblical concept to experience and not just read about. When my vision of Christ is within from past experiences and I know Christ is always with me and guiding me, my expectation for the future is full of hope. How can I become a more effective prayer warrior? How can I be better equipped for ministry? Why am I not more faithful memorizing scripture or visiting widows, orphans, or those in prison? Why am I so lacking in worldview outlooks? They are of no more interest to me than a passing shower. Andy is trying to drag me into twenty-first-century realizations, although it's a real struggle. But spiritual complacency? How can that be with so much more to learn and understand? Lord, please don't give up on me. I don't ever want to be spiritually satisfied until I see You face to face! Please forgive me that my prayers seem so repetitive and unimaginative. Please read my heart and not my limited vocabulary.

Our church service this morning consisted of a very loud, visiting rock band and was annoying rather than worshipful. The sermon was a very good history lesson taken from Revelation, but my heart had not been prepared. Please, Lord, lead us. We are seldom so woefully out of tune with the church culture of our day. My friend says, listen to the words and respond to words rather than the music. What if I can't hear the words over the music? Sigh. Lord, please help me. If I have a spirit of unrest or "judgmentalism" because something or someone does not live up to my expectations, please knock me over the head or something to let me know. "Judge not, that you be judged." I know, I know! I really do not want to be so set in my ways that I cannot see Yours. Help me, Lord. Help me see with Your eyes what I cannot find with my own.

> "So do not fear for I am with you; do not be dismayed, for I am your God. I will strengthen you and help you. I will uphold you with My righteous right hand." (Is. 41:10)

Thank You, Lord. So many times, You have answered me with Scripture. That this verse jumped out at me was nothing short of miraculous! I stand amazed! Enough journaling, and on with our reading of Matthew. Only one chapter today, because it is my prayer day of intercession. If I am not intentional about this, it will not happen.

### *Chapter 22*

In chapter 22, Jesus teaches about the resurrected life and that there are no marriages in heaven, the "hereafter." He was speaking to the Sadducees, who had no hope or belief in an afterlife. No wonder "sad" is in their name! But Jesus very clearly quotes the voice of His Father, saying, "'I am the God of Abraham, the God of Isaac, and the God of Jacob. God is not the God of the dead, but of the living'" (Mt. 22:32).

The story of the transfiguration tells us these Old Testament saints live on, and so will we. The only question is where. We have a choice, and I will get out my prayer cards over my friends who don't know You now. Here are my favorite scriptures to use:

> Lord God, I am not responsible for their salvation, but I am responsible to bring their names before You. And I do with every expectation You have a plan for each of them. A plan for good and not for evil, to give them a future and a hope. (Jer. 29:11)

(Sisters and) Brothers, my heart's desire and prayer to God for my friends, whose names I will insert among these verses, is that they may be saved. (Rom. 10:1)

Likewise I say to you, there is joy in the presence of the angels of God over one sinner who repents. (Lk. 15:10)

There is a way that seems right to a man, but in the end it leads to death. (Pr. 14:12)

Pray [for them] without ceasing. (1 Thess. 5:17)

For the Son of God has come to save that which was lost. (Mt. 18:11)

I also have a list of precious Jewish friends who don't know You and offer the following:

Jesus said "I am the way, the truth and the life. No one comes to the Father except through Me." (Jn. 14:6)

Jesus said, "Believe also in Me." (Jn. 3:18)

He [God] has blinded their eyes and deadened their hearts so they can neither see with their eyes, nor understand with their hearts, nor turn, and I would heal them. (Jn. 12:40; Is. 6:10)

He who believes in Him [Jesus] is not condemned, but he who does not believe is condemned already because he has not believed in the name of the only begotten Son of God. (Jn. 3:18)

Forget the former things; do not dwell on the past. See, I am doing a new thing! Now it springs up; do you not perceive it? I am making a way in the desert and streams in the wasteland. (Is. 43:18-19)

Salvation is found in no one else [but Jesus] for there is no other name under heaven given to men by which we must be saved. (Acts 4:12)

There is no difference between Jew and Gentile . . . the same Lord is Lord of all and richly blesses all who call on Him, for everyone who calls on the name of the Lord will be saved. (Rom. 10:12-13)

Moreover, the Father judges no one, but has entrusted all judgments to the Son, that they may honor the Son just as they honor the Father. He who does not honor the Son does not honor the Father who sent Him. (Jn. 5:22)

Lord, with the previous verses, I offer each name up to You for Salvation, that they might come to know You as never before. If I had a chance, I would ask them, "What do you have to lose? Don't tell me you can do a better job with your life than God can. Aren't you tired of trying yet?" Tony Campolo, a Christian pastor, author and evangelist, said, "If my faith commitment to what I believe to be true is erroneous, and there is no God and the Bible is false, I will not know it. When I die, all consciousness will cease to exist. On the other hand, if your atheism proves false, you will know it."

Something to ponder indeed. Realize:

*God loves you.* "'I [Jesus] came that they might have life and have it abundantly'" (Jn. 10:10).

*We are sinners.* "For all have sinned and fall short of the glory of God" (Rom. 3:23).

*We need a Savior.* "Jesus Christ is the Messiah and God's only provision for our sins. He died in our place. He alone bridges the gap between us and God" (1 Peter 2:24-25).

It's not enough to "know" any of the above verses. There are lots of "pew sitters" out there who know these verses, yet they have not acted on them by getting down on their spiritual knees and asking God for forgiveness and to come into their hearts. It is so simple and so profound.

> But as many as received Him, to them He gave the right to become children of God, even to those who believe in His name." (Jn. 1:12)

We receive Christ by personal invitation. Christ said, "Behold, I stand at the door and knock. If anyone hears my voice and opens the door, I will come in to him" (Rev. 3:20).

We have everything to gain and nothing to lose. This is a win-win all the way!

## CHAPTER 10

# MATTHEW TWENTY-THREE - TWENTY-FIVE

Dear God, I only want Your complete will for my two friends who are probably dying right now and don't know You. Help me never to let my own limited knowledge of a situation that concerns me enough to intercede get in the way of Your will for the person I am concerned about. I believe Your will for each of us is to know You in a personal way, and that is my prayer for my two friends . . . to somehow know You. I have no knowledge of the spiritual path of either one and have prayed fervently for both. Now, Lord, I give them to You, knowing You love them better than I ever could, and You want the best for both. I believe that choice is something I have no power over, and I ask You to send others to minister to each of them. Will my friends survive these illnesses? I can only ask for your mercy and grace. Amen.

Lord, a beautiful spring day on the prairie again. Blue skies, gentle breezes, doors and windows all open. Lovely. And good morning, Lord. Thank you for this day, for Your Word in scripture. Open my heart and mind that I might know You better. Be with us as we continue Matthew.

## *Chapters 23-25*

> Teach me Your way, O Lord, and I will walk in Your truth: Give me an undivided heart, that I may fear Your name. (Ps. 86:11)

Chapter 23 contains the most forceful condemnation of the scribes and Pharisees I have found in the Bible, and it reminds me we need to pray for discernment when we are sitting under a mentor's authority. Is the minister/pastor, shepherd, leader, elder, teacher clean on the inside? Does he or she display a lifestyle of the fruits of the Spirit outside the pulpit, lecture hall, or classroom that represents what I am being taught? There are so many really good pastors/teachers who are truly "walking the walk" with the Lord and not just "talking the talk." I am convinced my pastors in Lincoln, Palm Desert, and Frisco, Colorado are among those who have the utmost biblical integrity and wisdom in their ministries. I am always blessed when I take notes and follow their leadership. We are so fortunate in this country that we can readily sit under the teaching of men like Chuck Swindoll, Max Lucado, Charles Stanley, and David Jeremiah, just to name a few, by switching on Christian radio in our local areas. Books by these noted theologians, including Warren Wiersbe, are also readily available and always a blessing.

Before we leave chapter 23, I call your attention to the last paragraph in the chapter, which is beautiful and shows that the heart of Christ is so evident with the Jewish people:

> "O Jerusalem, Jerusalem, you who kill the prophets and stone those sent to you, how often I have longed to gather your children together as a hen gathers her chicks under her wings, but you were not willing. Look, your house is left desolate. For I tell you, you will not see Me again until you say, 'Blessed is He who comes in the name of the Lord.'" (Mt. 23:37-39)

I wish I had thought to include this with my prayer verses for my Jewish friends. It is so appropriate. And a beautiful lead-in for chapters 24 and 25 which is the fifth and last of Matthew's five discourses around which the book is written. This one is called the Olivet Discourse and contains some of the most important prophecies in the entire Bible. That being said, if you have not already, I hope you will grab your Bible and read these two chapters before another second goes by!

The questions were asked by the disciples. This could have been the twelve apostles, and it could have been many more, including women who believed in Jesus and followed Him wherever He taught. They were the original "groupies". The first question was, "When will these things be?" Jesus had just told them the beautiful temple begun by Herod and still a work in progress would be destroyed. The second was, "What will be the sign of Your coming and the end of the age?" They anticipated and wanted the time to be *now*. At this point, they had no idea there would be a second coming. They were told He would suffer on the cross, but they just could not wrap their minds around this concept. They were looking for a sign not only soon but now: a sign of their conquering King, charging into the spiritual and physical battle against Rome. Often when we are told something, we put our own interpretation on the story, depending on our own experiences and beliefs. These followers were looking for instant gratification! They had no idea a crucifixion and resurrection and "church age" must occur first. Surely this is human nature. Such selfish natures we are born with!

The things Jesus said to watch for starting in Matthew 24:4 are really interesting. The only one I have not heard of happening yet are the deceivers claiming to be Christ, the Messiah All the other signs have been ongoing during my entire lifetime. Wars and rumors of war: check. One nation will rise against another: check. Famines: check. Pestilence, earthquakes: double check. I live in the desert of California during the winter months and can attest that earthquakes are a frequent occurrence, much to the annoyance of our cat. To me, they are less scary than the occasional tornadoes that threaten the Midwest all spring. My daughter, Kim, disagrees. "Mom, we have warnings and a basement to go to in Nebraska." We have no warnings in the Coachella Valley, but we always have a Safe One to go to!

With apologies to my nondrinking friends, I will tell you Bob and I enjoy a cocktail or glass of wine almost every afternoon before dinner preparations as a time to relax, enjoy the scenery, and catch up with one another. We are frequently going twenty different ways from each other during the day. Last spring, we both had our heads in the refrigerator, looking for mix, cheese, and crackers, and so on, when a pretty good sized earthquake hit our area. We both looked at each other and said, "Drink fast!" Sometimes you have to have a sense of humor in the midst of the storm. We took our glasses outside, where we watched our pool water splash onto the deck because we never know what sudden calamities are in the offering such as a life threatening earthquake.

Now back to our subject at hand. Since all these signs have been taking place for a long time, I believe it is safe to say the end times have begun. Don't misunderstand me; I am not standing on a street corner with a sign saying, "The end is near." In fact, I think this end stage will continue for a long time. This doesn't bother me in the least, because based on my family's longevity, I may very well be in the final decade of my earthly life. But I do feel bad for my grandchildren, who will not have the world security and freedom my generation has always enjoyed and taken for granted. This reminds me of two things. First of all, I am eternally grateful my grandchildren are all saved and safely walk hand in hand with the Lord. Second, it reminds me to number my own days, so I may not waste any of them.

> Lord, make me know my end, and what is the measure of my days, that I may know how frail I am. (Ps. 39:4)

> All the days ordained for me were written in Your book before one of them came to be. (Ps. 139:16b)

I haven't seen any false prophets yet either, and even in the best preaching/teaching I have ever heard, not one claim. "Lawlessness will abound", Mt 24:12. Certainly this is escalating, especially in the larger cities. When I was growing up in Omaha, in a safe suburb called Dundee, we rarely locked our house, and we never took the key out of our car's ignition for fear we would lose it. I don't remember my parents ever purchasing a new car, and secondhand cars rarely came with a second key. Now we not only lock every window and door, we have security systems and hide behind gated communities. We don't know our neighbors anymore, because when we come home from auto trips, we put down our garage door and hurry into the house with our groceries. We don't sit on our front porches anymore, because they don't build front porches anymore. They build back decks and patios that are carefully screened for privacy. Bob and I walk in our neighborhoods all the time, and we seldom see a neighbor out in the yard or out walking. Yes, times are changing, especially in Europe, I'm told. But here is encouraging news: "And this gospel of the Kingdom will be preached in all the world as a witness to all nations, and then the end will come" (Mt. 24:14).

The last understanding I had from Wycliffe Bible Translators, located in Texas, say there are very few countries left that do not have the Bible in their native language. But, of course, this verse does not say "written word," that is, "Bible." It says "preached," which doesn't take into account mission trips going on all over the world literally all the time! Two of my three churches are extremely active in sending mission groups to third world countries and planting churches where they travel.

Matthew 24:15 gives us a greater problem than I can ever solve, because it talks about the "abomination of desolation." But it is understood that the "holy place" would be the yet again rebuilt temple in Jerusalem. This cannot be readily achieved, because that location is already covered by the Dome of the Rock. Then again, nothing is impossible with the Lord. I have heard rumors for many years that many of the gold and bronze fixtures for the temple have already been copied to God's exact specification in Exodus and hidden near Jerusalem, waiting for God's timing. I don't know this to be true, but it is an exciting thought.

The remainder of this verse describes the terrors of the tribulation to come. Many of us believe the church will be taken up in a cloud before this happens (the "pretrib" theory), but the final sentence in this verse possibly negates that theory when it says, "But for the sake of the elect those days will be shortened" (Mt. 24:22). The "elect" are true Believers—members of God's household. The church. I don't define "church" by denomination. I define it as those of us who claim Jesus as our Lord and Savior and walk according to His doctrines, not according to which door we enter on Sunday mornings. Or not. I think of church as simply being the "icing on the cake," a place to unite with others of like mind to continue to learn, praise, and worship as a community. Certainly not a necessity for salvation. The verse goes on to say, "Even the Elect will be deceived" (Mt. 24:24).

We need to pray fervently for wisdom and discernment. Now! We are not to wait until we see definite signs and wonders. These kinds of global cataclysms will appear immediately before Jesus' second coming. This is a no-brainer, because they didn't appear before His first coming, so all we can do is look at the future and prepare our children and grandchildren, so they will know there is a successful end of the story. Matthew 24:29 tells of the phenomena that will happen on the "Day of the Lord," the second coming. Matthew quotes from the Old Testament, Isaiah 13:10, also reported in Ezekiel 32:7, Joel 2:10, 31, 3:15, and Amos 8:9. When Jesus comes again, the entire world will know and see Him. "For as lightning that comes from the east is visible even in the west, so will be the coming of the Son of Man" (Mt. 24:27).

And,

> Then the sign of the Son or Man will appear in heaven and then all tribes of the earth will mourn, and they will see the Son of Man coming on the clouds of heaven with power and great glory. And He will send His angels with a sound of a trumpet, and they will gather together His elect from the four winds, from one end of heaven to the other. (Mt. 24:30-31)

I'm going to back up this good news with another quote, this time from 1 Thessalonians 4:16-18, written by Saul of Tarsus, Paul:

> For the Lord Himself will descend from heaven with a shout, with the voice of an archangel and with the trumpet of God. And the dead in Christ will rise first, then we who are alive and remain shall be caught up together with Him in the clouds to meet the Lord

> in the air. And thus we shall always be with the Lord. Therefore, comfort one another with these words.

The "tribes that will mourn" will be those that did not accept or recognize Jesus from the telling of the "good news." The elect will be celebrating to the hilt! Those two verses from Matthew tell us that wherever the Lord decides to return—I'm assuming it will be Jerusalem, the Holy Land—we will all see it happen supernaturally, wherever we are at the time.

Now the "last trump" in Hebrew history is Rosh Hashanah, and the "great trump" is Yom Kippur, so I don't believe we are done with the symbolism or importance of these two Jewish feast holidays. Belief has always existed that the rapture of the church will come on the first of these holidays, and the second coming of Christ on the second. Since these two Jewish holidays always come in the fall of the year, it's a real good idea to be prayed up and confessed up before that happens every year.

Notice in these readings that during the rapture, the Lord only comes as far as the clouds before He takes the church up with Him. What good food for thought! Every time I see a huge, puffy, cumulous cloud, I think about how the Lord will appear to us. Wow!

Verse 25 of Matthew contains the final parables in the book. The parable of the ten virgins is illustrative of God's judgment, which is unequivocal and irreversible. This is written in a language that would be fully understandable to the first-century citizen for a Jewish wedding. What it means to us is we cannot know assurance without the oil of the Holy Spirit, and we cannot succeed on borrowed religion. The saying "God doesn't have grandchildren" pretty much applies here. We cannot get by on the beliefs of our parents or those borrowed from our friends. The "born-again" birth process must occur with each of us as we seek a personal relationship with our Lord. It doesn't matter what kind of a household you grew up in, and it surely doesn't matter what church you attend. Neither will compensate for the personal relationship you establish with Jesus Christ, who is our advocate to the Father and gives us the gift of the Holy Spirit, who, in turn, gives us the talents, or spiritual gifts, to use and expand or to bury in the ground with no significant growth.

Don't miss the judgment that will take place on the second coming of Christ discussed in Matthew 25:31. I don't know about you, but I'm praying pretty hard to be a sheep and not a goat, and we certainly can't achieve that without the wisdom and guidance that only comes with prayer and a personal relationship with Jesus Christ. The spiritual "ball" is in your court! Romans 14:12 says, "For each one of us will give an accounting of himself to God."

O Lord, help me to always remember this while on my present journey. Amen.

## CHAPTER 11

# MATTHEW TWENTY-SIX - TWENTY-EIGHT

Thank you, Lord, for a lovely rainy day today. It feels like You are washing down the earth, and it smells so good! It is too cool this morning to open doors and windows, but I could smell that lovely "rain smell" when I went outside to get the morning paper. Your creation in all of nature is so very beautiful! The cloud formations look like we are in for a day or two of wet weather. Good job, Lord, of watering our lawn. Kiki wants no part of going outside this morning. Smart cat! It's a wonderful day to get into our last three chapters of Matthew. Let's do it!

> Seek the Lord while He may be found, Call on Him while He is near. (Is. 55:6)

Chapter 26 continues the last teachings of Jesus to His apostles. Starting in the sixth verse, we are told a woman anointed Jesus' head with a very costly perfume. We are told in Mark the value was nearly a year's wages, and it had been in an alabaster jar, which broke apparently while it was being opened. They were in the house of Simon the Leper in Bethany, a very small village just outside of Jerusalem, when this happened. We know Mary, Martha, and their brother, Lazarus, also lived in Bethany, and we assume Mary and Martha (not named here) were helping their neighbor serve this meal as Simon entertained them. The gospel of John tells us Martha "served," and Lazarus was a guest at the table with Jesus and the apostles. Simon would have been healed of his leprosy, or he would not have been in his house in Bethany. Perhaps this was an "appreciation" meal for his healing.

Matthew tells us the woman anointed Jesus' head, but John tells us she included His feet as well and then dried them with her hair. None of the apostles understood this act of pure worship, and most commentaries agree Mary probably didn't understand the symbolism or knew she was preparing Him for death. She was just following her heart. Jesus understood it implicitly. I thought it ironic that Jesus said whenever this story is told, it will be a memorial to her, yet only the gospel of John identifies the anointer as Mary, the sister of Martha and Lazarus. Let's give this New Testament "saint" all the credit she deserves!

This chapter is difficult to read, filled with the betrayal by Judas, the Passover celebration with the twelve, and the powerful words of the Last Supper celebrated for the first time—and which we are to emulate until we reach heaven ourselves—and Peter's incredulousness that he was accused of denying his Savior and Lord. Jesus took the remaining apostles to Gethsemane, and asked the three closest to Him (Peter, James, and John) to come deeper into the garden with Him. There He speaks the unforgettable words, "My Father, if it is possible, let this cup pass from Me" (Mt. 26:39). The arrest, false witnesses, accusations, and finally, Peter's denial round out this difficult chapter. In the final sentences, Peter remembered the words of Jesus, "'Before the cock crows you will deny Me three times'" (Mt. 26:75). So, he, Peter, went out and cried bitterly. Can't you just feel his despair? I can hardly read these words without weeping myself. Not just for Peter but for my own weakness, which would be my worst possible nightmare! Thank You, Lord, for the faith you have given me. Keep me strong until my own earthly journey is over. Amen

I cannot get through the twenty-seventh chapter of Matthew, leading to and experiencing Golgotha and the cross, without the vivid pictures of the film *The Passion of Christ* in my mind and heart. The sign above Jesus' head read, "THIS IS JESUS, THE KING OF THE JEWS," which was the charge of blasphemy against Him. The sign was written in Latin, Greek, and Hebrew, which symbolizes the representation of the political, cultural, and religious world of His day. Matthew tells of the supernatural signs that appeared after His death. The signs alone are so compelling as to His identity and deity, it would be impossible to ignore their validity. The veil of the temple was double thickness, woven horizontally, and separated the people from the Most Holy Place, where God resided throughout Hebrew history. The tearing from top to bottom could only have been done by God and signified the way into God's Presence was open to all and not limited to the Hebrew priests. The earthquake actually opened burial chambers where "saints" (read "believers") walked out and went home! Can you imagine not believing after all these signs? It actually blows my mind!

Matthew tells us three women were at the crucifixion. He mentions by name Mary Magdalene, who had been healed of seven demons; Mary, the mother of James and Joses who was no doubt Jesus' mother, and Salome, the mother of James and John. Matthew also tells us there were "many women watching from a distance." We know from the Gospel of John that John the Apostle was also there. This is one of the only occasions that we don't know where John's brother, James, was. He had no doubt "scattered" with the other apostles, who were all fearing for their lives, as well as in deep grief.

The celebration of the twenty-eighth chapter is such a relief, so miraculous, almost unimaginable in its glory. I always try to imagine myself with the two women who knelt at Jesus' feet at His resurrection and to feel what they must have felt. I can only imagine!

The last paragraph also has a triangle tucked into the margin of my new Bible, instructing us to "Go." The marching orders for our lives! And the ever-present loving words of Jesus to us:

> "I have commended you, and lo, I am with you always, even to the end of the age." (Mt. 28:20)

Tuck these words into your mind and heart, and know how real and true they are! Experience His Presence for yourselves. It's so easy . . . just . . . say, "Here I am, Lord. Forgive me. Come into my heart. I love You, Lord. Amen."

# PART II

# MARK

# CHAPTER 12

# MARK ONE - THREE

We have successfully navigated through the gospel of Matthew, and I do hope it blessed you as much as it did me. Because it was written by and for a Jewish audience, this might be the recommended gospel for Jewish friends to start with if they are curious about our faith. Hopefully, they are familiar with the Old Testament references.

The next gospel is Mark, and this is the same John Mark who was the cousin of Barnabas, who accompanied Paul and Barnabas on their first missionary journey but dropped out part way, much to the consternation of Paul, who was so angry he wouldn't consider taking him again. But Mark grew up both physically and spiritually and became a trusted friend of Paul's toward the end of the book of Acts, with Paul even calling for him when he was imprisoned in Rome.

Mark was not an apostle but became good friends with Peter during the years following the resurrection. In fact, it was to Mark's mother's house in Jerusalem that Peter fled after he was miraculously released from prison. John Mark's mother's name was Mary, and we are told in Acts 12 that the believers were together in that house, praying for Peter, when he unexpectedly arrived at the door. The believers were very frightened at this point, because the apostle James had just been killed on the orders of Herod Agrippa, the grandson of Herod the Great. A really bad dude!

I have a completely unproved theory that it was a teenage John Mark who was in the garden of Gethsemane the night Jesus was arrested, was grabbed (probably by Roman guards), and got away from them only in his "birthday suit." This story is told only in Mark, and who else would vividly remember something this frightening and embarrassing but the author? I know, I know; Jesus only took his apostles with Him that night to wait and pray with him, but when the Roman guards came to arrest Jesus, it is my feeling many people—especially believers, who were fearful for Jesus—followed them to see what the commotion was about. It doesn't take rocket science to know the Sanhedrin, chief priests, and scribes were all determined to hush up this growing band of believers who were about to upset their apple cart!

Mark was probably one of those believers who had followed Jesus through his mother's teaching from a young age and grew to know Peter well enough to record Peter's sermons and recollections that we have in the gospel of Mark. It is believed by most Bible scholars that the words of Mark are all stories given directly by Peter, who, you remember, was one of the inner circle of intimates walking with Jesus. As the "lead apostle" ("Upon this Rock I will build My church", Mt.16:18). Why didn't Peter write his own gospel? The answer is I don't know. Maybe he was too busy with evangelism. Maybe because of Mark, he didn't have to. We do have his words in 1 Peter and 2 Peter in the New Testament, right after Paul's epistles, Hebrews, and James.

Because the book of Mark is the shortest of the Gospels, I have also begun reading the Psalms, which I often love to use as devotion. I usually cover three to five in my daily reading but have been known to be "stuck" on one indefinitely, depending on my need and the Holy Spirit's teaching.

> But I know that the Lord has set apart for Himself him/her who is godly; the Lord will hear when I call to Him. (Ps. 4:3)

> Your Word says that we who believe in Your Name are set apart, and I do claim that sanctification as a process begun with my salvation and ending with You in Heaven. I know You hear my prayers before I can even give them words. Before a word even reaches my tongue, You know it. O Lord, thank you for the prayer cards offered to You this morning as the rain makes a wonderful sound on the French doors behind me. Be with us as we begin the gospel of Mark. Open our minds and hearts to what we may learn from Your Word.

## *Chapters 1-3*

Unlike the epistles, each gospel begins with the stories the authors are about to tell rather than a greeting to whomever they are addressing with information about the writer. Matthew's gospel started immediately with the genealogy of Jesus; Mark starts by telling about the forerunner of the Messiah, whom the Jews always expected to be Elijah. The prophecy is found in Malachi 3:1 and Isaiah 40:3, and is repeated for us here in Mark 1:2-3. Surprise! His name is John. He came preaching in the wilderness of Judea and baptizing in the Jordan River. His message was, "After me will come One more powerful than I, the thongs of whose sandals I am not worthy to untie. I baptize with water but He will baptize with the Holy Spirit" (Mk. 1:7-8).

John wore camel's hair and a leather belt; he ate locusts and wild honey. His hair was not cut. He probably looked like an adult hippie from the sixties, but here was a man on a holy mission for sure and with an impressive heritage as well. John's father, Zachariah, was a Jewish priest from the lineage of the tribe of Abijah, serving in the temple in Jerusalem. His mother, Elizabeth, was from the priestly tribe of Aaron. This couple was well past the age of childbearing, but here is where the supernatural part comes in.

Zachariah was privileged to light the incense just in front of the veil that divided the Holy Place from the Most Holy Place in the temple. It was an honor that would probably only come about once in a priest's lifetime, if that. So this duty, in itself, was huge. (The story about tying a rope around a priest's ankle in case he died while on this duty, because no one else was allowed in this space, is entirely false, by the way.) I always pictured this couple as being white-haired and retired-age old, but God put something in my mind today. Men from priestly tribes such as Aaron and Levi could start their training for the priesthood at the age of twenty-five, and after five years of education, started their duties as priests. (I always thought this was one of the reasons Jesus didn't start His ministry until the age of thirty.)

But the Old Testament also tells us priests would retire from their work at the age of fifty. I remember this specifically from one of my Old Testament studies many years ago, but now that I am writing about it, do you think I can find the reference? Of course not! Sorry. But remember, in those days, priests in the temple under the sacrificial system of worship had extremely difficult physical work to fulfill at the altar using lambs, goats, and bulls. Need I say more? So with this in mind, I am guessing Zechariah and Elizabeth were around the midcentury mark in years and thoroughly embarrassed and humiliated that they were childless. It was as if God had forgotten them. Now here is the exciting part. When Zachariah was performing his duties, probably with his mind on how close he was to the actual Presence of God given his present responsibility, he was shocked and frightened to find an angel on the right side of the altar of incense. The angel told him his wife would become pregnant and would have a son they would name John. "He will be a joy and delight to you. Be great in the sight of the Lord. Will not drink wine or fermented drink" (Lk. 1:14-15). But here is the most exciting part: "He will be filled with the Holy Spirit, even from birth . . . will also go before the Lord in the spirit and power of Elijah' (Lk. 1:17). And guess what? The angel's name is Gabriel. Yep . . . the same Gabriel who came to Mary.

Zachariah became incredulous and is rendered mute until after the miracle baby is born, because he didn't believe the angel. Most of this information comes from Luke, but because Mark is such a short gospel, this seems like a good place to fill in some blanks. All the gospel writers honor John as the forerunner of our Lord, and since we will meet him one day, he is one New Testament saint I don't want to ignore. I don't even know if Zachariah and Elizabeth knew what the Holy Spirit was at this point. Don't forget, the third party of the Trinity wouldn't be mentioned in the New Testament until the next paragraph in Mark, where we see John baptizing Jesus in the Jordan and a "spirit descending on Him like a dove" (Mk. 1:10). The Holy Spirit was indeed given to Old Testament people on a "need" basis. For instance, those working on the temple with implements of bronze and gold were given the Spirit, so they could perform their jobs according to God's exact specifications. If Zachariah had known his Talmud, he would have remembered the fourth word in the book of Genesis is the Hebrew plural of the word "God": Elohim: "More than one, less than many." This is our first clue of the Trinity: "And the Spirit of God was hovering over the face of the water" (Gen. 1:2). Yep, He was there in the beginning. So was Jesus. Genesis 1:25 also confirms the plural characteristics of a triune God.

Following the baptism of Jesus, the Holy Spirit was not given until after the resurrection, and this happened at Pentecost (the Jewish Feast of Weeks), which is why I mentioned earlier this was an important date for both Christians and Jews.

Jesus' baptism in Mark 1:9-13 is essentially the same as Matthew's and deserves a triangle in the margin of your Bible. Directly after this event, Jesus goes into the wilderness and has his first direct encounter with Satan, during which time John the Baptist is imprisoned. Both paragraphs are short and to the point. Jesus was alone with only angels to minister to Him. I don't mean to lessen the importance of the angels with the word "only." What I mean is no one else with human skin was with Him while He fasted in the wilderness for forty days, which is probably symbolic of the forty years the Israelites wandered in the desert. Directly after these two events, Jesus' preaching and teaching ministry took off in full stride.

The beginning of choosing the apostles coincides with the beginning of Jesus' earthly ministry, and the same four apostles are always mentioned first. They went into Capernaum on the Sabbath, and I have noticed that Jesus really didn't go back home to Nazareth after His ministry began. Capernaum seemed to be His home base during His three years of ministry, though He would always be known as "Jesus of Nazareth." His only trip back "home" was met with unbelief, so He could do very little while there.

Two things interest me in the first chapter of Mark: after the four newly chosen apostles and Jesus left the synagogue, they went into the house of Simon and Andrew, who were brothers, where they found Simon Peter's mother-in-law ill. Of course Jesus healed her; after her fever left, she got up and waited on them.

The amazing things about this story is that my Catholic friends tell me their church dates back to St. Peter as the first pope. My question was if he could be married and still conduct his religious duties, what happened to change this in later centuries? I have a hard time with many things "man" changes that I can't find in the Bible.

The second thing I noted was Mark 1:38, when Jesus said: "'Let us go somewhere else . . . to the nearby villages, so I can preach there also. This is why I have come.'" This reminds me of the verse in Matthew 18:11, which says, "For the Son of Man has come to save that which was lost."

Do these two verses contradict each other? Of course not! They explain one another. A person cannot be saved unless he or she knows the truth . . . the whole story. That's what Jesus was doing: telling the whole story. He said, "'I am the way, the truth and the life. No one comes to the Father except through Me" (Jn. 14:6). How could they know if He didn't tell?

Chapter 3 brings us to the final selection of the twelve apostles, which was completed "up on a mountain", Mk 3:13. No wonder churches have so many committees! The Lord initiated the practice of a leadership team from the very beginning of His ministry and showed us how to follow by example. Whenever the twelve are mentioned in Scripture, Simon, whose name was changed to Peter, is always mentioned first, with the brothers James and John following. Jesus called James and John "Sons of Thunder," probably referring to their intense, outspoken personalities. Funny, I don't understand that from reading Scripture. I "get" the personality of Simon Peter, who often spoke without thinking and is definitely a strong leader. I "get" the personality of John, because of his many writings—the gospel in his name; 1, 2, and 3 John; plus Revelation—but I have never perceived a personality for brother James. In fact, it surprised me he was the older of the two. He was the first of the twelve to be martyred, so he must have been very strong and a threat to the establishment.

One of the questions I always had about the apostles was why their names were often different in the Gospels. The reason for this is that some of them had different names depending on how they were described. Thaddaeus is also called Lebbaeus in Matthew, and he is also called "Judas son of James," all being correct but confusing to the reader. John, the apostle writer, calls him Judas (not Iscariot). So if you are as curious about the twelve apostles as I have always been, remember Lebbaeus (Mt.), Thaddaeus (Mk.), and Judas (Lk.) are the same person. Now if that isn't confusing enough, the gospel writer

John calls Bartholomew by the name of Nathaniel, who is always paired with Phillip. I have charted these names so many times, and I still get confused. If you think about it, though, it's not that unusual to be known by more than one name. Okay, here's an example: my name is really Joanne Marie (Carlson) Weigel, but I have been Jody since about the age of nine or ten. A few people who know me from early childhood still call me Joanne, several call me Mrs. Weigel, my children call me Mom, and my grandchildren call me Grammie Jody. I am all these names, depending on who is speaking and how they know me. Clear as mud? Many times in life you just have to have a sense of humor and go with the flow. Let's move on.

## CHAPTER 13

# MARK FOUR - SIX

> But let all who take refuge in You be glad; let them ever sing for joy. Spread Your protection over them, that those who know Your name may rejoice in You. (Ps. 5-11)

We begin chapter 4 of the gospel of Mark with the parable of the soils, also written in the Synoptic Gospels of Matthew (13) and Luke (8). I particularly like this parable, because all three gospel writers took the time to explain it as Jesus taught it. I can look back on my own life and remember times that I "heard" the Word, but as soon as I was away from the source, it was out of my mind, and I was off shopping, getting ready for a party, or driving children somewhere. I had a hard time reconciling biblical truths to the reality of the life I was living. They didn't mesh; nor did I want them to. I just wasn't interested. I was simply one of those people who God had to hit over the head so I had nowhere to look but up. Be sure to read this parable in terms of your own life, and see what you come up with. I hope your memories are better than mine. The remainder of chapter 4 are parables, and getting into chapter 5, we again find the demons cast into swine, which we discussed during our reading of Matthew.

The amazing thing about Jairus' daughter in chapter 5 is that she had actually died by the time Jesus got to her. Again we see Jesus taking the inner circle with Him: Peter, James, and John. The first thing Jesus did was to empty the house and not allow anyone but the child and her parents with them. The twelve-year-old child was restored to life as soon as Jesus took her hand and spoke to her, telling her to "arise."

I think it is significant that Jesus did not allow anyone with wavering faith in the room while He was performing the most miraculous healing He could do: to bring someone back from death as he did with Lazarus in the eleventh chapter of John and as He did with the widow's only son in Luke 7:11. This was a fairly private healing, whereas Lazarus was in-your-face-public for all the community to see. The difference was the timing. The more miracles, the more word spread about His signs and wonders, the closer He got to Golgotha.

Another point I want to make is when we have a problem and real prayer concern, I think we need to make sure we surround ourselves with people who really believe in Christ. When we ask for prayer, let's be sure we are asking of faith-based friends and not doubting thomases. It is important to bring God energy—not fear or doubt energy—into a crucial prayer situation. Remember, Jesus said, "Don't be afraid. Just believe" (Mk. 5:36).

Chapter 6 finds Jesus in His hometown of Nazareth but with so much unbelief He could do very little relative to His ministry elsewhere, and we don't find him returning to Nazareth again. The thing that really interested me in this chapter was the naming of his younger brothers—James, Joses, Judas, and Simon—and His "sisters" (plural). This was a local family in a town where everybody knew everybody, and they just couldn't buy into the reality that God's Son had grown up among them without their knowledge. Jesus must have kept a pretty low profile in Nazareth. And I have a theory about this. When Jesus was twelve years old, the whole family and the community caravanned to Jerusalem for the Passover. This would be the year Jesus would prepare for His bar mitzvah, and because of His preparation for His life's ministry and intense interest, He ended up staying in the temple, listening to and talking with the priests and rabbis. This story is told in the second chapter of Luke. His parents found Him after several days of worrying and searching. Jesus was repentant and immediately went back to Nazareth with them to enter into family life. This incident is the last time we read about Jesus' earthly father, Joseph, so we can only assume he died when Jesus was a teenager, which left Jesus with a huge responsibility. As the oldest son, He would have had to help train four younger brothers in a profession . . . we assume carpentry, which could have included wood carving or making furniture. Not only did four boys have to be educated, the sisters (plural, at least two) needed to find suitable husbands with dowries secured. Without a father in the household, this responsibility would have fallen to Jesus. No wonder He didn't have time to begin His public ministry until He was thirty years old. Now remember, I am not a theologian, and this is strictly conjecture on my part, along with the theory He started His ministry at the same age as priests. I am just throwing out ideas to expand our thinking and make Jesus more real to us in His unknown years.

Another interesting thing about chapter 6 is when Jesus sent the apostles out for ministry, He sent them out "two by two" and told them to take nothing extra with them, to go to a house, and minister from one place. They were given the ability to have power over unclean spirits (verse 7), cast out demons, and anoint with oil many who were sick and to heal them (verse 13). I think about this verse every time I see young men in black pants and white shirts, going house to house and giving out the tract called *The Lighthouse*. I don't remember which "sect" this is, but apparently they have never read this verse in Mark.

We also have the feeding of the five thousand in chapter 6 and this verse, "For they [the Apostles] did not understand about the loaves because their heart was hardened" (Mk. 6:5).

Lord God, if the apostles didn't understand a miracle of this magnitude, how in the world are we here on earth to understand? They walked, prayed, and listened to You daily for three years . . . we walk by faith and not by sight (2 Cor. 5:7). But Holy Spirit faith can open doors of our limitations as well as our understanding. Thank you! How I wish I could have walked in the Holy Land with You, Jesus. Please don't let my heart be hardened. Today is our National Day of Prayer here in the United States, and for the first time since its inception, the White House is not honoring the occasion. Lord, You have commanded us to pray for those who have authority over us, and I do pray for our president, his family, and his cabinet. I especially pray for the dignity and ethics of the office of the president. But O Lord, "czars" in America? If my heart is not hardened, it is nearly broken! I do pray for You to still the hand that would take away our democracy and freedom. I pray for you to open the hearts of all our lawmakers in Washington, D.C., that they might know You and officiate with Your help as our forefathers did. I am so reminded of the Old Testament Israelites who often had an evil king ruling over them, who did not know You or rule according to Your precepts . . . without Your guidance or wisdom . . . and I believe there are no authority figures placed in Washington D.C., or elsewhere, without Your permission. I don't know what lesson we need to learn from this administration, but I surely hope we learn it soon. Please, God, open their hearts, minds, and souls to the Truth as modeled by Jesus, the Christ, Messiah Lord.

> If my people who are called by My name, will humble themselves and pray and seek My face and turn from their wicked ways, then I will hear from heaven and will forgive their sin and heal their land. (2 Chron. 7:14)

> Lord God, we have troops fighting on foreign soil this very day to protect precious freedom. Please bless them, protect them, and encourage them this day. Lord, forgive our entire country! We kill our babies with abortion and think nothing of it. We don't visit the sick, the orphans, the widows, or those in prison, and we forget to pray for them.

> Forgive us, Father, for thinking we are in charge of our lives and can make plans without even consulting You. Forgive me, Lord, for being such a poor wife to Bob. I know how much he values food and how important good desserts are to him. And Lord, I confess, I really have lost all interest in food of any kind. I really wish I cared more about menus and housekeeping skills, and I can't even imagine what to do to try to improve! Lord, all things are possible through You. Please give me a servant's heart toward Bob. He is such a good man; I just couldn't ask for better. He has provided for me in such a remarkable manner. I truly want for nothing, and my husband has given me the most precious and the most loving children in the world. I am so grateful for my family, and I know every good and perfect gift comes from the Father of heavenly lights (Jas. 1:17).

Please accept this plea for help. I lay this at the foot of the cross on this National Day of Prayer. I'm sorry to be so self-centered, and . . . what . . . melancholy . . . down? Help, Lord.

My last reading for the day:

"In my distress, I called upon the Lord, and cried out to my God; He heard my voice from His temple, and my cry came before Him, even to His ears." (Ps. 18:6) Amen

# CHAPTER 14

# MARK SEVEN - NINE

Another lovely spring day, and I awoke with a feeling of being cared for. Thank You, Lord, for taking my concerns. I actually get to play tennis today with Kim and two of her good friends, who have also become my friends. What a blessing! Kim has been so gracious to include me with her scrapbooking friends, who are all parents of teenagers. Another mom like me is included, and we have all become such good friends. Scrapbooking has become what quilting was in the past two centuries: an opportunity to gather weekly with friends to work on our own albums and experience just plain fellowship. I have not met many of the children in the group, but feel I know them well from their moms. Often during the week, something will come up to remind me to pray for one or two of the teens we have discussed among ourselves. It is certainly a Christ-centered group from several different churches, and they have been a blessing to me when I am home in Lincoln. Kim and I will be playing with two of these friends this morning. How fun!

I love getting up so much earlier than Bob in the morning, so I can get my quiet time in before the rest of the day begins. It somehow makes everything go so much smoother during the day, and I am often reminded of verses I have read earlier that I can apply to my life. The "knowing" part is the easiest . . . it's the "doing" part that gets harder. That's my will trying. I want Your will to be so automatic that at the end of the day I can look back and say, "Thank You, Lord. I did something with my hands for Yours and didn't realize it until right now." My daughter, Kim, just does things like that so automatically.

Every time I talk to her, she has fixed dinner for someone just home from the hospital, taken cookies to someone else, or is having a family over for dinner. It's just a way of life for her family, and I envy her for the ease she has in entertaining and cooking for people (me included). She definitely didn't get this talent from me, but I'm so glad she has it. Our son, Andy, also loves to cook and is really good at it. Fortunately for him, his wife, Sandy, is also a great cook, and they do have fun putting their talents together in the kitchen. Obviously, we love to be included at both our children's dining room tables. Wouldn't you think some of this talent would rub off on me? Okay, they are both in their forties, so they are not "children" anymore, but you know how us moms are! They will be our "children" no matter how old we all get.

Now on to our next three chapters in Mark.

## *Chapters 7-9*

> "All the ends of the world shall remember and turn to the Lord, and all the families of the nations shall worship before You. For the Kingdom is the Lord's and He rules over the nations." (Ps. 22:27) Amen.

Chapter 7 continues Jesus' teaching with several of the same stories in Matthew. What caught my attention is His statement in verse 5: "There is nothing that enters a man from outside which can defile him; but the things which come out of him; those are the things that defile a man" (Mk. 7:5).

He goes on to explain that what enters a person's stomach does not enter his heart and is eliminated, making all foods acceptable (Mk. 7:19). I'm not even going to touch what a cardiologist would have to say about that statement in this day and age. But the teaching goes on to tell us what really defiles a man, and it comes from his heart: evil thoughts, adultery, fornication, murder, theft, covetousness, wickedness, deceit, lewdness, an evil eye, blasphemy, pride, and foolishness. Lord, forgive me, I have not been guilty of what I consider the "big, awful" ones, but I have indeed been guilty of covetousness, pride, and foolishness. And I know *all* wrongdoing is sin. Jesus told us, "For whoever keeps the whole law and yet stumbles at just one point, is guilty of breaking all of it" (Jas. 2:10).

Thank You, Lord, that when we confess our sin, You are faithful and just to forgive us our sins and purify us from all unrighteousness (1 Jn. 1:9). Whew!

I cannot leave chapter 7 without commenting on the Greek, Syrophoenician woman who was frantic to have her demon-possessed daughter healed. I can only think this was an extreme mental disability of some sort. If you have children, think back to when they were young, when you had full responsibility for them, and you will recognize this woman would move heaven and earth to have her daughter healed. I'm sure when she heard Jesus was going to be in the vicinity, she made a beeline for His attention for healing and wholeness. Her daughter was probably in no controllable condition to accompany her, so this mother did everything she could—including begging. Jesus reply astonished me the first time I read it when He said, "'Let the children be filled first, for it is not good to take the children's bread and throw it to the little dogs'" (Mk. 7:27). The reason I was so surprised was because it seemed so apparent Jesus was calling this woman and/or her daughter "little dogs." Huh? Then I remembered two verses that were helpful for me:

> "I was not sent except to the lost sheep of the House of Israel." (Mt. 15:24)

> "For I am not ashamed of the gospel of Christ for it is the power of God to salvation for everyone who believes, first for the Jew and also for the Greek. "(Rom. 1:16)

Okay, change of attitude many years ago. Not being Jewish, I feel very fortunate and blessed that Jesus extended His ministry and salvation to all people. Me included! And this sweet, desperate mother had such a beautiful reply. She was not offended, but had an immediate comeback! "'Yes, Lord, even the little dogs under the table eat from the children's crumbs'" (Mk. 7:28).

Jesus saw her grief, faith, and respect for Him (she had called Him "Lord"), and the daughter was healed from that moment. Long distance. Sight unseen. Don't you know that family's faith and hope had changed from that day on? This is one mother I can't wait to meet in heaven. I love her already!

Chapter 8 continues the healing ministry with significant teaching to the apostles in preparation for Calvary, and including Peter's confession to Jesus, "You are the Christ", Mk.8:29, the long awaited Messiah. Something we all need to do when we come to Christ: acknowledge him as the Son of God.

Chapter 9 recalls the transfiguration and the amazing meeting with Elijah, Moses, and even Father God appearing in a cloud. Peter's fear was making him babble, and it was as if the Father was saying, "Peter, stop talking and listen. This is My Beloved Son. Hear Him" (Mk. 9:7). I relate to Peter. I would be totally flustered too. And when I am, it's as if God reaches down and says, "Be still and know I am God" (Ps. 46:10). And I am humbled. And I am still.

Jesus continues his healing and teaching in preparation for His death. Two phrases to remember and memorize in this chapter: a young boy who had a "spirit" within him that rendered him mute . . . detail found only in Mark . . . and the disciples could not heal the boy. The father appeals to Jesus and His compassion, and He heals the boy. Then comes this beautiful phrase: "If you can believe, all things are possible to him who believes" (Mk. 9:23).

And the honest reply with tears: "Lord, I believe. Help my unbelief" (Mk. 9: 24).

I've been there. Have you? When you come on hands and knees to the foot of the cross with this plea for help, the Lord always answers. Look for it. Always. The Lord wants us to have faith and belief, so when we pray this prayer to believe, we know it is in accordance with His will. And whatever is in accordance with His will, He is gracious to help us with. We pray many prayers that could have a yes answer, and when that happens, doors fly open to our request. Or it could be a no answer, in which case we keep on praying and lifting that loved one up to the Lord for His timing, not ours. "Therefore, my dear friend, continue to work out your salvation with fear and trembling, for it is God who works in you to will and to act according to His good purpose" (Phil. 1:12-13).

## CHAPTER 15

# PERSONAL

From Chambers' *My Utmost for His Highest:* "Faith is the supreme effort of your life . . . throwing yourself with abandon and total confidence upon God."

Yes! I can face anything in life without wavering, because I know God is always orchestrating this concern, and when I have some down days, they don't last very long, because Jesus, I know You . . . and that underlying faith is more than adequate to see me through a life of expectancy and truly, mostly joy. When and if I can't find the joy, it's not because the Lord has moved . . . it's me. And I know how to find my way back! Sometimes I just need a "pity party" and a venue to let loose. Thank You, Jesus, for Holy Spirit faith that has no end. I know that I know that I know . . . and it's not what I know . . . it's *who*. That will never change. You have said, "Never will I leave you nor forsake you!" Thank You. I believe that with all my heart!

I just noticed the date and am remembering another spring day on May 8, 1947, in Albion, Nebraska, where the sheets and quilts all smell fresh and good right off the outdoor line, and when morning doves coo me awake in the early morning cool with a promise of daytime warmth to come. The lilacs and spirea were all in bloom then too, along the alleyway in back of Grammie's house. My mother and aunts sent me to my cousins' house to spend the night. The call came while Patsy Ruth and I were having breakfast, and I heard her mother say, "I'll send her home right after breakfast." And I knew my Grammie Mansfield had died in the night. Tears blinded me as I ran to Grammie's house—my mother's childhood home, where she and her five sisters were raised.

Aunt Ora was vacuuming her newly installed wall-to-wall carpet, being careful not to scratch her beautiful Steinway grand piano, where she so faithfully taught many generations of Albion kids to play. Her eyes were all red as she gave me a weak smile. I could only think of the day before, when I had burst into Grammie's makeshift bedroom in the large dining room off the kitchen in a childhood snit because I couldn't get the curls out of my hair. My mother quickly quieted me and led me over to Grammie's bed, where she looked at my tear-stained face with those beautiful blue eyes with so much love and compassion, it filled me to the brim. Grammie had suffered strokes, and all six sisters were on deathwatch for her; my mom was the most crucial, because she was a retired registered nurse, a degree that provided the family with much pride. Grammie couldn't talk, but holding one of my hands, she used the other one to point to herself and then put her hand over her heart and pointed to me. I love you. Even as a ten-year-old, I got that message! I was so overwhelmed with emotions and tried to process everything around me, but I was mute. Speechless. Mother led me back into the kitchen. I was remembering this scene so vividly the next day, when the grief and guilt came. I didn't even tell her I loved her too. How could I not? I was stunned at my own inadequacies.

That was over sixty years ago, and I remember it like it was yesterday. I still cry at my stupidity. The smell of spring in Nebraska brings back so many memories, and sometimes I can't even remember what happened last week! Sheesh! It brings me great comfort to know that Mom is now reunited with her parents and all seven (one died in infancy) sisters. I'll always remember the kitchen stool that was "mine," because there weren't enough chairs to go around the old enamel table. Oh Lord, thank You for memories that are so very precious to me. Help me make sure everyone around me knows with certainty that I love them. I am no longer as reticent as I was as a ten-year-old, but sometimes I do forget. But as a ten-year-old, I was a long way from being a Christian or knowing anything about Jesus or the precious gift of the Holy Spirit to temper my selfish, self-centered character with the fruits I so desperately needed. It would be many years later that You would finally get my attention and fulfill a spiritual side in me. I often wonder why it took so long, but I believe that, too, was part of Your plan for my life. "I know the plans I have for you, says the Lord, plans for good and not for evil, plans to give you a future and hope" (Jer. 29:11). Thank You, Lord, for speaking to me right out of the pages of Your Word.

I want very much to remember Aunt Ora. I always knew Aunt Ora. She was the taller, thinner twin, who was the musician. One of my first memories was when I must have been around seven years old, and we were visiting Albion. It was dusk, and I was sitting at the bottom of the stairway leading up to the big screened-in porch, where Aunt Ora and Uncle Bob were quietly talking. They obviously didn't know I was near when Aunt Ora asked Uncle Bob if they could have me if my parents decided to get a divorce. I was so stunned; I don't believe I breathed for a while! Uncle Bob, who was the county treasurer and rubbed shoulders with attorneys in the courthouse all day long, answered that he was quite sure the courts would not allow me to leave the care of my mother should that event take place. As shocked as I was, the one thing I always remember from this incident is that my aunt Ora loved me and would have taken me. I never told a soul about this unfortunate bit of information, and the next year, my mother was pregnant with my sister Nancy. So although there were some rough years, my parents stayed together until death separated them. When Aunt Ora died, I asked to commemorate her at her funeral. This is what I said:

Dear Aunt Ora,

I'm so glad to pay tribute to you in your own church today. It's important for me to let you know one last time how dear you are to me, how much I love you, and how special you have always been in my life.

When I was growing up, my family always came to Albion for almost all holidays—Thanksgiving, Christmas, Easter—and at least several weeks during the summer. We always stayed at your house (that used to be Grammie's), and each time we came, you were so excited to see us that I could hardly wait to arrive. You made me feel like I was the most wonderful little girl in the whole world!

Aunt Ora, you are one of the people who taught me about God when I was growing up, even though I couldn't see it at the time. You never talked theology with me; that wasn't your style. Instead, you modeled what it was to be a Christian woman living in the community. You accepted your God-given musical gifts and used them in every way you could through music lessons and playing the organ for this Methodist Church for so many years . . . and doing it with so much dedication and real joy. I saw all that as I grew up, Aunt Ora, and I was always so proud of you, sitting right behind the minister at your organ. I remember when Aunt Alice was dying in California . . . how you grabbed your Bible and went to her. How I envied your strength and faith on that trip! I hope someone was here for you too, in your last days with a Bible in hand.

But the real lesson in theology I learned from you was your unending love for me. You didn't have to tell me you loved me; I could feel it in your hugs and see it in your beautiful blue eyes. And the amazing thing was no matter how naughty, selfish, or undeserving I was, you hung right in there, loving me, being proud of me, and seeing all the good qualities I couldn't even find . . . the whole time. That's how you helped teach me about God. I came much later in my life to learn that He loves me the same way. How can I ever thank you for showing me that?

And Aunt Ora, you showed me even more by letting me know through your life that it's! acceptable not to be accomplished in the kitchen . . . that it is o.k. to pursue other God-given gifts, and to be grateful other people are talented in the cooking department! You and I talked about our mutual specialties . . . crisp bacon and the "Mansfield Special": peanut butter sandwiches! I still think of your house in Albion every time I smell bacon frying. I can close my eyes and feel the fresh, line-dried sheets and the soft, handmade quilts wrapped around my body. And I can picture you in the kitchen, fixing your specialty, that I know you always prepared for us with so much love . . . even as you were thinking ahead to a wedding or funeral to play for or special music for Sunday morning. Your house truly was my "little house on the prairie," even though it felt huge, safe, and snug with the big screened-in front porch where everyone gathered with ice cream on warm summer evenings.

I'm so grateful God didn't give you children of your own, because even though you had Hazel, your step-daughter, I watched you reach out to all eleven of us cousins and love us just like we belonged to you anyway. Not to mention all the children you nourished through piano lessons for years. Maybe some, like me, are not playing very much anymore, but I'll bet they still love the sounds of Bach, Beethoven, and Schubert that you introduced to us many years ago. I know I do.

I think one of my favorite memories of you involves the long talks and laughter we all shared, late at night around your kitchen table . . . often with popcorn and homemade fudge, a combination I learned to love in your kitchen. And how I hated to go to bed and leave you all up, talking and laughing together. I was so glad to finally grow up and not have to leave all the fun we had around that old enamel kitchen table! Weren't those the best of times, Aunt Ora?

Of the six of you sisters, there are only two left now—my mom, Ethel, and Aunt Erma! And neither of them are well right now. (If you could send each of them an angel, it sure would be great.) When its their time to join you, they won't be back here in this church where they all grew up, because they both live too far away. But I know you have gone ahead, just like Jesus did, to prepare a place for them and, indeed, for all of us who share the joy of knowing Christ as our Lord and Savior. So for me, this feels like a real ending for a part of my life without a reason to come back to Albion. And that makes me sad. For that reason, I need to say thank you not only to you, dear one, but to my relatives gathered here today and this entire community for helping me to grow up and cultivate values that are lasting and real and shared, as well as good, happy memories.

But I am really thanking the Lord for your pain-free death, and Aunt Ora, I am celebrating your "homecoming" last Saturday night. What a reunion party that must have been! I can almost hear the laughter. I just know when the Lord greeted you, He must have said, "Well done, my good and faithful servant. Welcome home."

I can't hear your music with my ears anymore, but Aunt Ora, I will always hear it in my heart. Save a place for me. You know how I hate to miss a good family party!

Lots of love from your niece, Jody

# CHAPTER 16

# PERSONAL

Good morning, Lord. Today is Saturday, the day I bring You authority figures and other friend's loved ones, so I will pause now to do that. And my wonderful country! How much we take for granted our freedom ! Thank You for hearing my prayers, Lord. I am forever grateful.

> "You have tested my heart. You have visited me in the night. "(Ps. 17:3) Amen

How many times, Lord, have I gone to bed with a problem and awakened with a solution, and a clear mind? You are so awesome!

> "The Lord rewarded me according to my righteousness; according to the cleanliness of my hands He has recompensed me, I have kept the ways of the Lord and have not departed from myGod.". (Ps. 18:20-21)

Dear God, surely the above verse is my prayer for me. I always desire clean hands and to keep all Your ways. Only with Your help, Lord. Only with Your help. I know I have not reached sanctification, as it must be a lifelong process of great strides forward (mountaintop experiences) and ugly falls backward into the valley of despair. But I know I am on the path, and I am grateful beyond words for the numerous ways You have blessed me.

As usual, people always first among my blessings. And my kitty, Kiki, a stray who comes directly from You. She tells me every day she loves me, and when she does, it reminds me to tell You "Thank You" every day and how much I love and treasure Your presence in my life.

> "As for God, His way is perfect: The Word of the Lord is proven; He is a shield to all who trust in Him". (Ps. 18:30)

Please allow me to tell you about Kiki. Expecting luncheon guests from Denver and satisfied that all was on schedule in the kitchen of our Lincoln home, I walked out to my front garden to pick flowers for the table. A gray streak crossed my path, and the first thing I said was "Scat." With my mind on entertaining (not an easy thing for me), I did not have time to think about a stray feline. When my guests arrived, they informed me a small cat was sitting in my front garden, and I assured them it was not ours. We forgot about our outdoor visitor while in pleasant conversation indoors, but midafternoon, when my guests left, there she sat in my garden, keeping her distance and studying us intently as we said our good-byes. Before going back indoors, I got a better look at this animal and decided she was fairly pathetic in appearance: very thin and small, her ears were too big for her face, and her legs were too long for her body. I guessed her to be quite young, maybe six or seven months old, and resolutely shut the door, promising myself to forget this visitor my mother would have called an "alley cat." But her black stripes and white paws identified her more accurately as a "tiger" cat, hardly an elegant representative of the species.

The next day, while I was in our dressing room off our bedroom, I glanced out the window and much to my surprise, the little cat was sitting on the window ledge, watching me with great interest. I saw her little mouth form a "meow" as she humped her back against the window frame as soon as she caught my eye. *Oh no,* I thought, *I will not be taken in by this lost stray! If I ignore her, she will find her way home. Yeah* right!

A day later, I was completely surprised to notice that wherever I was in the house, the little cat would find a perch on a window ledge and watch me. By the third day, I was onto her antics, and when I awoke early to retrieve the morning paper, I first peeked around the corner of the dining room in the front of the house. And there she sat, waiting for me to make an appearance with another mouthed "meow." How did this cat know where I was going to be, and how in the world do I get rid of her? I finally presented the possible problem to my husband, who emphatically told me to find her a home . . . and do it within two days before our summer sojourn to Colorado. My husband rang every doorbell in our neighborhood, inquiring who might have lost a cat. I phoned Animal Control, the Humane Society, and every local radio station hoping to find someone looking for a lost kitty. I finally resorted to friends, and after the tenth call, found a family who had four young boys who had lost their last cat to a coyote and promised to come pick up the stay kitty the next day. Whew!

Since I knew this young cat was going to have a home, and she had been camping at our home for three days, I relented and searched my kitchen for something appropriate to feed her. It turned out to be a "nuked" half hamburger patty, which I presented to kitty on the front stoop, where I sat and watched her eagerly consume the meal. This was the closest I had been to the animal, even though we had definitely developed a relationship in the three days she had been stalking me. As she finished her meal, I stood up and leaned down to pet the top of her head, touching her physically for the first time. Before I could straighten up, kitty stood up on her two back legs and extended both front paws to either side of my face, looking directly into my eyes. I was so astonished at this "thank you" in response to my belated act of kindness, I almost backed up over the stoop!

*Well,* I thought, *those little boys are going to get a kind, gentle pet.*

The next day, our appointment for the adoption transfer was midafternoon, and since a crew of window washers were working on the outside of our house, I cautiously brought kitty into the library and shut the door to await her new family. With a book in my hand, I settled down in my chair and watched the little cat explore every surface of the room, after which she very gently hopped onto my lap, looked into my face, and napped while she purred. She had very successfully wrapped herself around my heartstrings at this point, and the thought of four very active, rambunctious boys with this gentle creature was painful.

But at the appointed time of transfer, I gave her over to the eager young family in a kitty carrier borrowed from my daughter, who already owned three cats and was well equipped for feline emergencies. As the new owner's van pulled out of our driveway, I was brokenhearted to see them leave. When my husband returned home and I told him about the farewell, we both had tears as he said, "Maybe we were too hasty to give her away." Sigh.

The next day we left for our home in Colorado for the summer, assuring each other that a cat, or any pet, was out of the question at this stage of our lives. It just wouldn't work to transport an animal from the Midwest to our home in the desert several times a year. How could we ever manage that? After all, we were at the stage of our lives to simplify and enjoy semiretirement years rather than assume more responsibility. It just didn't make sense. But I couldn't make my heart believe what my mind was saying.

All this was reported to our daughter, Kim, who had the responsibility of calling the new family to retrieve her carrier. In the course of the conversation, Kim asked if they had yet bonded with the new kitty and said perhaps we were too hasty giving her away. Our daughter asked if she could possibly come get her back. The mother was so gracious and said kitty had cried most of the night, and, of course, she would return her.

When our daughter's family arrived at our home in Colorado two days later for their pre-planned summer vacation (God's timing!) they had an extra bundle in the cat carrier. Kitty came into our great room, did some exploring while the family whooped and hollered our hellos and welcome, and as we all settled down on the sofas to watch, kitty took one look at me and settled down on my lap as we continued to chat happily around her, listening to the story of the near-escape at the security checkpoint in the Lincoln airport before our son-in-law, Mike, could outrun and catch her with security looking perplexed.

We named her "Kiki Kamper," because she responds when we call "kitty-kitty, and she "kamped" at our house for three days. Our rational minds told us it was not possible for us to have a pet, but Kiki told us otherwise. She chose us, and although she would not have been my choice of feline, I tell her every day how beautiful she is, and she tells us every day how much she loves us. She fits comfortably under the seat of airplanes and has learned the terrain around our homes. No doubt about it, we have been blessed by her presence. She is a very special gift. When our daughter took Kiki to the vet for a health certificate before they could take her on a United Airlines flight, we were surprised to learn she was a small eight-month-old and had already been spayed. Her paws were in good condition, and there were no fleas, mites, or ticks. Her origins will forever remain a mystery. That was nine years ago this summer. What a dear little blessing she has been for us!

The problem with journaling is simply that it is so easy to start looking back and remembering . . . especially after thanking the Lord for blessings and joys in our lives. I absolutely promise to get right back into the gospel of Mark tomorrow. Honest!

# CHAPTER 17

# MARK TEN - TWELVE

> "The judgments of the Lord are true and righteous altogether; more to be desired are they than gold, yea, than much fine gold". (Ps. 19:9b-10a)

Good morning, Lord. I know your judgments are true and righteous, and this morning in church we heard about the church of Thyatira and how a Jezebel was leading Your people astray with false teaching.

> "and I gave her time to repent of sexual immorality and she did not repent. Indeed I will cast her into a sickbed and those who commit adultery with her into great tribulation unless they repent of their deeds." (Rev. 2:21-22)

Father God, You know I have been praying for two friends who are very ill right now. Lord, I don't know if either has a spiritual belief, and I can only pray there is someone close to come near to each of them with a Bible in hand. This morning's sermon gave me much to think about, and for all I know, each of their illnesses may be in response to their own inability to repent or that neither of them knows it is necessary. It's so hard to know, but the thought did take a great deal of responsibility away from me. My job is to pray; Yours is to send a messenger. I absolutely trust Your plan for each of us, Lord. Forgive me when I try to take over Your job. It happens too frequently!

Oh, Lord, here it is in my reading . . . the Twenty-Third Psalm:

> "The Lord is my Shepherd, I shall not want. He makes me lie down in green pastures. He leads me beside the still waters.
>
> He restores my soul; He leads me in the paths of righteousness for His name's sake.
>
> Yea, though I walk through the valley of the shadow of death, I will fear no evil; For you are with me: Your rod and Your staff, they comfort me.
>
> You prepare a table before me in the presence of my enemies. You anoint my head with oil. My cup runs over.
>
> Surely goodness and mercy shall follow me all the days of my life, and I will dwell in the house of the Lord, forever."

Every single line is amazing . . . uplifting . . . an anointed writing that goes right to my heart! "The Lord is my Shepherd." What does a shepherd do for us? Everything! Protection, guidance, healing, nourishment, leads us home, and sees to our every need. Hears us when we cry. Gives us solutions to problems, restores relationships. Everything a sheep cannot do for itself. Thank You that You are my Shepherd. Thank You for this most beautiful Psalm. It fills me with a special feeling that I can't describe. It is so dear to me! Now, finally, let's go back to Mark.

## *Chapters 10-12*

Chapter 10 begins with the Pharisees question: "Is it lawful for a man to divorce his wife?" (Mk. 10:2; they were always trying to trip Him up.) Jesus answered with words as meaningful today as then. Let's look together. Jesus said:

> "Because of the hardness of their heart, he [Moses] wrote this precept. [Divorce] 'But from the beginning of creation God made them male and female.' 'For this reason a man shall leave his father and mother and be joined to his wife, and the two shall become one flesh.' Therefore, what God has joined together, let man not separate." (Mk 10:5-9)

I would say the hardness of heart is still a big issue of divorce in this day and age. But the above scripture was God's intent for all marriages. We have sin issues that are not dealt with properly, biblically, and the result in our present culture is a divorce rate rapidly climbing over the 50 percent range. And sadly, this includes couples who profess to be Christians. What a very sad statistic! And the saddest is the rippling effect divorce has on everyone involved. The fact is, we live in a fallen, sinful world, and divorce is something we will no doubt have to deal with for the rest of our earthly lives. Yes, God makes allowances and permits divorce under certain circumstances, but it is still painful and something I don't want to discuss or judge. And no, God doesn't want anyone to live in an abusive, addictive, or worse circumstance. I thank God I don't have to deal with this subject with either family or friends right now. We have all known friends whose divorce after many years of marriage has left devastation scattered everywhere. The pain, depression, and heartbreak extend beyond the immediate family. Extended family hurts just as badly.

The other stories in chapter 10 are repeated in the other Synoptic Gospels, but I draw your attention to the request of James and John in Mark 10:35. They have come to Jesus with a request to "sit at Your side in Your glory." Do you remember how, as children, we all had the "me first syndrome," rushing to the playground to be first on the swings or raising our hands to be the first one chosen in school? These brothers were having a "childhood moment," is all I can think. "Me first, me first, choose me!" This is no excuse for them, but in Matthew, it is their mother, Salome, who at first asks Jesus if her sons could have that privilege. Here is a mother who wants only the best for her two boys, and she knows Who the best is! Don't we all want the very best for our children? But really, Salome! Don't you think that's a little too over the top?

Jesus handled it so well, and told them yes, they would "drink the drink and be baptized with the same baptism," but they would go through many trials just like the ones ahead of Jesus. And as it turned out, James was the first to be martyred. But Jesus said it was not up to Him who would sit on His right and His left.

How do you think the other apostles felt about this self-serving request? Of course they knew. Of course the other ten were displeased and had a right to be! I'm a little put out with them as well, but what we learn about his story is servanthood. "Whoever of you wants to be first shall be slave of all" (Mk. 10:44). What a lesson to learn!

And now the "kicker" verse: "For the Son of man did not come to be served, but to serve, and to give his life as a ransom for many" (Mk. 10:45).

Lord, God, help my selfish nature! Help me to learn how to serve. I do it so badly! And, of course, I want to sit next to Jesus too. Don't you?

In chapter 11, we come to what is traditionally called "Palm Sunday," Jesus' final week culminating His three-year ministry. Nothing is done by chance or by circumstance. It was all carefully planned by Jesus to fulfill prophecy. The Gospels tell of the triumphal entry into Jerusalem. All four also tell about the feeding of the five thousand. Those are the only two events repeated in all four gospels, except, of course, for the crucifixion. Matthew reports the donkey had a "colt" with her, and Mark gives the additional information that "no one had sat upon" the colt. It was unbroken. The significance of this is that the Jews thought animals that had never been ridden were especially suited for holy purposes. How would we have known that? The quote from Zechariah 9:9 prophecy is:

> "Rejoice greatly, O daughter of Zion! Shout, O daughter of Jerusalem! Behold, Your King is coming to you. He is just and having salvation, gentle and riding on a donkey, on a colt, the foal of a donkey."

The Jews would have recognized this act as fulfilled prophecy, if not immediately, then certainly in hindsight. A donkey is a symbol of peace and humility, not pride. In my younger days of community volunteering, I served as a docent at our wonderful Folsom's Children's Zoo in Lincoln. I had the honor of taking third-graders on tours of the zoo and telling them facts about the animals exhibited. My favorite were the Sicilian donkeys, gentle, tame animals that tolerated petting. They were gray, but on their upper back, just where the mane started, was a darker gray perfect cross about four inches long. Myth says the cross appeared on this breed right after the triumphal entry, because this was the species that carried Jesus into the city. I had such fun telling children that story and seeing their surprise! And that was a year or two before Jesus found me. Okay, Jesus "found" me way back when; it was a year or two before I found Him. (The Lord had been working on me long before my spiritual eyes were open.) That Mark, Luke, or John do not tell us there were two animals tied up does not bother me one bit. It was the younger, unbroken one that was important. (This is not a kind of detail to nitpick in the Bible. What is important to one author may be superfluous to another.) Jesus even knew the two apostles He sent would be questioned about the untying and taking of the colt. He had it planned down to the last detail. "The Lord has need of it." Wouldn't you give all you had if you heard those words? Of course you would! What skill or talent do you have right now that your Lord has need of? Just thinking. Not prying, mind you.

Matthew and Mark both write about Jesus' cursing a fig tree whose abundant leaves indicated an expectation of fruit. We will never understand this seemingly indiscriminate act unless we know fig trees in the Old Testament symbolize the Jewish nation in Hosea 9:10, Nahum 3:17, and Zechariah 3:10 (those hard to locate minor prophets). What Jesus expected and hoped for, either in the fig tree or Jewish nation, was not to be. This reminds me, what kind of fruit are you producing? If you have the Holy Spirit within you as a result of accepting Christ Jesus into your heart, you will produce fruit that never spoils: love, joy, peace, patience, kindness, goodness, faithfulness, gentleness, and self-control (Gal. 5:22). If you don't find those fruits within yourself, maybe it's time for a long talk with a good friend. Let's make Him a really Good Friend!

The cleaning of the temple contains beautiful words for all denominations to defer to:

> "My house shall be called a 'House of Prayer' for all nations. But you have made it a den of thieves." (Mk. 11:17)

This is a direct quote from Isaiah 56:7c. Elsewhere, Jesus refers to His body as a "house" or "temple." I believe His House will eventually be the place of prayer for all nations. It is just going to take a while by the looks of the spiritual temperature of the world. Just think: if our bodies are a temple of the Holy Spirit, and they are (3 Co. 3:16, 6:19), doesn't that tell you Jesus' resurrected body is the whole enchilada? You better believe it! Not only did the first-century temple need cleansing before it was destroyed in AD 70, our "temples" need cleansing from time to time also. When I first realized that fact, it gave me a desperate desire to stop smoking in 1979. I just couldn't figure out how to do it on my own, because I was so addicted to nicotine. So back to square one. I prayed, "Lord, I have a real desire to clean my body of impurities that I am smoking, but I just don't know how to do it."

Within one week of that prayer, a good friend, Phyllis, whom I have known since grade school, called me and said, "Jody, I have signed us both up for a Seventh Day Adventist four-day no smoking clinic. I am picking you up Thursday afternoon at 5:30." I was so flabbergasted at the almost instant response to my prayer. I never told my friend. I just went with her, and we both quit. That was September 9, 1979. I guess now I will tell her. She is one of my favorite bridge buddies when I am home in Lincoln. The Lord works in mysterious ways, and I am always amazed at His creativity and ingenuity. Our Lord is an awesome God!

Chapter 12 repeats parables and teachings from the first gospel. The question of taxes is certainly relevant to us today. When Jesus says, "Render to Caesar the things that are Caesar's, and to God the things that are God's" (Mk. 12:17), just substitute the acronym IRS for "Caesar," and you've got basic instructions for April 15 of each year.

The question of resurrection is teaching for the Sadducees, or for any of us who think physical death is the end of our lives, ending with the words:

> "I am the God of Abraham, the God of Izaak, and the God of Jacob." (Ex. 3:60)

> "He is not the God of the dead, but the God of the living." (Mk. 12:26b-27)

The answer as to which is the greatest commandment comes to us through Jesus:

> "Hear O Israel, the Lord our God, the Lord is One. And you shall love your God with all your heart, and with all your soul and with all your mind, and with all your strength. This is the first commandment and the second is like it: 'You shall love your neighbor as yourself.' There is no other commandment greater than these." (Mk. 12:29-31)

No wonder our Jewish friends are concerned that we are worshipping three "gods." The answer is, we are not. We are worshipping one God with three different manifestations or characteristics. My view is if we love God the Father spiritually, emotionally, and intellectually He will reveal Jesus. And Jesus will, in turn, reveal and give us the Holy Spirit. I did not become a Christian until 1975, but I always believed in and prayed to God the Father. Something deep within me always knew God was watching over me. It was truly the "church" part that I didn't understand. It wasn't talking my language intellectually or spiritually. I thank God often and fervently that has been corrected!

## CHAPTER 18

# MARK THIRTEEN - FOURTEEN

My devotion this morning is from *My Utmost for His Highest:*

> "The first thing God does is forcibly remove any insincerity, pride and vanity from my life. And the Holy Spirit reveals to me that God loved me not because I was loveable, but because it was His nature to do so."

Good morning, Lord! It's another dark, gloomy rainy day. My Law Wives Group is coming today for bridge. I shall make it as cheerful and sunny inside as I can! The devotional this morning was on brotherly love—good timing and reminder for me today. Lord, please be with Andy and Sandy this day as they travel to meetings for You in Atlanta. Watch over their activities and bless their ministry. Thank You for Andy's worldview that far exceeds mine. Protect Gramma Dee and the boys and the pets in their absence. I love You, Lord, and I praise your Holy name:

> "So do not fear, for I am with you. Do not be dismayed, for I am your God. I will strengthen you and help you. I will uphold you with my righteous right hand." (Is. 41:10)

Thank You, Lord. Your promises throughout the Bible give me such hope and security. And such a glimpse into Your characteristics that never cease to amaze me.

## *Chapters 13 and 14*

Chapter 13 of Mark, starting in verse 3, contains what is known as the Olivet Discourse or the Little Apocalypse. We have discussed this discourse in Matthew, chapter 24, but in this story from Mark, we are told who the disciples were who came to Him "privately" (Mt. 24:3). They were the apostles Peter, James, John, and Andrew. Jesus had just told them the beautiful temple they were looking at would be destroyed down to the last stone, which actually happened in AD 70. Except for some pieces of stone that make up the Wailing Wall, nothing remains of Herod's temple except the foundation. A Roman siege by Titus committed atrocities greater than the Holocaust. Pretty much the same signs were elaborated with the additional warning that:

> Brother will betray brother to death, and father his child. Children will rebel against their parents and have them put to death. All men will hate you because of Me, but he who stands firm to the end will be saved. (Mk. 13:12-13)

Jesus repeats His warning of the celestial signs and again tells of His rapture of the Church. Also during this discourse, Jesus reminds us that "'Heaven and earth will pass away, but My words will never pass away'" (Mk. 13:31).

This is certainly a good reason to have our Bibles open every day with a prayer for understanding. Jesus tells us emphatically that only the Father knows when the second coming and ultimate judgment will be. We are given signs to watch for, and the very important commands from Jesus are, "Be on guard, be alert, keep watch" (Mk 13:32, 35), and ending the chapter with the word "watch." We have no desire for Him to catch any of us sleeping!

Incredibly in chapter 13, Mark repeats the story of Mary, sister of Martha and Lazarus, who anointed Jesus with the expensive perfume and breaking the expensive alabaster jar, with Jesus repeating His words of appreciation for her act of worship and love. She also is unnamed in the episode, but I may know what that mystery is. One of the books I am now reading has put forth the idea that the gospel of Mark may have been written and copied for church service use within fifteen years of Jesus' death and resurrection, and people still living during this time would need to be protected from Roman persecution. I don't know about you, but I feel better about Mary's name and identity not being made known for that reason.

This chapter pretty much follows the words of Matthew in telling about celebrating the Passover with the twelve apostles. Only Luke, however, tells us the two apostles who made arrangements for the upper room and the food were Peter and John. They would have had the responsibility for the roasted lamb, the unleavened bread, wine, bitter herbs, and sauce. The Passover meal was immediately followed by Jesus' initiation of the communion remembrance celebration, which we all still participate in and will until Jesus returns or we go to heaven first. We again hear the painful prediction of Peter's denial and his pain at the thought. The discomfort and anticipation of waiting at Gethsemane with the apostles unable to stay awake is recounted. We read of Jesus' arrest, triggered by a kiss from Judas Iscariot; Peter lopping off the ear of the High Priest's servant, Malchus (Jn. 18:10); and Jesus doing one last thing before his arrest (healing the ear; Lk. 22:51). And here is the story of the young man wearing nothing but a "linen garment" and having to run for his life without clothes. My New International Version translation commentary also suggests this nude young man "may have been Mark, and his linen garment suggests a person from a wealthy family." Yep . . . my bet is on John Mark himself! Since he is the author of this gospel, we assume he got over his embarrassment and put his priorities in order! But of course he never forgot! Nor would we under the same circumstances. After the arrest, both Matthew and Mark report, "everyone deserted Him and fled" (Mk. 14:50; Mt. 26:56b). Naturally, they were all scared silly and ran for their lives. But of equal importance, whether they knew it or not, they were fulfilling the prophecy Jesus had predicted and repeated:

> "You will all fall away," Jesus told them, "for it is written: 'I will strike the Shepherd and the sheep will be scattered.'" (Mk. 14:27; Zech. 13:7) But the next words are so important:

"But after I have risen, I will go ahead of you into Galilee." (Mk. 14:28)

Make no mistake: they were still clueless about what that statement meant. Jesus may just have well been talking a foreign language. I'm sure we have all had the experience of hearing something but not understanding it until after we have looked at it in hindsight. That reminds me of hearing a lecture in a physiology class at the university and not understanding it until the lab experience of actually doing it . . . in this case, dissecting a frog. Yep . . . I did. Nothing I want to discuss. We can often hear something with our ears but not comprehend. When Kim was just a toddler, we took her to the country club for a Fourth of July celebration. After our dinner, I told Kim to stay close to our table, because there would be fireworks . . . big bangs and very loud. She heard with her ears but had no understanding until after the first big bang, when she hurried back to my lap, trembling. I believe this is exactly what happened to the apostles and disciples—words from Jesus beyond their experience or comprehension. Hindsight is a wonderful teacher!

When the arrest takes place in the garden and everyone scatters to the four corners, the one observation I would make is that Peter did not scatter along with the others. He followed along as close as he could to watch and learn what he could. How many times are we tempted to bury our heads in the sand, because we are so frightened we don't want to know what is happening? Give Peter some credit for staying as close as he could. In fact, in the gospel of Luke, we are told after Peter's denial before the rooster crowed, Jesus turned and looked at Peter in the courtyard.

The trial of Jesus is so trumped up by a jealous Sanhedrin, illegal night gathering, and false witnesses who did not agree with one another that we get a slightly different slant with each gospel account. In order to get the entire story, we need to look at the Gospels and put them together. At one point, the high priest, who was Caiaphas, questioned Jesus, who did not answer the first several times, which was in response to the prophecy of Isaiah, which says, "He was oppressed and afflicted, yet He opened not His mouth; He was led as a lamb to the slaughter, and as a sheep before its shearers is silent. So He opened not His mouth" (Is. 53:7).

Finally, the high priest—in extreme exasperation, I'm sure—asked Him point blank, "Are you the Christ, the Son of the Blessed?" Mk. 14:61

He could not say the word God out loud or write it other than G-d. And here are the immortal words of Jesus: "I am. And you will see the Son of Man sitting at the right hand of power and coming with the clouds of heaven" (Mk. 14:62).

How many times have you heard unbelievers say things like, "Jesus never said he was the Messiah? People only tried to fit Him into a mold." Wrong! The words of Jesus here could not have been more explicit as to His identity and His deity. If you have not met with the Living Christ either in prayer, meditation, worship, dreams, or other forms, you may right now be reading something beyond your experience or understanding. I hope and pray that by now, whoever is reading this with me has a faith-based mentality to know the words of the Bible are so real and true that you can bet your life on them. Literally!

Chapter 14 covers the sham religious trial of Jesus, which is part one of his trial. We will cover part two, which is the Roman trial, in the next chapter. The Roman part was necessary, because the religious council did not have the authority to pronounce a death sentence. And the Sanhedrin would settle for nothing less.

# CHAPTER 19

# MARK FIFTEEN - SIXTEEN

Our devotion for this morning:

> "The secret of the Lord is with those who fear Him, and He will show them His covenant. My eyes are ever toward the Lord, for He shall pluck my feet out of the net." (Ps. 25:14-15)

Lord God, thank You for each bit of wisdom You give us through Your Word. There are so many sentences and paragraphs that act so well as a devotional . . . for wisdom, for meditation, for spiritual growth and understanding. Certainly this scripture is one of them for me.

A very busy day today . . . up early to prepare and pack for a long weekend in California with Kim and Mike to celebrate their new "digs" in Laguna Niguel tomorrow. We are so grateful they want us with them and are so looking forward to seeing this area through the experience of their eyes. Almost back to Mike's roots, where he grew up. Their family loves the beach so much. They have vacationed there every summer for the past four or five years, so this is a very exciting dream acquisition for them. How blessed are we! Hang onto me, Lord. This is a busy, busy day, and You know how distracted I get and how much I need You to protect and guide me. Prayer cards out by my bed for tonight so I won't forget. You know how tired I am at night. Forgive me, Lord, for being so rushed. Ephesians 6 protection, please!

## *Chapters 15 and 16*

Mark 15, with the civil trial of Jesus, is a very difficult chapter for me to get through. The Sanhedrin did their illegal "trial" at night and delivered Jesus at daylight, bound like a criminal, to Pilate, the Roman procurator (governor), who was in Jerusalem for the Passover. (Not because he was a Jew but to make sure order was maintained.) Pilate recognized the trumped-up charges for what they were: envy and fear of losing control of the power held by the Sanhedrin. Pilate tried to release Jesus as the one prisoner who would be set free. Pilate had been warned by his wife not to have anything to do with "that just man" (Mt. 21:19), because she had "suffered many things today in a dream because of Him." Here we go again with spiritual revelations coming in the form of a dream. This information, you may recall, is only told in the book of Matthew, and I wonder how Matthew came by this gem of information, especially after Pilate was forced into the decision to crucify by the chief priests, who had stirred up the crowd. In order to placate the growing unruly crowd, Pilate had Jesus scrounged and released the guilty prisoner, Barabbas, before handing Jesus over to the Roman soldiers whose duty it was to crucify the three prisoners. Rather than focus on the crucifixion itself, I ponder the participants of this shameful trial. We know that Pilate's wife had met Jesus, or at least knew the truth about Him from a dream. She would never be the same. Perhaps she even sought out some of the apostles or Matthew afterward to share information. I can only imagine. But we know that even Pilate was a part of God's plan that would fulfill the prophecies throughout the Old Testament.

When it was apparent Jesus was too weak to carry His own thirty—to forty-pound crossbar, they compelled a certain Cyrenian, Simon, the father of Alexander and Rufus, to carry the cross for Him to Golgotha, where He would be crucified. I had always thought Simon was probably a black man, because he came from Cyrene, which is in Libya in North Africa. Simon had probably returned to Jerusalem for Passover and got caught in the wrong place at the wrong time. But perhaps I should say he was exactly in the right place at the right time! My speculation that Simon was a black man is possibly affirmed by two prophecies as follows from the Old Testament. See what you think.

> "From beyond the rivers of Ethiopia My Worshipers, the daughter of my dispersed ones, shall bring my offering." (Zeph. 3:10)

> "Fear not, for I am with you; I will bring your descendants from the east, and gather you from the west. I will say to the North [Russia?] 'give them up!' And to the south [Ethiopia?], 'do not keep them back!'" (Is. 43:5-6)

Now bear with me here. These two predictions of Jews returning to their homeland came true! In his book *The Signature of God,* Grant R. Jeffrey writes, "In the later part of the 1980's especially in 1991, over eighty-five thousand black Jews returned home to Israel from Ethiopia in fulfillment of the ancient prophecies" (p.187). Who knew there were "black Jews"? And, of course, they couldn't come back home to Israel until after 1948, when Israel miraculously became a nation again. Yep, I think Simon was probably one of the many people of color named in the Bible. And really, it doesn't matter, but if I were black, I would want to know that and be proud of my heritage. I just love seeing fulfilled prophecy, especially in the last century!

While Jesus was hanging on the cross, a three-hour phenomenon happened: "Now when the sixth hour had come, there was darkness over the whole land until the ninth hour" (Mk. 15:33). Jeffrey's research confirms the writings of a third-century pagan historian who wrote in his book, *The Third History of Thallus,* "There was an unusual darkness that blotted out the sun for a number of hours at the time of Passover in the year A.D. 32, the year of Christ's crucifixion."

Although Thallus speculated this was the result of an eclipse, "Any astronomer could tell you it was impossible for an eclipse to have occurred at that time because Passover was carefully calculated to occur at the full moon, which would have made an eclipse impossible" (Jeffrey, p. 180).

Jesus died. He "breathed His last" in the thirty-seventh verse of Mark 15, and that's when the veil of the temple split lengthwise down the middle. Mark also tells us many women were watching from a distance, I'm sure in shock and horror.

Joseph of Arimathea, a prominent Sanhedrin council member, claimed the body, brought fine linen, wrapped His body in it, and placed it in his own tomb, which had been hewn out of rock. One can only wonder where Joseph was during the night when his own council was meeting illegally. Luke tells us Joseph had not agreed with the council's decision (Lk. 23:51), so we can only assume he had been there. Now the linen cloth Joseph brought became known as the Shroud of Turin, and through some metaphysical means, an imprint of a man's face and body were "burned" into the fabric. Whether this shroud is actually the burial cloth of Jesus has yet to be proven scientifically. It is in the custody of the Roman Catholic Church and buried in a sealed vault, which is only raised and opened every twenty-five years. Real or not, it is incredibly exciting to think it may be the real burial cloth.

In the late 1970s, Bob and I were on a tour of the vineyards of West Germany when we came upon the fairly intact remains of a magnificent castle in Trier, Germany. During the Middle Ages, the castle had been occupied by monks. Because it was bordered on two sides by rivers and two sides by moats, the castle was thought to be impregnable by enemy forces. Whenever Rome deemed herself to be in trouble from an invading army, the shroud was taken by messenger to the castle of Trier for safekeeping until the danger passed. It was just thrilling walking around that wonderful place and thinking about monks protecting what they thought—and what might be—the burial cloth of Christ. It is a very compelling memory for me, as a "young" Christian at the time.

And now, of course, the Good News. Chapter 16 recounts the resurrection of Jesus. I don't know why Matthew only reports two women discovering the empty tomb, and Mark includes Salome, the mother of James and John, along with Mary Magdalene and Mary the mother of James the Lesser. The women had prepared spices and ointments to further prepare Jesus' body for entombment, since the Jews do not believe in embalming. Matthew tells us the young man who greeted them was an angel, dressed all in white, who had rolled away the stone. Mark simply tells us the "young man" was dressed in a "long white robe" and sitting on the right side of the open tomb. The words spoken by the young man were similar to those recorded in Matthew, but there is a difference. He said, "'Go and tell His Disciples . . . and Peter . . . that He is going before you into Galilee and there you will see Him, as He said to you'" (Mk. 16:7). There is no report of worshipping at His feet or that the women told anyone, because they were too afraid . . . probably terrorized and confused. But note the wording: "tell His Disciples . . . and Peter." Jesus had already forgiven Peter's denial and was even now preparing him for future ministry.

At this point, the gospel presents a mystery to us, as Mark apparently stops writing after Mark 16:8. Bible scholars through the ages agree the style and vocabulary change abruptly starting in Mark 16:9. No one knows who finished the gospel or when or why. They only know the very early manuscript scrolls do not contain the ending paragraphs, which does not mean they are not valid, only that they are not Mark's writing. The wording agrees that Jesus met first with Mary Magdalene, who tried to spread the Good News that Jesus was alive, and she had seen and talked with Him, but no one believed her. Then Jesus appears to the two disciples on the road to Emmaus (Lk. 24:13), and even though they hurried back to Jerusalem, the two were not believed either. The gospel ends with powerful words credited to the resurrected Jesus:

> "Go into all the world and preach the Gospel to every creature. He who believes and is baptized will be saved, but he who does not believe will be condemned. And the signs will follow those who believe: In My name they will cast our demons, they will speak with new tongues, they will take up serpents, and if they drink anything deadly, it will by no means hurt them, they will lay hands on the sick, and they will recover." (Mk. 16:15-18)

The ending paragraph says, "after the Lord had spoken to them" Mk. 16:19, a period of forty days later, He was taken up into heaven and sat at the right hand of God. Maybe those aren't Mark's words, but they surely are beautiful and meant to be thoroughly enjoyed.

Before we leave the gospel of Mark, I would like to add a postscript so you can be looking for further information in the world press. Okay, I'm always the optimist! Many years ago, most of us read about the marvelous discovery of the Dead Sea Scrolls in caves outside of a place named Qumran, where the third sect of the Jews, called Essenes, had a large settlement. I hope you remember in Matthew we discussed the three Jewish sects. The miracle is back in 1947, an Arab youth threw a stone into a cave near the Dead Sea and heard it bounce off an object that sounded like pottery. When he investigated, he found copies of ancient scrolls that had not been handled or touched since the Essenes had been killed in AD 68. That was before the temple had been destroyed, which happened in AD 70. The only information the press gave us initially was a "partial copy of Isaiah had been found," and historians and biblical scholars were delirious, because the scraps found matched entirely with the copies we have today, with only a few minor spelling differences that would not affect the meaning of the sentences. This was huge evidence of the accuracy of at least one book of the Old Testament. Word began to trickle down that the entire Old Testament had been found in the caves, with the exception of the book of Esther, and that in some cases, several copies of scrolls were found in their entirety. The word came out that in almost fifty years, only a small percentage of the scrolls had been translated and identified! Remember I wrote back in Matthew that it was my opinion the Essenes were the closest group who might embrace Jesus and believe His claim of being the Son of God. And there in the caves are hundreds, if not thousands, of scrolls that might give additional insight as to life and beliefs in the first century. My point is whenever this information is shared with the biblical world of scholars, we may find much more about why the gospel of Mark was unfinished. Very exciting! In the words of Jesus, "and what I say to you, I say to all: Watch!" Mk. 13:37

# CHAPTER 20

# PERSONAL

Today I read in *My Utmost for His Highest* by Oswald Chambers,

> "We have to get into the habit of carefully listening to God about everything, forming the habit of finding out what He says and heeding it. If, when a crisis comes, we instinctively turn to God, we will know that the habit has been formed in us."

Chambers also reminds me today to get in the habit of doing character-building exercises and that we need to "Work our own salvation with fear and trembling, for it is God who works in you to will and to act according to His good purpose" (Phil. 1:12).

Perhaps this is a good time to tell you why I have the incentive to write a book of this kind, not only to encourage you in the Word, but to tell you where I am coming from. I seldom teach a class without letting them know I really am a born-again Christian, which is the only reason anyone would have to listen to what I say . . . or in this case, write. Thank You, Lord, for Your continued Presence with me in the form of the Holy Spirit. There was a time when this was completely beyond my understanding, and I admit I have no "fear" of my own salvation.Please let me tell you why: That was decided once for all in the spring of 1975, when I was ill with a terrible case of the flu. Stomach, respiratory; all parts of my body were sick. I was in bed for three weeks in our upstairs bedroom at Calvert Place in Lincoln, Nebraska. It was such a wonderful, elegant, and graceful three-story Georgian house built in 1916 and 1917 on three acres of wooded grounds in the heart of the city. My life could have been described as "perfect": gorgeous home; handsome, hardworking husband, Bob, who is a self-employed, focused real estate attorney/developer. Our children were also "perfect" and the delight of my life: a thirteen-year-old daughter, Kim, and a ten-year-old son, Andy. Our family was complete with a Lhasa Apso named Chan and a calico Persian named Pechou. My parents were happily retired in Florida, and we had a wonderful relationship with them. They visited us every summer for a month, staying in the guest cabin in our backyard. Bob's mother was widowed, living in Lincoln, and was an important part of our lives. My social life was filled with wonderful friends who shared my interests of volunteering, bridge, tennis, and dance club. On the outside, looking in, there was nothing that could be added to make my life more complete.

But I had a hole in my heart, and I didn't know why. I had contemplated several times going back to the university to complete my education, but that didn't work out. I had been searching for a spiritual life I did not have or know anything about. My search included new age ideas; I had read most of Shirley MacLaine's books. My search had not included churches, because they had meant very little to me in the past. I had grown up a Methodist, with spurts of attending Presbyterian churches in Omaha as I was growing up, but my heart must have been so hardened nothing spoke to me. I never heard a sermon that made sense to me. Oh, I loved Christmas, especially when we traveled to Albion, a small town where my mom grew up. Albion was special. My Grammie was there and many aunts, uncles, and cousins. I often got to sleep in the big bed with my Grammie Mansfield. Those were special times, because she told me stories about lost kittens and Indians coming to the house asking for food around the time Albion was being settled. But the best remembrance was falling asleep and listening to Grammie whisper her prayers every night after our talk. I could never hear much, except the 'dear God' part, and hard as I tried, I never heard the "amen." I thought my Grammie must have had the longest prayers of anyone in the whole world! She and most of the family were Methodists. My great-grandfather, who helped lay out the town, had donated the land for the Methodist Church, and my aunt Ora was the organist for as many years as anyone could remember. (You've already met her.) So church was a requirement in Albion, but sporadic at our home in Omaha, where I grew up. I had attended Sunday school occasionally but could never figure out what those felt figures of Noah and Samson had to do with me! That was too much of a stretch.

Back to my life in Lincoln in 1975 and an upstairs sickroom. My illness was getting tedious and difficult for the whole family. Each morning, Bob would somehow get the children off to school, feed the cat and dog, bring me tea and toast, put the phone on the bed between our pillows, and leave for his office. And I lay in bed, watching the fine cracks in the bedroom ceiling of our house. (I told you it was old.) The master bedroom was en suite (meaning it had a bathroom), way ahead of its time, located on my side of the bed. I could usually make it the twenty feet or so when sickness overwhelmed me. Two trips to a family friend-doctor led to no answers and this was very difficult for me to handle.

I had three girlfriends who knew how sick I was, and two of them called regularly to check up on me. The first one was an acquaintance through the junior high PTO. She knew I was not a Christian, and when she heard I was ill, she prayed. One of the other friends, Kathy, has been my good friend since law school days. She had been a Christian for a long time and just assumed I was also, because we were both on a quest for spiritual answers. Maybe one of the problems was I didn't have the right question. Anyway, Kathy also checked on me by phone often, and I know she prayed for me. Was I brain dead too, back then? Sheesh! But the third friend is the most amazing story. Her name is Judy, and she is the adopted daughter of my parents' best friends. We grew up together in Omaha—birthday parties, family dinners, Sunday afternoon visits, and so on. She was a year older and attended different schools, so as we grew older, we grew apart with different friends and interests altogether. I was a tomboy and loved the outdoors; she was a born housekeeper even as a child. Judy ended up pregnant as a junior in high school and married when she should have been a senior. The marriage was a disaster, and after the second baby, it ended in divorce.

So here we were, nearly twenty years later, and Judy and her new husband had moved to Lincoln. She called me on the phone, trying to reconnect. And my husband, who also knew her from Omaha, was having no part of this friendship! "Her boys are unruly, and I don't want to meet her new husband", who happened to be a lay Baptist preacher! This was totally beyond our level of understanding. So our renewed friendship took place mostly over the phone, and especially when Judy found out I was so sick. She prayed. But she didn't just pray . . . she talked. She asked embarrassing questions, like, "Do you know Jesus?" Huh? "Have you ever asked Jesus to come into your heart?" Double huh? She might as well have been speaking a foreign language. And she laid out reasons why I needed to know Jesus: (1) I'm a sinner. "For all have sinned and fall short of the glory of God" (Rom. 3:23). I'm a sinner? To me, this seemed like the pot calling the kettle black. (2) Results of my sin: "For the wages of sin is death, but the gift of God is eternal life in Christ Jesus our Lord" (Rom. 6:23). (3) Jesus loves me and wants me to know Him. "But God demonstrates His own love for us in this: while we were still sinners, Christ died for us" (Rom. 10:9-10). Judy wasn't giving me Bible verses; that probably would have freaked me out. I would often have to hang up on her and crawl to the bathroom to be sick before getting back to bed—to again study the ceiling cracks and think about what Judy had told me.

On the twenty-first day of my illness, Judy called me and asked, "Do you know where you are going when you die?" and, "Do you want me to pray with you to accept Jesus?" No to both questions. I told her it was personal (a cop-out phrase if I ever heard one), and I needed to take care of this myself. Alone. My own words. No "Christianese" or "church" language. I needed to be real with the Lord . . . who I did not know.

I slipped out of my bed and onto my knees. I grabbed a handful of wrinkled sheets, closed my eyes, and "got real" with God. I told Him I didn't know Jesus at all, and I wanted to. I told Him I was a sinner and confessed every awful, selfish, bad thing and thought I could think of. (It turned out there were plenty!) The tears came freely then, and the sheets in my hands became the robe of Jesus. He sat on my bed and held me as I cried . . . and cried . . . and cried. I asked Him to come into my heart and apologized over and over for not knowing Him . . . for not learning about Him. And gradually, as I stopped crying, the bright light that had been in the room became normal bedroom light, and the robe I had been clutching was once again wrinkled sheets. Dry sheets, even though I had cried buckets of tears into them. For some unknown supernatural reason, I ended my prayer by saying, "Jesus, if there is something else I should be asking for, I want it!" Such a miracle I would voice that last prayer. I knew absolutely nothing about the Holy Spirit, but I had inadvertently asked for Him. I crawled upon my bed, totally exhausted and cried out, and incredulous that Jesus Himself had ministered to me that afternoon. It was Holy Week of 1975. As a matter of fact, it was Maundy Thursday, and later I was to realize I had been born on Maundy Thursday of 1937 and born again on Maundy Thursday of 1975. As I sat on my bed, pondering what had just happened to me. I realized for the first time in twenty-one days, I did not have a fever! I grabbed my thermometer to make sure. And on top of that, I was hungry! What a miracle. And just a few weeks ago, I read, "And as many touched [the hem of His garment] were made perfectly well" (Mt. 14:36b).

I was well. I didn't ask for healing. I think I had been sick for so long, hope for healing was no longer an issue. I was simply asking for Jesus. He gave me His all. How could I not give Him my all? I don't know about the "fear and trembling" part of the verse we started with, but I know without any doubt whatsoever my salvation is secure forever. The Lord is still in the business of working out my sanctification, and I can help Him by intentionally being in the Word every day and by intentionally having a devotional book by my Bible with journal notebook, pens, and prayer cards to remind me who to give to Him daily. I have been blessed. It feels so good.

Now as we finish Mark, we are getting ready for the gospel of Luke. Please excuse me for getting so personal in this chapter, and grab your Bibles for meeting the physician who gives us a marvelous account of the Great Physician. God bless you as you read.

# CHAPTER 21

# PERSONAL

From *My Utmost of His Highest:*

> "Remember that you have been saved so that the life of Jesus may be manifested in your body . . . You did not do anything to achieve your salvation, but you must do something to exhibit it."

Wow! The only thing I did to achieve my salvation was to submit my will, body, soul, and spirit to the Lordship of Jesus Christ, ask Him to forgive my sins and my sinful nature, and to come live in my heart, a concept totally foreign to anything I had heard or read.

> "I beseech you, therefore brethren, by the mercies of God, that you present your bodies a living sacrifice, holy, acceptable to God, which is your reasonable act of service." (Rom. 12:1)

Yep . . . it's there in the Bible. It seems to me even what we do to exhibit our salvation must come from the Holy Spirit. I can't love the unlovely or cantankerous, but He can through me; I can't control my impatience with a slow driver or an inept clerk while standing in a line while shopping, but He can through the fruits of the Spirit in me. I can't find joy in all circumstances, but He can through me. Praise the Lord, indeed!

We are just back home from a weekend in Orange County seeing Kim and Mike's new "villa," their townhouse in Laguna Niguel. Andy and Sandy came over for two days. What fun! We laughed, we played, we hiked, we ate delicious meals, but mostly we just loved being together. We got to see an amazing video of Strategic Resource Group, a Mission group providing money and resources for third world missions, with both Andy and Sandy featured in a roundtable discussion that was beautifully done and so good! Thank You, Lord, for their vision; thank You for using both of them in such a mighty way for Your Kingdom. This was the first time in fifteen years we have had time with our adult children without our grandchildren. All four of them are still in school for several weeks, which is how this trip came about. And as much as I love all four grandchildren, it was so special to have time with their parents. Very precious time. Thank You, Jesus, for Your presence with us, for Your protection over us, and for special protection for the children.

Oh, coming back to Nebraska, I head the flight attendant of our UAL plane tell us we were on flight number 316. Jesus. You are in *all* the details of our lives. Joy!

# PART III

# LUKE

## CHAPTER 22

# LUKE ONE - FOUR

*Introduction to Luke*

Let's see what we know about Luke, the third gospel. First of all, the author's name is Greek, from Lucas, or Lucanus. He was probably born in Antioch in Syria and was taught the science of medicine. We know nothing about who his sponsor was, but most physicians in the first century and before were slaves owned by wealthy families for their exclusive use. Ancient historians also tell us Luke had the creative gift of painting. His excellent writing ability in both the gospel and his second volume of Acts (the complete history of the Christian church) indicates he was highly intelligent and had great respect for the gentleman to whom he was writing, whose name was Theophilus. There is no doubt Theophilus was a Roman dignitary of power and wealth, and he may have been the person who originally published Luke's writings. Other than the fact Luke was Italian and probably lived in Rome, we are clueless. The most significant thing I can think of about Luke is he is the only writer in the New Testament who is not Jewish. His good friend and at times missionary colleague was Saul of Tarsus, Paul, the "missionary to the Gentiles." We know how intelligent Paul was from his writings and his extensive education in Jerusalem under the impressive teacher/rabbi Gamaliel, which would have been comparable to several PhDs all wrapped up in one.

So friends, grab your Bibles and read with me the first four chapters of Luke.

And dear Lord, as we get into this very familiar Christmas story, please open our spiritual eyes to grasp truth and facts we have not been aware of in the past. Amen.

## *Chapters 1-4*

The very first thing we learn is that Luke gets his information from eyewitnesses and "ministers of the Word." This wasn't just hearsay writing, and he had a perfect understanding from the first. We don't know how old Luke was, but since he became a contemporary of Paul, it is not beyond reason to assume he was born not too long after Jesus. His gospel was written between AD 58 and AD 60, so let's say roughly twenty-six to twenty-eight years after the Resurrection. Think of your own life. I can easily remember details that took place thirty years ago, and I'm sure you can, too, depending on your age, of course. So there were lots of witnesses (to Jesus and ministry) still around at the time of his writing. James, the first martyr to be killed, had not died yet, so it was before AD 62. Luke had many detail-oriented people to interview, including the apostles. We don't know how or when Luke became a believer, only that he left us an outstanding work of history that brings us closer to the details of Jesus' life here on earth.

We did a pretty good job of covering John the Baptist's story of his birth and parents in our previous gospels, but read this section to find that John was filled with the Holy Spirit even from the womb. This is the only person in history who this can be said of, so it is certainly worth noting. A careful reading tells us his parents were both filled with the Holy Spirit also.

In this section we have the wonderful story of the angel Gabriel, visiting Mary and giving her the news she was pregnant. He also told Mary that her relative, Elizabeth, was in her sixth month of pregnancy. We also have the words, "For with God nothing will be impossible" (Lk. 1:37). Tuck these words into your heart and mind. They come in very handy!

What a good place for Mary to go . . . visiting her also pregnant relative. They both had miraculous pregnancies and both knew God had touched them for a special, still unknown reason. As Mary entered the house of Zacharias and Elizabeth and called out a greeting, the baby John leaped in the womb, and Elizabeth was "filled with the Holy Spirit" (Lk. 1:41). Both women had beautiful songs of praise as they considered and shared their unusual circumstances. Verse 56 tells us Mary stayed three months with her cousin and then returned to her house. Many years ago, I read that in the early years of Jewish history, virgins were not allowed to be present during a birth. I thought that was a wonderful idea. No sense in giving Mary more than she could handle. She knew God was in total control of her and had great trust in His ability to bring this miracle birth about however He pleased. Notice we are not told in this gospel how an angel came to Joseph in a dream to reassure him about Mary. We were told this in Matthew: another example of why we need all four gospels to get the entire story.

After John was born, his father's tongue was loosed, and when he named the baby John, he was also filled with the Holy Spirit and gave a lovely prophecy of praise, the Benedictus, for the rest of the chapter." I call your attention to verses 1:68-69, where Zacharias praises the Lord for the "horn of salvation in the house of His servant, David." Now Elizabeth and Zacharias were both Levites (she from the house of Aaron), so they were referring to the child in Mary's womb, since she was from the house of David through her mother.

Chapter 2 of the book of Luke is possibly the most well known in the entire Bible, with the exception of John 3:16. We have the story of the angel visiting the shepherds, and after the angel had given the birth announcement, we read, "And suddenly there was with the angel a multitude of the heavenly host praising God and saying, Glory to God in the highest and on earth peace, good will to men" (Lk. 2:13-14).

These verses are called *Gloria in Excelsis Deo*. I can almost smell pine branches and hear "Silent Night" and "Oh Little Town of Bethlehem" every time I read this chapter. Can't you? The shepherds wasted no time telling their story to anyone who would listen. Actually, it's a wonder the Holy Family escaped from there, because Bethlehem is so close to Jerusalem. They really stayed for nearly two years. After eight days, Jesus was circumcised according to the laws of Moses. The miracle of the eighth day was confirmed by the medical community in the past few decades. On the eighth day of a child's life, his immune system and blood clotting ability are fully developed for the rest of his life. When I shared this information with Kim fourteen years ago, after we knew she was pregnant with a baby boy, she made arrangements with her pediatrician to have her son circumcised in the doctor's office on the eighth day. Fortunately, their doctor is a Christian and understood immediately their request and was happy to comply.

As an aside, several months into Kim's second pregnancy, when we returned to our home in Lincoln, Kim told us she had an appointment for an ultrasound, and we were invited. Bob immediately balked but was persuaded to join us, so Kim, Mike, Bob, and I crowded into a tiny examination room with a technician. This was all new technology for us, and when the machine was turned on, the baby cooperated beautifully by turning in such a way that all four of us shouted at once, "It's a boy!" We all walked out of that office with tears flowing down our faces. We knew that God had given us a gift that day.

After Mary's forty days of confinement following the birth, they took Jesus to the temple to present their firstborn to the Lord as directed by Moses (Ex. 13:2, 12-15). It was then they met a man named Simeon. The Holy Spirit had revealed to Simeon that he would not die until he saw the Messiah. A really sweet story. Simeon's prophecy was a good news/bad news thing for Mary. And here we also have a prophetess named Anna, who apparently spent all her time at the temple praying and fasting, and she recognized the Christ-child when she saw Him. Who says all babies look alike?

Chapter 3 gives us the story of John the Baptist, who must have had a very powerful ministry to have brought multitudes into the wilderness for baptism. The Jews were familiar with baptism, but it was only used for Gentiles wanting to become Jews. John proclaimed that everyone needed to be baptized for the remission of sins. He said, "'One mightier than I is coming whose sandal strap I am not worthy to loose'" (Lk. 3:16).

I see the triangle sign in the margin of my Bible by Luke 3:21-22, indicating the baptism of Jesus, the Holy Spirit descending like a dove, and the Father's voice from heaven saying, "You are my beloved Son; In You I am well pleased" (Lk. 2:22b).

This is the start of Jesus' public ministry. The remainder of the chapter is Jesus' genealogy through Mary, moving backward from Jesus to Adam. No, Mary's name is not mentioned, but hers is the strong connection to the Son of David and the Son of Judah.

Chapter 4 recounts the temptation in the wilderness for forty days. Note that Jesus was now filled with the Holy Spirit and scripture verses and wisdom to withstand the devil's wiles. This is a lesson for us. If Jesus needed all these defenses, don't you suppose we need them as well? I think we are often attacked by evil forces and don't recognize where they come from, which makes it very difficult to withstand. We truly do need to put on the full armor of God every day, for ourselves and for our families (Eph. 6:10).

When Jesus returned to Galilee from the wilderness, He was accepted. He taught in their synagogues regularly. But when He returned to Nazareth, His hometown, and especially when He read from Isaiah 61:1-2, He assured them that "Today this scripture is fulfilled in your hearing" (Lk. 4:21), They just could not believe what they were hearing. They actually tried to run Him out of town. His supernatural escape was a nice touch. I loved it.

The remainder of the chapter includes His time back in Galilee, where they were more accepting, and the same healings recorded in Matthew and Mark. The chapter ends with the crowds begging Him not to leave (a far cry from Nazareth!) and His words, "'I must preach the Kingdom of God to the other cities also, because for this purpose I have been sent'" (Lk. 3:43).

# CHAPTER 23

# PURELY PERSONAL

From *My Utmost for His Highest:*

> "Never sympathize with someone who finds it difficult to get to God; God is not to blame. It is not for us to figure out the difficulty, but only present the truth of God so that the Spirit of God will reveal what is wrong. The greatest test of the quality of our preaching is whether or not it brings everyone to judgment. When the truth is preached, the Spirit of God brings each person face to face with God Himself.' Oswald Chambers

This reminds me of a story. My mom gave me such a gift on her last day on earth. It was December of 1986, and Mom was dying of uterine cancer in Florida. It had been a long, three-year struggle filled with both hope and despair. The last year was the worst, with my sister and me taking turns visiting Mom and Dad for a week or ten days at a time to help out where we could. Mom was eighty, Dad eleven years older, and they still lived alone until we finally moved them into a lovely retirement home complex on the Caloosahatchee River in Ft. Myers. It was too little and too late. Mom could do nothing but languish, and Dad wouldn't leave her side to go meet people. My turn of being with them ended when my sister, Nancy, and her husband arrived with their travel trailer to spend the winter. I needed desperately to return to my home in Lincoln. Bob felt very strongly that I had deserted him. Christmas was coming, and Andy was coming home from Pepperdine for his break. I got a call from my sister on December 22 that Mom had slipped into a coma, and the end was near. I spent a sleepless night, praying for peace for both Mom and Dad and for angels to comfort them in their greatest time of need. The next morning, I called their apartment to find my sister out for a while with her husband and a hospice nurse on duty. I identified myself to the nurse, whose name I never knew, and asked her, "Could I please talk to my mom?"

The reply was, "Mrs. Weigel, your mother is in a deep coma."

"I know that, but if you could please just put the phone to her ear so I could talk to her, I would be very grateful." I could not understand why this simple request was met with such resistance! She was probably trying to protect her patient from me, but I persisted in my request until she finally comprehended that I would not give up and go away. When I was told the phone was in place, I started talking. I don't know how I did it without breaking down, which certainly would have been counterproductive, but I was able to tell Mom how much I loved her and to thank her for her unconditional love for me for forty-nine years. I told her how proud I was of her . . . especially in the three years of her terminal illness. I told her Jesus was waiting for her, and one day we would be together with our Lord and our loved ones. She was just going ahead of me, just like Jesus did. I ended simply, saying, "I love you, Mom." And then I heard it. Mom cleared her throat and whispered, "I love you, honey."

That's when the tears started. When the nurse came back on line, she was crying too, as she asked, "Did you hear, Mrs. Weigel?" Oh, yes, I heard loud and clear. What a gift! I got the call that very afternoon that Mom had died . . . just hours after I talked to her. Of course, there were tears—there still are—but there was also joy and relief that her ordeal was finally over. That kind of joy underlining all of life's circumstances can only come from the Lord. He is in all the details of our lives.

I knew Mom was with the Lord, because at least five years before her death, we had a long talk while sitting on the picnic bench by the guest cabin in our backyard in Lincoln. Mom said something to me that almost broke my heart. She said, "Jody, I don't have what you have with the Lord, and I don't know why." Needless to say, we sat at that table for a long time. Yes, she had asked for forgiveness and for Jesus to come into her heart. But she still felt she was "missing something," which was exactly how I felt when I had a hole in my heart. I inquired about her experience with the Holy Spirit, and yes, she had asked, but nothing seemed to have changed. I reminded her of scriptures from Luke and Matthew:

> "Ask and it will be given you, seek and you will find, knock and the door will be opened to you, for everyone who asks, receives, and he who seeks, finds, and to him who knocks the door will be opened" (Mt. 7:7)

> "Draw near to God and He will draw near to you." (Jas. 4:8)

> Jesus said, "When the Helper comes, whom I shall send to you from the Father, the Spirit of Truth who proceeds from the Father, He will testify of Me." (Jn. 15:26)

I felt in my spirit something was blocking Mom from the fullness of experiencing the Holy Spirit, but I couldn't discern what it was, and neither could she. We prayed about it, sitting on that old picnic bench, and I think we both felt better about asking God for help.

I know most of us probably feel this way about our mothers, but really, my mom exhibited every single fruit of the Holy Spirit, all nine of them, and every single day! Her compassion and love for people were legendary in her retirement community. I won't know until I get to heaven how far Mom got on her spiritual journey here on earth, but I do know the only thing I need to: she was saved! And so was my dad.

In their latter years, it was our habit to talk on the phone at least every Saturday morning, and several times in between, depending on health and activities. One Saturday morning, Mom called and said, "Dad wants to tell you something." That was most unusual, and I was curious what it could be.

When Dad got on the phone, he said, "Last night I asked Jesus to come into my heart." I couldn't believe it! I started crying the minute the words were out!

"Dad, after all these years [he was ninety], how did this come about? I am so happy for you." As it turned out, he had watched a Billy Graham Crusade on TV the night before and responded to the altar call. Halleluiah, and God bless Billy Graham! That was a day I didn't think would ever happen. My father was the most prejudiced, hardheaded, opinionated unbeliever I have ever known. He was the original "Archie Bunker." He used to refer to me as his "religious daughter" to his retiree friends in Florida. I very much dislike the term "religious," but coming from my father, it was a compliment. At least he knew where my heart was.

A very strange thing happened the morning after my mom died. Andy was home from college, and Bob was making hasty plans for us to fly to Florida. It was Christmastime, so we were lucky to get two tickets for December 25, leaving our grown children home to have Christmas with Bob's mother. Bob had left for his office very early on the twenty-fourth, and I was downstairs in the living room, having some quiet time before our trip, when Andy came racing down the stairs, saying, "Mom, Mom, didn't you hear the phone?" I assured him I had been sitting in the living room for forty-five minutes, and the phone had not rung, but he assured me otherwise.

"Mom, it was Grammie, and she said, 'Andy, honey, is that you? I just wanted you to know I'm just fine.'"

I can't explain the story. I only know it happened, and I also know my mom had died the afternoon before. It is a gift. That's all I can think. I can't even begin to explain this in a logical, theological manner. I can only call it a gift.

Thank you, Lord, that you have my family. Some in heaven with You, some here on earth with our eyes on the goal and joyful anticipation in our hearts. The knowledge of eternal life spent with you is almost more than I can comprehend . . . but also spent with my precious family and extended family . . . almost sends me over the moon! Lord, You are so good! Now, let's get back to Luke with the next four chapters. Amen.

# CHAPTER 24

# LUKE FIVE - EIGHT

Lord God, open our spiritual eyes, minds, and hearts to Your stories we are about to read. Amen.

## *Chapters 5-8*

Chapter 5 tells us Jesus was by the Lake of Gennersaret (also called the Sea of Galilee and sometimes the Sea of Tiberius). Sigh. Here we go with all these different names again. Don't let it bother you; we are still in Galilee, where people are mostly fishermen, love Jesus, and are thrilled by his words, His ways, and His countenance. He meets Simon (Peter) in a most unusual way: by using his boat as a platform to speak to the crowds who have gathered to hear Him. After His message, he directed Simon's boat out to deeper water, where the incredulous fisherman caught so many fish he had to call his partners for help. This is when we learn that James and John, the brothers, are partners with Simon Peter. Peter knew a miracle when he saw one and was immediately struck by his own sinfulness. That's what happens to all of us when we come into the Presence of Holiness. We see our own dirt, which we try desperately to sweep under a rug. But Jesus pulls it all out into the open where He can cleanse and forgive one and all. We assume when He called Simon, He called James and John also, with these words, "Do not be afraid. From now on you will catch men. So when they had brought their boats to land, they forsook all and followed Him" (Lk. 5:11).

The healings continue, with both a man with leprosy and a paralytic, who was lowered through the roof of a house in order to get to Jesus and was healed by the forgiveness of his sins. Wow! What a testimony on the importance of asking for forgiveness! And Jesus confirms this by saying, "'But that you may know that the Son of Man has power on earth to forgive sins'" (Lk. 5:24.) And the paralytic picked up his bed and walked, and the people were amazed to say the least!

The only other apostle called in the fifth chapter is Levi, a tax collector called Matthew after his conversion. He was so excited to be chosen, he gave a banquet for his friends, who were all a bit on the seedy side. When the scribes and the Pharisees saw what kind of people Jesus was dining with, they were critical. I love the answer Jesus gave, "'Those who are well have no need for a Physician, but those who are sick. I have not come to call the righteous, but sinners to repentance'" (Lk. 5:31).

The only trouble is there are so many different kinds of "sickness," and some of us don't know who we need or when. I certainly did not, and I was sick physically, emotionally, and spiritually. Sometimes we have to come to the end of our rope before we can lose our pride and look up for healing.

Chapter 6 gets Jesus a really bad reputation with the zealots because of His healing and work on the Sabbath. Sheesh! There are some people you can never please, because they just don't get it! They are stuck in their own time frame and not willing to open their minds and hearts to something they don't understand. In chapter 6, we also have Luke's account of choosing all twelve apostles. He had many disciples out of whom He called the twelve and gave them authority to act on his behalf. Don't let the names confuse you; remember the explanation from our account in Matthew.

We also have a slightly shortened account of the Beatitudes, which are called the Sermon on the Plain here. He had been on a mountain, where He "prayed all night" (Lk. 6:12), chose His twelve apostles, and came down to a "level place." There was such a multitude that I imagine it was safer and more comfortable than on the side of a mountain. Bob and I usually go to Colorado each summer to escape the Midwest heat and humidity, and I assure you it is more comfortable to stand on a level place than having to watch your footing on rocks and inclines! Especially when you really want to concentrate on what is being said. The Beatitudes are definitely commands for our daily attitudes. And who knew the Golden Rule was a Bible verse located in both Luke and Matthew (Lk. 6:31; Mt. 7:12)? I think most of us learned it in grammar school but didn't know how to carry it out in our lives until we achieved some maturity. A handwritten notation in my Bible says, "Maturity in Christianity is when you stop looking for an example and start being one." Wow! Marching orders.

Chapter 7 gives us the story of the Centurion's servant, who was ready to die, and the faith he had in Jesus' ability to heal him, which He did and used as an example to the crowd. Jesus' words about the Centurion: "'I say to you, I have not found such great faith, not even in Israel'" (Lk. 7:9). What a goal for all of us to have such great faith! I'll bet the widow whose only son was raised to life on his way to the burial chamber had that kind of faith. How could she not? They all glorified God, saying, "A great prophet has risen among us: and God has visited His people" (Lk. 7:16).

A difficult question has come about in Luke 7:18, where John the Baptist sent two of his disciples to Jesus to ask Him, "Are you the Coming One, or shall we look for another?" Sheesh! What's going on here? Don't you think John had heard all his life about Mary's miraculous baby? John was related to Jesus on their mother's side and had recently baptized Him and watched the anointing of the Holy Spirit. Now he's doubting?

I think John's expectations were for something climatic to happen after the baptism, and when life went on as usual, he began to wonder. In his defense, John was in prison at this point, out of circulation, and had not seen Jesus in action. So Jesus' answer to the two messengers was to show them His power and His healings, which proved the fulfilling of prophecies from Isaiah 35:5-6 and 61:1. John's daddy, remember, had been a temple priest, and he had no doubt grown up well grounded in Old Testament verses and prophecies. Plus, he had been filled with the Holy Spirit from the womb. His human nature just needed reassuring. I'm sure he got it when his disciples returned to him. And Jesus gives John the highest accolades possible: "'For I say to you, among those born of women, there is not a greater prophet than John the Baptist'" (Lk. 7:28).

The anointing of Jesus' feet, which also involves an alabaster flask, is not at all the same as the anointing done by Mary in Bethany. This woman, who apparently had access to the Pharisee's house, was undoubtedly a prostitute. As she stood behind Jesus, she wept freely, and her tears washed His feet as she ministered to Jesus as the host had not. This is a wonderful story of judgment, forgiveness, and restoration. This unnamed woman may have come into the house as a prostitute, but she left it forgiven, clean, and restored. We will meet her in heaven. Count on it. What a story!

Chapter 8 begins by telling us about the women who ministered to Jesus and apparently traveled with the twelve as they preached through every city and village. Don't mistake Mary Magdalene for the prostitute; they are not the same, and Mary Magdalene was the one who was healed of seven demons. We really don't know exactly what this means. What it meant in the first century could be very different than how we understand it today. We may say it was a form of mental illness—the demon of fear or demon of gluttony; that kind of demon. We just don't know, but we can appreciate she was one of several who honorably served Jesus and cared for His needs, such as good clean clothes, and so on. The author Dan Brown would have us believe there was a romantic interest between Mary Magdalene and Jesus, to which I would say "Poppycock!" Yes, Jesus had a fully human side, as well as fully God, but His last three years were focused on telling the Good News and proving He was the fulfillment of over 90 percent of the prophecies in the Old Testament, which He fulfilled to believers' complete satisfaction. The only prophecies not fulfilled right now are the ones still pointing to the second coming. I can't wait! But going back to Mary Magdalene, what if she and Jesus were romantically involved or even had a secret marriage? Would it change anything at all about His ministry or mission? I don't think so. (I don't believe this; I'm just throwing a what-if out there.)

The remainder of the stories in chapter 8 are the same ones we read about in Matthew and Mark. I am always captivated by the story of Jairus' daughter, who died surrounded by people of so little faith. This is where Jesus puts them all outside, with only her hopeful parents, Peter, James, and John in attendance to watch and celebrate the healing. This was a more private healing, and Jesus warned them not to tell anyone what happened. Yeah, right! This twelve-year-old girl is going to contact her friends just as soon as she can get out of the house, and her parents are going to praise Jesus' name until they are taken into heaven! There are just some things you don't keep secret for long. I would say raising the dead would be right up there at the top. Wouldn't you?

# CHAPTER 25

# LUKE NINE - TWELVE

From *My Utmost for His Highest:*

> "If you want to be of use to God, maintain the proper relationship with Jesus Christ by staying focused on Him, and He will make use of you every minute you live . . . yet you will be unaware, on a conscious level of your life, that you are being used of him."

Wow! Chambers almost always gives me something really profound to think about, pray about, and ponder. Take a minute and then let's start the middle chapters of Luke.

## *Chapters 9-12*

Chapter 9 of Luke contains pretty much the same stories we have read in Matthew and Mark, with a few interesting embellishments. Of interest to me is the statement by Jesus in Luke 9:26-27:

> "If anyone is ashamed of Me and My words, The Son of Man will be ashamed of him when He comes in His glory and in the glory of the Father and the holy angels. I tell you the truth, some who are standing here will not taste death before they see the Kingdom of God."

Verse 26 is talking about Jesus' second coming and how and why he will judge us, but verse 27 is the fulfillment of the following verses about the transfiguration. In these verses He is talking with all His apostles, but in the following story of the transfiguration, the "some who are standing here" turn out to be the inner circle of Peter, James, and John. And if the transfiguration isn't the exact replication of the "Kingdom of God" in the presence of Moses, Elijah, and the voice of God the Father, I don't know what else it could be.

The following words are not in our previous two gospels, so let's point them out: "Two men, Moses and Elijah, appeared in glorious splendor, talking with Jesus. They spoke about His departure, which He was about to bring to fulfillment at Jerusalem" (Lk. 9:30-31). Now we women know what "glorious splendor" is all about and can use our imagination for their clothes, fabrics, colors, etc. You just know these two ancient prophets were dressed to the hilt! And yet they paled in comparison to the bright light splendor surrounding Jesus. It's no wonder Peter started to babble!

The first story in Luke 10 is unique to this gospel and tells us about Jesus sending out more disciples (called "others" here) with pretty much the same instructions He previously gave the twelve apostles: "Go, heal the sick, preach the Good News that the Kingdom of God is near." Lk 10:9 They were given all the authority the apostles had for a specific ministry, and it worked

They were told to "heal the sick and proclaim the Kingdom of God has come near." They returned really "pumped" that "even the demons submit to them in Jesus' name ", Lk 10:17. The only thing we don't know is how many "others" went out. The King James and the New King James editions tell me there were seventy. My New English Bible and New International Version tell me there were seventy-two. We are told through commentaries that certain differences in early text manuscripts make it unclear which number is correct. Does it matter? Of course not! Jesus used other people whose hearts were committed to Him and gave them authority and gifts to get the Word out. He will do the same for you and me. All we have to say is "Here I am, God. Use me." Have you? Will you?

We cannot leave the tenth chapter without a word about Jesus' friends in Bethany, where Martha, Mary, and Lazarus lived. If you haven't already, please stop and read this story in Luke 10:38-42. Let's look at the setting. Martha is entertaining Jesus and His disciples (probably just the twelve, but there could have been more). Jesus is teaching, probably in the main room, with lots of people sitting at His feet, listening raptly to His words. Martha discovers her sister, Mary, sitting at Jesus' feet, listening, while she, Martha, is tending to the roast lamb and lentils and counting silverware . . . or pewter ware or ironware . . . errr . . . place settings. So Martha interrupts the teaching, which one of my pastors called "an explosive act," and vents her displeasure at having to do all the work. Jesus answers with a gentle rebuke, "'Martha, Martha, you are worried and upset about many things, but only one thing is needed. Mary has chosen what is better and it will not be taken away from her'" (Lk. 10:41).

Whew! What a valuable lesson for all of us. Martha simply got out of balance with her entertaining skills and forgot her priorities. Been there, done that! Oh not with Jesus, but sometimes I've gotten so distracted with what's in the oven (or should be) and how my table looks I have forgotten to use my listening skills to greet the arrival of guests. I very much want to be more like Mary in my priorities. Thank you, Lord, for this lesson on hospitality and priorities.

In the eleventh chapter of Luke, we find the disciples asking, "Lord, teach us to pray, as John also taught his disciples" (Lk. 11:1). Lord, teach me also to pray. I feel so inadequate in this regard. I have my prayer cards for my family, extended family, and those I want to be in our family, and I give them to You regularly and frequently. But it seems to be so surface, so routine, so rote. I hope You know my heart is overflowing with what my vocabulary is too limited to express. Just spending this time with You each morning is a joy and a privilege. Thank You, Lord, for taking all my limitations and loving me anyway. It truly blows my mind!

When I first started journaling, it was simply because I had a need to talk with someone about what I was discovering in my Bible readings, and other than one day a week for ladies' Bible study, I really didn't have another person-with-skin who was reading the same material I was reading. Thus, I began talking to God with pen and paper. It was never fancy; the vocabulary was always limited. But there were also few interruptions, and when there were, the written word reminded me of the thought pattern I was trying to express. It was, for me, a way to learn how to worship individually and personally rather than corporately. I often learned to worship with a hymn book in my lap,—"Oh Lord, My God, when I am in awesome wonder . . . consider all the works Thy hands have made." I still cannot, to this day, hear that opening line without tears of joy and gratitude sneaking down my cheeks. Until recently, our church in Frisco, Colorado, had printouts of all the songs sung during Sunday services. Fortunately, they were mostly praise songs we knew and loved, so I would bring the printouts back to our cabin and use them for personal worship in my quiet time, while my Bible, pen, and notebook rested quietly in front of me. By the time I opened my Bible for daily readings, my heart was so prepared and hungry for the Word that my time with the Lord just flew by! We discovered this year our little church in Colorado has gone "high-tech" with large screens in front of the congregation, and I am grateful I have saved so many song sheets from previous years. We are looking forward to and planning our annual trip to the mountains to discover what other changes have taken place.

I usually have something specific to pray about for my husband . . . usually for his wisdom and guidance in handling a business situation the way the Lord would have him handle it. But if nothing specific comes to mind, the following is a special prayer for my husband or any family member who needs prayer. I've said before, you can't go wrong when you use words directly from the Bible.

> "And this is my prayer, that your love may abound more and more in knowledge and depth of insight, so that you may be able to discern what is best and may be pure and blameless until the day of Christ, filled with the fruit of righteousness than comes through Jesus Christ . . . to the glory and praise of God" (Phil. 1:9-11)

Or more prayer suggestions:

> "I keep asking that the God of our Lord Jesus Christ, the glorious Father, may give you the Spirit of wisdom and revelation, so that you may know Him better. I pray also that the eyes of your heart may be enlightened in order that you may know the hope to which He has

> called you, the riches of His glorious inheritance in the Saints, and his incomparably great power for us who believe. "Eph. 1:17-19) NIV

> "With this in mind [God's justice], we [I] constantly pray for you, that our God may count you worthy of His calling, and that by His power He may fulfill every good purpose of yours and every act prompted by your faith. We [I] pray this so that the name of our Lord Jesus my be glorified in you, and you in Him, according to the grace of our God and the Lord Jesus Christ.' (Thess. 1:11-12)

> "Therefore, my beloved brethren [husband, son, daughter], be steadfast, immoveable, always abounding in the work of the Lord, knowing that your labor is not in vain in the Lord." (1 Cor. 15:58)

No matter what words you use in prayer for intercession, remember God looks at your heart and not your syntax. He wants the best for your loved ones—even more than you do! A prayer that often works for me is to ask the Lord to allow me to see the person I am praying for through His eyes . . . not mine. What a world of difference that makes! I had a mother-in-law I always perceived did not like me. That was very hard for me to try to accept, and before I became a Christian, I didn't do a very good job of succeeding with my efforts. But after I became acquainted with Jesus, I asked Him to reveal to me what I could do to have a better relationship with Bob's mother and to allow me to understand her better. What He revealed to me was an eye-opener and allowed me to see through His eyes and not my own. She was not a "warm, fuzzy, huggy" person, because she had never learned how to love from her parents. When you don't know love from your family of origin, it's very difficult to experience it and almost impossible to pass it on. The "problem" wasn't me at all; it was my perception of how she felt about me. As soon as this was revealed to me, I could encourage our children—and myself—to greet her with hugs and joy.

When you look at someone through the eyes of the Lord and not your own, all kinds of changes can take place, whether it's in the home, on the tennis court, in an office situation, or in church! Try it, and see how it works for you.

And now, farther on in Luke, Jesus chastises the Pharisees, telling them, "'The outside of the cup and dish are clean, but your inward part is full of greed, and wickedness'" (Lk. 11:39).This verse reminds me of an experience I had several years ago when we returned to our home in Lincoln from our winter stay in the desert. Our home is quite nice, very comfortable, and the décor has always been pleasing to me. It's always nice to be home, No matter where that home is. They are only temporary anyway, but wherever they are, we are stewards of our properties. The morning after our arrival, Bob left for his office, and as I was cleaning up the breakfast dishes, I was admiring my home. The cleaning ladies, whom I could not function without, had recently been there, and I was thoroughly enjoying the soft sheen of the wood floors and every surface dusted, cleaned, and polished. After all, we hadn't been home long enough to mess it up, and I was truly relishing this state of tidy, clean, bliss! Then I opened the dishwasher to put in our coffee cups and cereal dishes and got such a shock! We had company for dinner five months before, and the dishwasher had not been started. Mold almost reached out to grab me! I thought of the above verse and absolutely howled with laughter. My kitchen, which had looked so perfect from the outside just a few minutes before, was full of . . . I don't know about greed, but surely wickedness, germs, and dirt on the inside! That's an example of us! I can clean myself up to look pretty good, hair trimmed regularly, nails trimmed, clothes clean and (usually) unwrinkled, but if I'm not clean on the inside, I am no better than the Pharisees, whom Jesus called a "whitewashed wall." And that means prayed up, praised up, and confessed up every day. I thought about that the whole time it took me to remove every item from the dishwasher, hand wash in hot suds with bleach, and run the dishwasher several times with extra detergent. Yuk!

What was almost worse was when I reached into the kitchen drawer for a clean dish towel and exclaimed aloud, "Who spilled the wild rice?" Yikes! Not wild rice . . . mice! The top drawer had been full of cough drops, each one separately wrapped in a little yellow wrapper. You know what some top drawers of kitchens look like. This one contained pencils, pens, unidentified keys, rubber bands, and so on. Commonly called "junk" drawers, the one in our house also contained cough drops. All were empty except for the little yellow wrappings left behind. And droppings in the next drawer down to let me know we had critters. Fortunately, they had vanished for the time being, and within a few days, Bob became my hero (once again!) by trapping three of them in the walk-out basement. I did not inquire as to their demise, nor did Kiki. She was oblivious! I had a talk with her about her function in our household, but she wanted to no part of my instructions. Sheesh!

Lord, I don't want to be clean on the outside and not on the inside! Jesus, thank You for Your cleansing blood on the cross . . . for Your forgiveness, for redeeming me at such a time of my life that was so spiritually empty, for loving me right into Your kingdom whether I deserved it or not. I am so grateful to have the privilege of experiencing just some of Your glory right here on earth. Hold onto me, Lord. I need You.

Luke 12 has a verse close to my heart, and of course another story. Let's start with the verse: "Take heed and beware of covetousness, for one's life does not consist of the abundance of the things he possessed" (Lk. 12:14).

My life and my treasures here on earth, I hope, have little to do with what I possess. My very greatest treasures are my family and my extended family . . . those precious friends who know me with all my faults and love me anyway. Lord, save me from covetousness. I have needs and I have wants, and they are not the same. I am so aware that You have provided for me so well through the gifts and intelligence of my husband, Bob, who has such a generous heart, and I do thank You for that and him, but I also see Your hand all the time. "Every good and perfect gift comes from the Father of heavenly lights, Who does not shift like shifting shadows" (James 1:17). How well I have learned that! Five years ago, we watched a new house being built in our neighborhood in the desert. Almost every evening Bob and I would take a walk and inspect the new house after the workers had left. We loved it from the beginning. Perfect lot . . . on a small lake . . . view of the mountains surrounding Coachella Valley, and that one extra bedroom for our granddaughter, Marisa. As the workers were putting the final touches on the new house, we called Valerie, our realtor, and listed our house. If, perchance, it sold, we would make an offer on the new house, which was a "spec" home. This was the very beginning of the economic turndown, so we were not willing to own two houses at our winter retreat location. As luck would have it (and Lord, You know I don't even believe in the concept of the word "luck." You are the Author and Finisher of every detail of our lives) our house did not sell. The day the new house went on the market, a nice family from Washington State bought it. When I realized how disappointed I was, I was also convicted of my feelings of covetousness and was once again on my knees asking for forgiveness and counting the many blessings I had already received from His hand. Forgive me, Lord, when I mistake my needs with my wants. Will I ever stop being so selfish? Please, Lord, don't give up on me. Ordinarily I look around and am astonished at the material things You have blessed us with.

Last year, when we returned to the desert, our neighbors told us the "new" house was back on the market. Their youngest son was graduating from high school, and they didn't need the extra bedroom we had been wishing for. And they wanted to sell fully furnished, with many improvements and even more upgrades. "Mrs. Seller" was the most imaginative and creative interior decorator I have ever seen. At Bob's urging, we made an appointment with the listing agent, saw the house, and, of course, we loved it all over again. But it was 2008, and the real estate market for high-end residential homes in Southern California was nonexistent. Many homes were going back to the lenders, and it was a very fragile market, at best. I was very grateful for my husband's foresight in never having a mortgage on personal property. If we couldn't afford it, we didn't buy it. Simple. We made an offer to trade their house for our house in the same neighborhood, free and clear, plus cash for the upgrades. The agent was reluctant to even submit the offer but did because it was the law. She had to. It was rejected immediately. At this point, I thought I could see God's hand all over this transaction. It had to have been His hand who opened this door once more. But with the rejection, I was disappointed. It was Bob who said, "Don't give up. Just wait. This isn't over yet." He was right, and I put it on the back burner. Four months later, the owner called and asked if our previous offer was still on the table. It was. Within three weeks, we traded houses and moved. We both got to stay in the same neighborhood we loved, got the extra bedroom for our granddaughter, and I got the home of my dreams.

Yep . . . God's hand was all over this transaction! It reminds me so much of the phrase, "Delight yourself in the Lord, and he will give you the desires of our heart" (Ps. 3:4). No, I didn't ask for that house. I asked for wisdom and guidance for both families and for God's will to be done. Then I started thanking Him, and every single time I walk into our new home, I remember to thank God (How could I not?) and to mentally thank the former owners for taking such good care of it. Good grief! I absolutely know a gift from God when I see one!

Now let's move on with this verse from chapter 12 in the gospel of Luke:

> "And do not seek what you should eat or what you should drink, nor have an anxious mind. For all these things the nations of the world seek after, and your Father knows that you need these things. But seek first the Kingdom of God, and all these things shall be added to you." (Lk. 12:29-30)

Thank you, Lord. I'm having a hard time getting past the twelfth chapter of Luke, there is so much to mediate on, including:

> "Do not fear, little flock, for it is your Father's good pleasure to give you the kingdom. Sell whatever you have and give alms; provide yourselves money bags which do not grow old, a treasure in the heavens that does not fail, where no thief approaches nor moth destroys. For where your treasure is, there your heart will be also." (Lk. 12:32-34)

Thank You, Jesus. You are my treasure! The special gifts You have given me are the people in my life: my husband, Bob; our adult children, Kim and Andy; and their spouses, Mike and Sandy, who are as dear to me as my own. I prayed for both of them long before we met, so when it did happen, it was almost like, "Oh there you are!" What blessings they are to us! And our four precious grandchildren: Marisa, our first and only granddaughter, our little princess; her younger brother, Kipper, who I had the privilege of watching come into the world. What an awesome gift! Both children are Kim and Mike's and live in Lincoln. They are sixteen and thirteen this spring. Oh my! Andy and Sandy have the two little guys . . . Joshua, who is now eleven and a half, and his brother, Jared, now ten. Such loving little boys! Such blessings. These are the treasures who will follow me right into heaven, along with my darling sister, Nancy, and our dear friend Dee, Sandy's mom. Lord, these and the treasured friends are my blessings and for sure where my heart is. Thank you. I feel like the richest person in the whole world with these blessings. This is surely where my heart is!

> "For everyone to whom much is given, from him much will be required, and to whom much has been committed, to him they will ask the more" (Lk. 12:48b)

> Thank You, Lord. Please help me to use all I have been given for Your Glory in any way that I can. Material gifts, spiritual gifts, physical energy . . . let them be for Your Glory and for Your harvest. With all my heart I desire to do Your will and not to let any of my friends be left behind. I give them to You often, Lord, and ask again for you to soften their hearts and open their minds to the truth of Your Word. Amen.

## CHAPTER 26

# LUKE THIRTEEN - SIXTEEN

Dear Lord, today is my friend Jill's birthday. Please bless her, Lord, and reveal Yourself anew to her.

I am actually cooking today, because my sister, Nancy, is coming from Florida just for the weekend with her friend and neighbor, Boo, who we have not yet met. I think our cousin Cindy will be here tomorrow. How fun! Bless our time together, Lord, no matter how short.

From *My Utmost of His Highest,* our devotion for today:

> "Whenever His hand is laid upon you, it gives inexpressible peace and comfort, and the sense that "underneath are the everlasting arms" (Deut. 33:37), full of support, provision, comfort, and strength. And once His touch comes, nothing at all can throw you into fear again.

This Old Testament quote reminds me so much of Elizabeth Elliott, a multi-media Bible teacher, author and speaker. It is one of her theme verses. I listened to her for years on Christian radio and learned so much from her. Bless her, Lord, wherever she is right now.

A verse from Psalms keeps coming back to me: "Create in me a clean heart, O God, and renew a steadfast spirit within me. Do not cast me from Your presence, and do not take Your Holy Spirit from me" (Ps. 51:10-11). Amen. Oh Lord, can there be a better prayer? I pray this for me always. I can think of no greater calamity than to lose Your Presence, and I thank You and praise You that I know You are with me. If anyone has moved between us, I will know it is me and not You. If that should ever happen, I don't think I could stand it!

Nancy and Boo arrived yesterday and Cindy will come today. I woke up feeling ill with allergies this morning. I really don't want to be sick! This afternoon was better (Yes, I'm writing this at night. Sometimes with company you just do what you have to do!), but I still had a headache behind my eyes. Rats! Thank You, Jesus. I need to hang on to You right now. I take my health so much for granted and have had a relatively healthy life, notwithstanding breast cancer in 1989 and two strokes in 1999, but I forget to thank You when I am feeling well and full of energy. But when illness strikes, I am on my knees, asking for mercy and healing all over again.

Oh dear, today is Sunday Sabbath morning. I was up and almost dressed but just couldn't make it beyond tooth brushing. Back to bed with Charles Stanley on TV for my corporate worship this morning. Bob and Nancy went off to church without me. Rats! Feeling better this afternoon, so I could go to Kim and Mikes' for a pleasant afternoon by the pool and Kipper charcoaling chicken for all of us. Delightful! Kim's family loved Boo as much as we did. Nancy is so blessed to have wonderful neighbors and friends in her Florida community.

Monday morning, and Nancy and Boo are leaving today. Please, Lord, help me to function vertically until they leave this afternoon. We are having such a good time, but I feel so awful! "I can do all things through Christ who strengthens me" (Phil. 4:13).

Thank You, Lord. I feel so responsible for people around me. I am such a "controller." I'm sorry, Lord. Help me to "chill out" a little. Oh yes, headaches and chills. Sigh! I took the girls to the airport and then came home for a nap on the sofa. At lunchtime, Kim suggested I might have a sinus infection. That resonated with me the more I thought about it, so off to Urgent Care I go. Yep . . . sinus infection . . . temperature of 101.2. Darn! Prescription for ten days. I'm so relieved to get help, and thanks to Kim for suggesting the correct diagnosis today. She is so wise. Thank You, Lord, for my daughter.

Two days later and feeling much better. Bridge today at my house. I don't have to drive and am not contagious, so will not cancel. Thank You, Lord, for friends who will accept me, unwashed hair, messy house, and all.

Now we will move on with Luke's gospel.

## *Chapters 13-15*

The first three stories in chapter 13 are all beyond my comprehension. The first has to do with repentance and a story of the evil nature of Pilate, which was just one of the reasons the Jews rebelled against Rome and what ultimately led to the destruction of Jerusalem and the temple in AD 70. The bottom line of the story, in my opinion, is twofold: life is not fair, and we all have to repent. Confess. Turn around and go the other way.

The parable about the man with the fig tree is also unique to this gospel. The fig tree has often been a symbol of Israel, but we can all relate to this parable in that God will not wait forever for us—or Israel—to produce fruit.

The crippled woman being healed on the Sabbath was forever a bone of contention with the rabbis and chief priests, and in this case, the ruler of the synagogue. In this life, we will meet people who are so fanatical they don't understand that mercy and grace trump rules and regulations. God alone will have to deal with these types. I cannot.

The other parables are repeated in Matthew and Mark. This chapter ends with Jesus again and forever lamenting Israel's lack of faith in Him:

> "Oh, Jerusalem, Jerusalem, the one who kills the prophets and stones those who are sent to her! How often I wanted to gather your children together as a hen gathers her brood under her wings, but you were not willing. See, your house is left to you desolate, and assuredly I say to you, you shall not see Me until the time comes when you say, 'blessed is He who comes in the name of the Lord.'"
> Lk. 13:34-35

This is a good place to stop and pray for any Jewish friends you may be praying for. I can feel the longing in Jesus' words, and it breaks my heart!

The parable of the ambitious guest in Luke 14:14, reminding us to be humble in social situations (and elsewhere), reminds me of:

"Humble yourselves before the Lord and He will lift you up." (Jas. 4:10)

"He who exalts himself will be humbled, and he who humbles himself will be exalted." (Mt. 23:12)

Haven't we all seen people who hurry to get the best of everything, never mind who is in their way? Now we know what God thinks of these kinds of self-serving actions.

The parable of the great supper in Luke 14:15 tells us what excuses we give to Him when He calls. One excuse was "work," one excuse was "wealth," and another excuse was a "spouse." What excuse do we give when the Lord beckons us? Are we too busy being "Marthas"? When we are too busy to come when He calls us, He will replace us. He will send His servant for others. And perhaps it was Israel who originally did the refusing, and we Gentiles are the others who Jesus found. The bottom-line lesson for us: if you are invited by the Lord, accept! Don't even give it a second thought; don't wait for a spouse or children or a friend. Go to Him.

The next story about discipleship is similar. If called, don't hesitate: "Whoever, does not forsake all that he has cannot be My Disciple" (Lk.14:33).We're talking about priorities here . . . not loss. When the Lord is your first priority, He strengthens all your other relationships into a bond that cannot be broken. He is not asking you to give up, but to put Him first.

In chapter 15 we are given a precious verse: "I say to you that likewise there will be more joy in heaven over one sinner who repents than over ninety-nine just persons who need no repentance" (Lk. 15:7). So don't give up on that person (or people) on your prayer list who just don't get it. The angels in heaven are holding their collective breath, waiting! "Likewise I say to you there is joy in the presence of the angels of God over one sinner who repents" (Lk. 15:10).

The remainder of chapter 15 is devoted to the parable of the lost son: the prodigal. If you have not read it, please stop right now, and read this tragic story only told in Luke. It starts at Luke 15:11 and continues to the end of the chapter. This is the story of sin, loss, degradation, repentance, and restoration—all in one fell swoop! God turns a prodigal around many times by chastisement, and disciplines those He loves. The father's immediate forgiveness and joy is a picture of how the Lord feels and reacts when we return to Him if we have fallen away in disbelief or discouragement. For any of you who have sons, daughters, or other family members who have fallen away for any reason, this is a story of hope. It is interesting that the older son, who stayed home, is just as sinful in his disrespect, disdain, judgmentalism and lack of compassion and forgiveness as the younger, who ran away and came to his senses. Oh my. So much to consider here. If this story brings you sadness, may God bless you and encourage you with hope and joyful expectation for a future reunion just out of sight!

Chapter 16 has the parable of the unjust servant with two memorable verses by which to live:

> "He who is faithful in what is least is faithful also in much, and he who is unjust in what is least is unjust also in much." (Lk. 16:10)

> "No servant can serve two masters; for either he will hate the one and love the other, or else he will by loyal to the one and despise the other. You cannot serve God and mammon [money" (Lk. 16:13)

Jesus spoke to the Pharisees who were lovers of money: "'You are those who justify yourselves before men, but God knows your hearts: For what is highly esteemed among men is an abomination in the sight of God'" (Lk. 16:15). I have a very dear friend whose beautiful, intelligent daughter is currently serving a prison term, because she didn't learn these concepts about money and God. How terribly sad! Everything we ever need for a successful, fruitful, and satisfying life is written in the pages of this book. Whether we get it or not is the entire question. It is not for me to judge.

The parable of the rich man and Lazarus, the poor beggar, always takes my breath away! It is so shocking in its directness and simplicity about heaven and the torments of hell in flames of fire. Do I believe them? I do. What I have trouble with is believing one can see from the depths of hell into the loveliness, peace, and contentment of heaven and vice versa. I do believe there is a fixed gulf between the two that cannot be breached in either direction. But I'm not sure I believe one can actually "see" from one place to the other for the simple reason I believe if I could see into hell, it would break my heart, and I know there are no heartaches or tears in heaven. Fascinating that the rich man thought his family would respond if someone would come back from the dead. But Abraham said to him, "'If they do not hear Moses and the prophets, neither will they be persuaded though one rise from the dead'" (Lk. 16:31). Oh, Abraham, you wonderful prophet of old, how wise you are! I can't wait to meet you!

Have you noticed how many different parables there are in Luke compared to Matthew and Mark? Taken together, they give us a more complete picture than just one gospel at a time. We are almost adding precept upon precept. Oh doesn't that sound just like the beloved Kay Arthur, author, teacher and founder of Precepts Ministry? Bless her, too, Lord, wherever she is.

Thank You, Lord, for opening our minds as well as our hearts to Your Word. Amen.

# CHAPTER 27

# LUKE SEVENTEEN - TWENTY

From *My Utmost for His Highest:*

> "Pray without ceasing." (1 Thess. 5:17)
>
> "The correct concept is to think of prayer as the breath in our lungs and the blood from our hearts."

I think prayer is a natural response to loving and knowing Jesus. But like everything else, it has to be practiced to become as natural as breathing. Natural for most of us is a do-it-yourself concept, or prayer only when nothing else works. A last resort. The Lord wants us to pray as a first resort . . . unceasingly. When we have Jesus in our heart and are so aware of the Presence of the Holy Spirit, it is easy to be in communication with Him all the time. When we begin our day with prayer, His Presence stays with us all day long. The feeling of being connected, . . . of being protected, . . . and yes, of being loved. We are chosen people, a royal priesthood, when we are under the shadow of God's wings. It's true some of us have to be hit over the head or really taken down in life—physically, mentally, or spiritually—before we give up and give our broken, sick lives over to Christ and ask for His help, His Presence, and His healing. I was one of those broken sick people, so full of pride I thought I could handle my life all by myself. Oh my was I wrong!

The Bible says, "Pride goes before destruction, a haughty spirit before a fall" (Prov. 16:18). My pride stayed with me right up to the "destruction" that sent me to my knees in 1975 and allowed me to hang onto the robe of Jesus and ask for forgiveness. That illness was absolutely allowed by the Lord to send me to my knees. I am convinced it was the only way He could get my attention.

One of my very favorite verses that I come back to time after time is:

> "Do not be anxious about anything, but in everything, by prayer and petition, with Thanksgiving, present your request to God, and the peace of God, which transcends all understanding, will guard your hearts and minds in Christ Jesus.' (Phil. 4:6)

Dear Lord, You know I am an anxious person. I'm wired so that I just can't wait to see what the next thing is. It is never in my nature to be late for anything, especially if it has to do with spiritual matters. I can't think how many times Bob has asked me to slow down and wait for him. I have really tried to do that, but my mind just races on ahead as I try to slow my body down. I am just anxious. But tonight got me out of bed when I heard on the ten o'clock news one of my medications was put on a list of drugs suspected of weakening bones, and I can't take a statin drug without it. And I just found out my cholesterol level has gone up slightly this year. I knew it had. I stopped taking it for a while and then cut way back. My doctor has just prescribed a different, stronger statin that I haven't even picked up from the pharmacy yet. I know I can't take it without stomach acid protection, which apparently is now suspect. Help, Lord! It's so hard to grow old and have all these prescription problems! I know there must be natural remedies that will get me off all the meds that can't help but have harmful side effects. Lord, Your Word says if we need wisdom to ask, and it will be given: "If any of you lacks wisdom, he should ask God who gives generously to all without finding fault, and it will be given to him" (Jas. 1:5).

Thank You, Lord. I am for sure asking now for wisdom and also thanking Your Holy Spirit for suggesting through Kim what was wrong with me recently. Thank You, for using her to let me know. I am very grateful for the mysterious ways in which You work! I am even more excited when I realize them—and not necessarily in hindsight. Wow!

What an awesome God You are! Just last night, bored with TV (the news did me in!) and channel surfing, I happened to catch a program on natural healing. I *never* watch programs of this kind and seldom stray away from *Jeopardy, Wheel of Fortune,* and the Christian channel. Oh yes, I also like the Weather Channel. Sheesh! I'm showing my simplicity. Anyway, I wrote down the author's name and will purchase his book ASAP. I am determined to get a handle on my own health, asking first of all for God's wisdom and healing touch.

Oh, Lord, I need You, how I need You, every hour I need You, most holy precious Savior. I come. I come. Thank You, Lord. I know You will give me wisdom on how to handle this health issue and the peace of God, which transcends all understanding and is already guarding my heart, my mind, and my physical problems in Christ Jesus, my Lord.

Lord, yesterday, just hours after asking for protection for my family—aware that what I am writing just now means I need to ask for daily protection for my family especially—because if just one of is hurt, the rest of us hurt also. Our thirteen-year-old grandson, Kipper, was in an accident not entirely of his own doing. Please God, these are precisely the kinds of minor, mind-boggling incidents that we desperately need protection from. I can only thank You that it wasn't worse and no one was hurt, and crucial lessons were learned, including Kipper isn't old enough to drive yet, and we are under the shadow of Your wings.

> "And we know that in all things God works for the good of those who love Him, who have been called according to His purpose. "Rom. 8:28)

Thank You, Lord, for giving us protection, wisdom and perspective through all we do and say and think. Amen.

Let's continue with our reading of the gospel of Luke.

## *Chapters 17-20*

Since Luke is a physician, I suspect he must have been very interested in all the healings performed by Jesus, and chapter 17 gives us a group healing of ten lepers who were calling out for mercy. "Have pity on us," they shouted. Jesus did have pity on them and told them, "'Go, show yourselves to the priests.' And as they went, they were cleansed" (Lk. 17:4). Note this was not an instantaneous healing. It was a process they had to participate in. They needed faith to go, since they still had the disease. Still infected, they started, and it was on the way that they were healed. And only one returned to thank Jesus, and he was a Samaritan, not even a full Jew; he was someone the community often looked down on. Ninety percent of the group went on their way, healed and whole, without looking back to thank and praise the Lord. Is this indicative of our society as a whole? Are we so self-absorbed that we don't know or care who our Creator, our Healer is? Oh Lord, forgive us! Open our eyes to the miracles You do all around us every single day for which we forget to thank You.

The next question is one we all want to know: When will the Kingdom of God come? Jesus answered, "'The Kingdom of God does not come with your careful observation, nor will people say, "here it is," or "there it is," because the Kingdom of God is within you'" (Lk. 17:21). Huh? Didn't we just recently read where Jesus said repeatedly to "be on guard," and "watch"? Didn't He give us all kinds of signs to look for, most of which are occurring this minute? There must be more to this saying. Oh yes, let's explore a passage in Romans:

> "For the Kingdom of God is not a matter of eating or drinking, but of righteousness, peace, and joy in the Holy Spirit, because anyone who serves Christ in this way is pleasing to God and approved by men" (Rom. 14:17)

We think of the Kingdom of God as the time Jesus will return to this sinful, dirty, fallen world and straighten us all out again. But what Jesus is saying here is, we don't have to wait for that to happen; we can enjoy the Kingdom now. We just have to spiritually dig a little deeper and look within ourselves to find that kind of joy in the Person of the Holy Spirit. Here Jesus talks about His return:

> "For the Son of Man in His day [the second coming] will be like lightening, which flashes and lights up the sky from one end to

another. But first, He must suffer many things and be rejected by this generation" (Lk. 17:24-25)

I would say He has most definitely been rejected by our generation also, when you look at our liberal media and that prayer is no longer allowed in public schools. And don't get me started on limitations at Christmastime! Whatever happened to our Judeo-Christian heritage? Back to our chapter 17, don't miss Jesus telling about His return and how life will be going along as normal everywhere on earth when He comes again. One thing I notice is that he talks about "on that night." I don't think of Jesus coming back at night, because I think of Him coming back on big, puffy, white clouds visible to all of us, no matter where we live. This is the chapter where He indeed tells about those unbelievers who are left behind. This is incentive to increase our prayers for our unsaved, unbelieving friends.

Chapter 18 continues with the same subject, telling about the widow who persists in her requests to a judge until he finally relents because of her persistence. Of course this is encouragement to keep praying for that lost person or family member who might think you are a little "over the edge" with your love for Jesus. We read, "And will not God bring about justice for His chosen ones, who keep crying out to Him, day and night?" (Lk. 18:7).

I admit, I don't cry out day and night. My unbelieving friends tend to be on my Saturday prayer card, because they are not on my mind that often. The concerns of my family and extended family always take precedence with my intercessions. That's why I have to write down the other names to offer them up to God . . . lest I forget. And I would. It's human nature to forget all those except those closest to us. And I do.

Stories revealed in previous gospels make up the remainder of chapter 18. But when we get into our last reading for this day, we have a new and interesting story about a tax collector named Zacchaeus, who was quite short, a chief tax collector. and very wealthy. He climbed up a sycamore/fig tree. I don't know about the "fig" part; we don't have those kinds of trees in Nebraska, but we had a marvelous sycamore tree in the front yard at Calvert Place, where we lived for twenty-one years. It had whitish bark and very sturdy limbs. It had allowed my imagination to picture a small tax collector climbing up for a better look. This is a story of an instant conversion experience, rather one that takes some time to process and where one needs to hear more facts. When Zacchaeus experienced the Living Lord, he was willing, able, and fell all over himself to "come clean." While it was the law that he pay back four times the amount to anyone he had cheated, it was because of his heart and his sudden generosity that he gave half of his possessions to the poor. The last sentence of this story is the key phrase of the entire book of Luke: "'Today salvation has come to this house, because this man, too, is a son of Abraham; for the Son of Man came to seek and to save that which was lost'" (Lk. 19:9-10).

When the head of a household comes to the Lord, the entire household is blessed! I don't know about you, but I have several husbands on my prayer list who are precious, powerful husbands and fathers, but they don't know the Lord. And I keep thinking when the Lord finally reaches them, what a change it will make in their extended families, who all look to the patriarch for guidance. I'm not for a minute putting down the prayers of a wife and mother. On the contrary; if it wasn't for a mother named Monica, Augustine would not have come to the Lord and brought Christianity into Europe in mid-centuries. I just think the head of the household has a huge influence on his entire family. Keep praying!

The story about the ten minas is also fascinating. The nobleman who went away to be made a king gave ten of his servants ten minas. When he returned, he called his servants to him to find the first one had doubled his money. "Well done, my good servant. Because you have been trustworthy in a very small matter, take charge of ten cities" (Lk. 19:17). The next servant had earned five minas, and likewise was put in charge of five cities. But the last one had buried the money, not invested it, and lost it to the first servant, who was the most successful investor. Curious minds want to know what happened to the remaining seven servants, but we are not told.

What do we learn with this story? It seems to be saying there are two classes of people: fruitful and unfruitful. We are to leave more behind than we found, and if we don't, we have missed the message! To be cautious and careful, simply picking up after ourselves, is not good enough. When the Spirit of the Living God is in us, to be fruitful, we must invest our lives, our jobs, our money, our reputations, our security. Otherwise, we decrease and die. It is not enough to preserve what is. We must use the gifts God has given us. Have you? Are you?

The remainder of the chapter is the triumphal entry into Jerusalem on the day we call Palm Sunday. It marks Jesus' last week before the crucifixion. We weep along with Jesus at His words as He surveys the city He loves:

> "If you, even you, had only known on this day what would bring your peace . . . but now it is hidden from your eyes. The days will come upon you when your enemies will build an embankment against you and encircle you and hem you in on every side. They will dash you to the ground, you and the children within your walls. They will not leave one stone on another, because you did not recognize the time of God's coming to you." (Lk. 19:41, 44)

Chapter 20 of the gospel of Luke contains the same stories and parables we found in Matthew and Mark. In the parable of the tenants, Jesus tells about the owner of the vineyard (God the Father) sending his representatives (the prophets), who were badly treated, beaten, thrown out of, and killed. He finally sends His Son, who also was not respected and killed. This parable is a no-brainer, and the prophecy and bottom line are, "What then will the owner of the vineyard do to them? He will come and kill those tenants and give the vineyard to others" (Lk. 20:15b-16).

## CHAPTER 28

# LUKE TWENTY-ONE - TWENTY-FOUR

Today's reading from *My Utmost for His Highest:*

> Lord, I will follow You, but .............(Lk.9:61)
>
> "Trust completely in God, and when he brings you a new opportunity of adventure, offering it to you, see that you take it. We act like pagans in a crisis, only one out of any entire crowd is daring enough to invest his faith in the character of God."
>
> Oh, Lord, I want to invest my faith in Your character. Show me how. Lead me in the way I should go. Always and forever. When Victoria suggested last spring that I start writing, it seemed like a "new opportunity of adventure," and it has been. With You, Lord, every avenue is a new adventure. I am grateful. Amen.

And good morning, Lord. Thank you for a brand-new day and any opportunity I may have to serve You. Today Bob and I are celebrating our fifty-first anniversary. We will celebrate by going to Marisa's dance recital at a local high school. We have not seen her dance for several years and are especially looking forward to the performance, because she has a solo number for the first time. What fun!

Lord, God, thank You for my husband, for his loyalty and love for me and our family, for his wisdom and strength. Especially, Lord, be present in our marriage, reminding me that a cord of three cannot be broken. Help me, Lord, to be sensitive to his needs—especially in the kitchen. That is so hard for me.

Memorial Day, and a day to pray for our troops in the Middle East. Lord, I know peace will not come in my lifetime unless You come back soon, but I do ask You to protect our young men and women who are in the armed forces and in a foreign land protecting our freedom. Be with them, Lord, and protect them until they can return home to their loved ones. A picnic today at Kim and Mike's pool. Mike's mother is here from San Francisco, and her good friend is also here from near New Orleans. What fun! Also a celebration of Marisa's amazing performance yesterday. We were so proud of her talent, her grace, and her poise!

Now Lord, open our hearts and minds to the last four chapters of Luke's gospel.

## *Chapters 21-24*

Chapter 21 talks about two destructions: the first prophecy of the temple, which took place in AD 70 (Lk. 21:5-6), and the signs of the second coming, which we discussed at length in Matthew. It's a little disturbing to read: "When you see Jerusalem being surrounded by armies, you will know that its desolation is near" (Lk. 21:20).

To see the animosity of the surrounding countries in the Middle East today, it makes us wonder. Since we know the entire story ends with Jesus' return to earth, it is also quite exciting to see this played out and to contemplate. I might remind all of us that things might get very fragile for us, even here in the United States, on global issues, and if that happens, let us be reassured with Jesus' words: "'Make up your mind not to worry beforehand how you will defend yourselves. For I will give you words and wisdom that none of your adversaries will be able to resist or contradict'" (Lk. 21:14-15).

You can't plan ahead of time what you will say or do. Trust Jesus for that. Is that not one of the most reassuring paragraphs you have ever read? Especially in light of this entire chapter, which tells us to watch and pray, because so many signs are happening as I write this!

It is very encouraging to me to read, "'Heaven and earth will pass away, but My words will never pass away'" (Lk 21:33). We can *never* go wrong studying, reading, meditating on, and memorizing the words in the Book of Life. And here is the good news/bad news as we finish up this chapter.

> "Be careful or your hearts will be weighed down with dissipation, drunkenness and anxieties of life, and that day will close in on you unexpectedly, like a trap. For it will come upon all those who live on the face of the whole earth. Be always on the watch and pray that you may be able to escape all that is about to happen, and that you may be able to stand before the Son of Man." (Lk. 21:34-36).

Friends, these are our "marching orders." We've been told, so we will be prepared. Thank you, Jesus, we are not going into the future blindfolded.

In chapter 22, we have the betrayal by Judas, one of His Apostles, and then the story of the Last Supper. One or two extra tidbits thrown into Luke's account. Jesus kept the location of the Passover supper a secret from all but Peter and John, who were instructed to look for a man carrying a water jug and to follow him to his master's house. Jesus probably wanted to keep the location secret, so He could give last-minute instructions without being interrupted. A man carrying a water jug is almost an oxymoron! It just had never happened! That was culturally and traditionally women's or slave's work, so it was easy for them to find the house with the large upper room.

After the Passover meal and institution of communion, with instructions to "do this in remembrance of Me," we come very soon to the Garden of Gethsemane, where Jesus withdrew a "stone's throw apart" from the apostles and then gave a very powerful and poignant prayer: "'Father, if it is Your will, take this cup away from Me. Nevertheless, not My will, but Yours be done'" (Lk. 22:42). Jesus, in His anguish and preparation for what is to come, is still teaching, not only the apostles, who couldn't seem to keep their eyes open, but us as well. As our Mentor, Teacher, and Savior, Jesus is teaching us to never go into an unknown and/or dangerous situation without first going to the Lord. And the prayer that never fails is, "Your will, Lord, not mine." You can map out any kind of solutions you want and present it to God in prayer, but His will and His way are always going to be better than any solution we could come up with.

Verses 43 and 44 are unique to Luke's gospel. Luke is describing a physical condition: "Then His sweat became like great drops of blood falling down to the ground" (Lk. 22:44). In his commentary, John MacArthur's Study Bible, page 1561, tells us this condition is called hermatidrosis, a very dangerous situation in which capillaries dilate and burst, mingling with the perspiration, brought on by great anguish. I don't know about you, but I am in anguish just thinking about this stressful scene. Leave it to Dr. Luke to include this in his writings.

Luke also records the severing of the servant's ear, but he is the only writer who records Jesus' healing: "And He touched his ear and healed him" (Lk. 22:51).

We have recorded, starting now, the trials of Jesus. I am going to outline them for us according to my handwritten notes. I will give you chapter and verse, so you can follow along in your own Bible:

> Trial Number One
> Jesus was brought before the Sanhedrin (Jewish religious law) twice—once illegally at night (Lk. 22:54) and the second time at daybreak (Lk. 22:66). Judged guilty [implied] (Lk. 22:71).
>
> Trial Number Two
> Represents Jewish secular law in front of Pilate and then on to King Herod, who happened to be in Jerusalem at the time. Judged innocent. "So Pilate said to the Chief Priests and the crowd, 'I find no fault in this Man'" (Lk. 23:4).
>
> Trial Number Three
> Herod sent Him back to Pilate, who judged Roman law, who again found Him innocent (Lk. 23:14-16). Pilate said for the third time, "'I have found no reason for death in Him. I will chastise Him and let Him go'" (Lk. 23:22).

Finally, after the insistence of the chief priests and Jewish rulers, He was "delivered to their will" (Lk. 23:25) to be crucified by a Roman guard, along with two other prisoners, one on His left and one on His right. Only in Luke does one of the prisoners stop mocking Jesus and realizes who he is and what kind of injustice is being carried out. When this person realizes the truth of the situation around him, he believed in Jesus, and said, "'Lord, remember me when You come into Your kingdom'" (Lk. 23-42).

And Jesus answered him, "'Assuredly I say to you, today you will be with Me in Paradise'" (Lk. 23:43).

The word "Paradise" suggests a garden and was used to describe the Garden of Eden, but where it is used in the New Testament (2 Cor. 12; Rev. 2:7), it refers to Heaven. This is good news for us no matter how you look at it, because no matter how late in life you believe in Jesus Christ as Messiah, Lord, Savior, you are going to heaven with Him! Halleluiah!

This reminds me of a family story. Bob's grandparents, who I had the pleasure of knowing for maybe ten or twelve years before their deaths, lived in Omaha. The grandfather was a powerful patriarch of the Weigel family, a tall, proud, German man with snow-white hair. He was what I would call a master gardener. Whenever we visited their home, we were given a tour of Gramp's garden in the backyard. It was nothing short of meticulous! Row upon row of vegetables, with nothing between the rows but rich, dark soil. A weed wouldn't have a chance to grow under Gramp's watchful care. Gramp eventually developed diabetes and a heart condition, and one day ended up in the hospital with a heart attack. Gram Weigel (his wife), their daughter, Dorothy, and her husband, Jack, were visiting him when he suddenly died. Bells and whistles went off all over the place, and the family was banished to the hallway, while nurses and doctors rushed in to revive this well over eighty-year-old man! When he was revived, the relatives dried their eyes and went back to the room to finish their visit. They heard a wonderful story from Gramp. When he died, he found himself in a wonderful garden, full of light and beautiful plants. Bob's father, who had died ten years previously, and Arthur, a baby they lost as a toddler, were there to greet Gramp. He was pretty indignant that he had been revived and brought back to a hospital room. And when Gramp was indignant, everyone around him shook! The good news to this story is that he did die a couple of days later, and the family was left with a great story of a garden.

After I became a believer, I formed the habit of sitting very close to the front in the sanctuary in church. Bob was always perplexed by my choice, but I figured I had a lot to catch up on, and I didn't want to miss a word! When I asked Bob where his family liked to sit when he was growing up in Omaha, he replied, "The back row . . . with Gram, Gramp, aunts, and uncles . . . the whole family. If Gramp didn't agree with the minister, he simply stood up and left, and the whole family was expected to follow him." I still chuckle over the absurdness of that story! It's hard to imagine such arrogance, or that the whole family would actually follow his lead. But to be fair, I don't know what stand the minister might have taken to have been so offensive to Gramp. Maybe it was justified. I'm still chuckling.

Joseph of Aramathea fills out the remainder of chapter 23, as he claims the body and takes it to his own newly hewn tomb. A fulfillment of prophecy.

Chapter 24 devotes itself entirely to the resurrection and appearances of the Risen Christ. Each gospel gives a little different slant on the same story, depending on who remembered what. In Luke, the first appearance was to the two disciples on the road to Emmaus. One of the disciple's names is Cleopas, and his companion may have been wife. (I think I got that note from a sermon many years ago. I don't remember who said it, and I don't know if it's true.) They rushed back to Jerusalem to tell the apostles, who had already heard Jesus had appeared to Simon (Peter), an appearance we were not told about. But as they were excitedly discussing these events, Jesus Himself stood in the midst of them and said, "'Peace to you'" (Lk. 24-36). They were terrified and thought He was a ghost. He had to reassure them with these words:

> "Why are you troubled? And why do doubts arise in your hearts? Behold My hands and My feet that it is I Myself. Handle me and

> see, for a spirit does not have flesh and bones as you see I have." (Lk. 24:38-39)

And,

> "He opened their understanding that they might comprehend the Scriptures." (Lk. 24:45).

Jesus was talking with His apostles and disciples. We don't know to how many, but what He does for others, He will also do for us. This is good to remember as we end the third gospel and prepare for the last one.

> Thank you, Jesus, for opening our hearts and minds that we might understand as never before . . . with Your eyes, Lord, not ours. Amen.

# PART IV

# JOHN

# CHAPTER 29

# JOHN ONE

*Introduction to the Gospel of John*

For some reason, in starting the fourth gospel, I have a need to stay in the Psalms rather than a devotional. While I do appreciate Chambers, as well as other devotional authors, I feel closer to God in the Psalms, and it is always a good place for me to begin again. My meditation this morning goes back to Psalm 27, where I lingered over the following excerpts:

> "One thing I have desired of the Lord that I will seek: That I may dwell in the house of the Lord all the days of my life, to behold the beauty of the Lord and to inquire in His temples. [Oh the privilege!] For in time of trouble He shall hide me in His pavilion, in the secret place of His Tabernacle he shall hide me. He shall set me high upon a rock" (Ps. 27:4-5)
>
> "I will sing, yes I will sing praise to the Lord". [This is a promise I am so excited about!] (Ps. 27:6c)
>
> When You said, "Seek My face, my heart said to You, Your face, Lord, I will seek." (Ps. 27:14)

Thank You, Lord, for Your words to us this morning! Thank You for bringing us safely to our summer cabin in Colorado, although it was somewhat a surprise to wake up this morning to several inches of snow covering the trees and forest floor . . . something that never ceases to amaze me in mid-June! And it reminds me why we seldom come in winter months, even though the beauty of Your creation—summer or winter—is awesome beyond description! This morning as I was getting my coffee, I glanced outside to see what I thought was a dog racing across our back forest area. Fortunately, Bob was in the den and called out "coyote" in time for me to recognize it. Not a good sign for our Kiki. We will have to be very cautious with her this summer. Thank You, Lord, for protecting her when we cannot.

I am about to start the gospel of John with great anticipation, excitement, and doubt that I can ever do justice to this masterpiece of divine literature. To say this is my favorite book in the Bible is hardly strong enough. To say it inspires and encourages me each time I read from its passages is an understatement. After I became a Christian, I called my friend Judy the next morning to thank her and tell her I finally understood what she had been trying to convey to me. She was so happy for me, and almost the first thing out of her mouth was, "Do you have a Bible?" Well yes I did, but it was a King James that my grandmother purchased for me when I was a child. I had tried to read it several times but could not get past the "these," "thys," and "begats." She advised me to go to a Christian bookstore and purchase a Living Bible paraphrase and to read the gospel of John, which I did the following week, right after Easter. It was good advice, and I was totally mesmerized! It took me all spring and summer to "inhale" the Living Bible. In the fall, when Bible study classes resumed in our Presbyterian church, I learned a paraphrase version was not acceptable for serious study, so my first "serious" study Bible was the New English Bible. The New International Version, my personal favorite, had been published in 1973, but it would be several years before it was available to me in Lincoln. (One of our pastors here in Colorado calls this version the "Nearly Intellectual Version," tongue in cheek. I have since forgiven him.) It is still my favorite, although the New King James is growing on me. Daily. Let's go back to the introduction to John so we'll know who, what, where, and why. I don't think it matters much which version of the Bible we use, as long as it is compatible with our intellects. Maybe that's why I like the New International Version so much!

We are already well acquainted with John, the younger brother of James. Both were partners with Simon Peter in the fishing business (Lk. 5:7-10), which means he was also from the Galilee region. His real claim to frame was his closeness to Jesus as the "Apostle Jesus loved" (Jn. 13:23) and his inclusion in the "inner circle." His father was Zebedee, a successful businessman also in the fishing industry, and his mother was Salome, who we met when she wanted her sons to sit "one on Jesus' right and the other on His left" (Mt. 20:20). Salome was thought to be a sister of Jesus' mother, Mary. The first-century lineage was more interconnected than we can imagine. If this is true, and most commentaries accept this relationship, James and John were at the very least first or second cousins to Jesus. Communications have improved so vastly in our day and age that we find it hard to believe people in the first century did not know their extended family, but that's the way it was. James and John were called "Boanerges," which translates to "Sons of Thunder." They were completely exclusive and intolerant (Mk. 9:38; Lk. 9:49) with tempers so violet they were prepared to blast a Samaritan village out of existence because it was not hospitable to them on a journey (Lk. 9:54). That was even hard for me to write, because I could see none of these very strong characteristics in John's writing, which, of course, is the power of change that takes place after walking with and being taught by Jesus.

After the crucifixion and resurrection (we don't know exactly when), John took Mary, Jesus' mother, and presumably the remainder of his family away from Jerusalem and to live in Ephesus, where he wrote the gospel we are about to read. John wrote this book, called the *Spiritual Gospel,* from his own memory and from what he had been teaching for perhaps as long as seventy years. William Barclay, in his *The Gospel of John,* puts a date of AD 100 on the writing. It was written to a different church than the Synoptic Gospels, in that the church had now become mostly Gentile (Greek) in its makeup rather than mostly Jewish, and Greek believers had a different mind-set than Hebrew believers. Also, a false belief by the name of Gnosticism was creeping into the church and needed to be addressed. The basic doctrine of this heresy is that matter is essentially evil and spirit is essentially good, therefore, God could not have created the world, since the world would be untouchable for Him. To say the Gnostic did not believe the first paragraph of Genesis would be an oversimplification of their disbelief, so John countered this with his opening statement of the prologue of John (Jn. 1:1-180) with the words so familiar to us: "In the beginning was the Word and the Word was with God, and the Word was God. He was in the beginning with God" (Jn. 1:1).

William Barclay reasons this gospel was written at the urging of John's friends in a group (church) community and with their help and the leadership of the Holy Spirit. A. H. N. Green Armytage, in his *John Who Saw,* compares the four gospels of Jesus' life as:

> "Matthew suits the teacher with his systematic account of the teaching of Jesus; Mark suits the missionary with his clear-cut account of the facts of Jesus' life, Luke suits the parish priest with his wide sympathy and picture of Jesus as the friend of all, and John is the Gospel of the contemplative.

Armytage also compared the gospels of Mark and John:

> They are in a sense the same Gospel, only where Mark saw things plainly, bluntly, literally. John saw them subtly, profoundly, spiritually. We might say that John lit Mark's pages by the lantern of a lifetime's meditation. (William Barkley, *The Gospel of John,* vol. 1, revised edition, p. 22)

It has also been said of the gospel of John that "It is a pool in which a child may wade or an elephant may swim" (Roger Fredrikson, *John, The Communicator's Commentary,* p. 17). I love that description, because when I first read this gospel, I did not know anything about the Bible. I was a "child" (at thirty plus) and needed an index page to find the book. Yet it spoke to me in such a profound way, I knew joy and anticipation at each reading. That has proven true over the last thirty-five years. It has been said that in his elder years, John was urged to write this book not only by his friends and fellow bishops in the church, because after thinking about Jesus' words for so many years,

John could say with powerful insight, "Yes, those were His words, and He meant . . ." He had incredible insight in his senior years!

By the end of the first century and the beginning of the second, when this book was written, the church had changed completely and, as mentioned previously, had shifted to mostly Gentile believers. These two cultures, the Hebrew and Greek, were so different from each other, John needed to think of a way to unite them. "The Jews were traditional, righteous and struggling to be faithful to the Law, while the Greeks were sophisticated, inquisitive and philosophic" (Fredrikson, p. 30).

## *Chapter 1*

John brought both cultures together with his opening phrase: "In the beginning was the Word" (Jn. 1:1). The reason this was brilliant is because this wording had significance to both cultures. The Jews saw the word of Genesis and knew that God "spoke a word" to begin creation, and once a word was spoken, it would stand forever . . . never to change. To the philosophic Greek, the word "Word" (*Logos*) meant the very Reason of God . . . the Mind of God. So John was saying in his brilliant prologue that Jesus was demonstrating the mind—the reason of God in human form. Not identical, but alike in characteristics and minds.

Please get out your Bible and read the prologue, the first eighteen verses. We learn that Jesus has always been, is eternal, was on the first pages of Genesis, and has always been with God . . . even when he was born in a stable and came to us in human form. He was and is always connected. We have the same connection to the Lord (all three manifestations) as soon as we become born-again believers. He is always here for us. Not even a whisper away.

The reason John also writes about John the Baptist is because there was another heresy at this time that said the Baptist was the true messiah and was worshiped as such. This needed to be addressed and corrected, which John (the author) does in the prologue in verses 6-9. Verse 10 picks up with John describing Jesus again with such significance and continues with, "He came to that which was His own, but His own did not receive Him. Yet to all who believed in His name, He gave the right to become children of God" (Jn. 1:11-12).

Whew! I'm one. Are you? The closing verse of the prologue tells us Jesus is now at the Father's side, and He has made God the Father known to us. Oh yes! Go ahead and read the first chapter, please.

When we get to verse 29, I will point out that John the Baptist and Jesus had already met (other than when they were both in wombs) at the Jordan River, and the baptism had already taken place. John calls Jesus the "Lamb of God." I had always assumed this referred to the Paschal lamb of the Passover feast. The Jews would have recognized this term as the sacrificial system of placing sins and/or burdens on a sacrificial animal, which had been part of their culture and religion until the temple was destroyed in AD 70. At that time, this practice was discontinued. Maybe on some level they knew the ultimate sacrifice had already taken place and it was no longer necessary. One can only hope. And pray.

Here again in this passage, John the Baptist proclaims that Jesus had always been "before Him," referring to His Eternalism. You may remember from Luke that Jesus was born in a stable just three months after the Baptist's birth, and even though they were related on their mothers' side, they had grown up apart. John's words at the conclusion of this segment are so significant: "I have seen and I testify this is the Son of God" (Jn. 1:34).

Nothing in the Baptist's speech or demeanor would indicate his wish to be worshipped or to take glory away from the Lord Jesus. On the contrary, his sole responsibility was to testify as to Jesus' true identity, which he did unerringly throughout the four gospels and throughout his short lifetime.

In the next segment, we have a slightly different rendition of choosing the first apostles, and this is where we learn John and Andrew had been disciples of John the Baptist before they met Jesus. They had been on a spiritual quest before they were even chosen. This reminds me that it is easier for the Lord to direct you and me if we are moving—doing something worthwhile—rather than playing a waiting game. It is easier to direct and guide a moving person than to budge a "couch potato." When we are on the right path, doors fly open, ideas come rushing into our mind and consciousness, and we act on our instincts as if we have been guided, because we have been! People who say, "God can't use me . . . I have nothing to offer," either haven't tried or haven't realized the power of the Holy Spirit and the privilege of having such a creative and powerful "boss" calling the shots!

Getting back to Scripture, did those two apostles ever have such a great day! They followed Jesus, but He turned around and met them, and they got to spend the whole day with Him. This is the author of the book we are reading right now! Is that a goose-bumper or what? I just love that after their initial meeting, Andrew hurried to find his brother, Simon. Once you've met and know Jesus, you want everyone special in your life to know Him also.

I can't read this story without remembering when our son was born forty-five years ago. We didn't have ultrasound then, so whatever came out was a surprise we simply took home and loved. We already had a daughter, so we were hoping for a boy, but I remember specifically telling God it was fine if this was another girl, because I already knew how to love a little girl baby. But if it were a boy, he would have to help me; that was out of the realm of my experience. (I wasn't a Christian at the time but always believed in God, and talked to Him often.) We had a hard time with names, and if this were a boy, we settled on the name Sanford Charles. When our son was born, we hesitated to name him, and when Bob came back to the hospital the next morning, I told him we could not name him Sanford. He was an Andrew, not a Sanford. Bob agreed with me, and it was a good choice, because our son married a Sandy, and that would have been confusing. But when our Andy came to know the Lord as a teenager, he never looked back and did the same thing the apostle did; he brought people to the Lord as fast as he knew how. And he's still doing it today! Thank You, Lord, for our precious son, who is also precious to You. I now believe his name was a prophetic choice.

Now back to our newly chosen apostles. Notice that each chosen man went out and found a special friend to bring to Jesus., After Jesus found Philip, Philip went out and found Nathaniel, who is probably also known as Bartholomew. We just have to assume John went out and found his brother, James. The author doesn't tell us who or how the other apostles were chosen. It wasn't pertinent to the point he was getting across, and I'm quite sure by this time they were no longer alive. We are now told the first thing Jesus did after meeting Simon was to change his name to Cephas, which translates to Peter in Greek. Peter was actually impetuous, unstable, and talked a lot without thinking first. But Jesus knew Simon would grow into his new name and become stable as a rock. And he did. In the Old Testament, a change of name is indicative of a change in stature with God. Remember Abram to Abraham, Sarai to Sarah, and Jacob to Israel. All had significance.

When I was a child, my parents purchased a home in Omaha, closer to my grade school, and we became friends with a family who had previously owned it. Occasionally they would stop by for a visit, and on one of those visits, the lady said to my mother, "Why do you call her [me] Joanne Marie? It doesn't fit her."

I realize in retrospect this was quite rude of her, but I was all ears, waiting to hear what would come next. My mother, always the polite hostess, asked Mrs. Wilson very nicely, "What would you call her?"

The answer came back, "I would call her Jody."

"Mom," I leaped out of the corner, "I love that name. Can I be Jody?" I didn't want to be *called* another name; I wanted to *be* that other name. And eventually I was. There is nothing wrong with the name Joanne—I have two special friends in the desert by that name—but it just wasn't a name that seemed to fit me at that young age. I had an opportunity to re-create myself and was very grateful for it. I think it perplexed my dad, but he got over it. So I know firsthand a new name can make a world of difference to a person . . . for whatever reason.

You may notice that chapter 1 of John ends with Jesus calling Himself the "Son of Man," which was His favorite title for Himself. I'm sure you noticed it in the other gospels as well. It comes from the prophet Daniel, chapter 7, verses 13-14, who prophesied about a Messianic figure "like the Son of Man," coming with the clouds of Heaven, who had been given, "Authority, glory and sovereign power: all peoples, nations and men of every nation worshiped Him. His dominion is an everlasting dominion that will not pass away and His Kingdom is one that will never be destroyed."

The "clouds of heaven" tell us this refers to His second coming, which seems to me Jesus is promising every time He calls Himself the Son of Man. Isn't that an interesting thought to end this chapter with? Thank You, Lord. We are on a journey with John.

# CHAPTER 30

# JOHN TWO - FOUR

Devotion for today:

> "Into Your hands I commit my spirit, Redeem me, O Lord, the God of truth" (Ps. 31:3)
>
> "But I trust in You, O Lord; I say, "You are my God, my times are in Your hands; Deliver me from my enemies, and from those who pursue me; Let Your face shine on Your servant, save me in your unfailing love." (Ps. 31:14-16)
>
> "How great is Your goodness which You have stored up for those who fear You, which You bestow in the sight of men for those who take refuse in You." (Ps. 31:19)

This is such a remembrance for me.

Oh Lord, aren't there times when we all come crawling to You to ask for a reprieve? I know I have, admitting I have no control over the days assigned to me, and throwing myself upon Your mercy. These verses bring back so many memories of time spent on my spiritual knees doing just that, asking for mercy and healing. Somehow I thought I had dodged a bullet when I successfully went through breast cancer in 1988 and emerged healed and whole in 1989. I breathed a huge sigh of relief and went on with my life as if nothing had happened. No, that's not accurate. No one faces stage 4 breast cancer with a recommendation of immediate mastectomy without fear, trepidation, and lots of questions!

I was literally and figuratively on my knees for long periods of time. But maybe that's human nature to arrive on the other side of illness and forget the fear and just be grateful for health and energy once again.

I guess that is why in December of 1998 I was blindsided by a stroke while Bob and I were watching a football game at our home in Rancho Mirage one Monday evening. Through a series of guessing games and denial ("I'm fine. I don't want to go to a hospital!" "Maybe we should go to ER at Eisenhower Hospital after all."), and a long night in emergency while the stroke diagnosis was finally confirmed, I was once again calling on the Lord, praying, "You are my God, my times are in Your hands." We sent Andy and Sandy home; Sandy was ready to deliver Joshua in just a few weeks, and everyone was frantic to get her out of the germ-laden area. Very early the next day, I was wheeled into more diagnostic proceedings that confirmed I'd had a stroke the night before. Doctors actually "saw" another one happening as I was being examined. While the test was being administered, the tech kept saying, "Look at her eyes . . . look at her eyes . . . she's having another stroke." Not a warm-fuzzy moment in my life.

And there I was again, Lord, begging for Your Presence . . . Your healing . . . Your mercy. No, life is not fair, but it certainly is an interesting journey. It wasn't a question of "Why me?" so much as "Why not me?" and "Here we go again, Lord. Hang onto me, because I am reaching for You with every bit of energy and faith I have!"

Back in my room, I had more questions than answers. I was wearing a heart monitor without a clue why. It was my brain that had two strokes, not my heart. I hit my call button for a trip to the bathroom, but after twenty minutes, I remembered how very early that morning a nurse carefully walked me with my IV into my private bathroom, just a few feet away. The door was even open. It couldn't be that difficult! I very carefully swung my legs over the side of my bed made sure my IV pole was moving, and successfully maneuvered my way into the bathroom. I was so proud of my success, but as I sat on the commode, I passed out. I didn't fall; I was well planted! I just put my head down on my chest and fainted. I told you I was wearing a heart monitor, and I woke up with three livid nurses yelling at me. One took the pole, and the other two each took one of my arms as I was firmly and quickly escorted back to my bed—with a very strict scolding! As I sputtered my apologies, I was astounded to find the sides of my bed being raised, and my arms being wrapped in canvas and tied to the railings! The tears started then, but I soon found this to be counterproductive, because they were rolling into my ears and I had no way to stop them. I must have dozed off, because when I woke up, my hospital-assigned neurologist was untying me and telling me what a case study I was, because they were able to watch me have a second stroke. He told me they would start me on Coumadin immediately. I came to find out that meant a blood test every few hours.

Oh dear. I think this was the lowest point for me. I was having a hard time trying to process all that was happening, and everything was just going too fast for me to truly comprehend. And I was only in my early sixties. Still young! (Everything is relative!) One of the administrators of the hospital was a good friend of Andy's and when she saw the name Weigel come through admissions the night before, she called Andy to confirm my relationship, which was how I got such a beautiful private room. Each day that I was there, Debby Dahl swept in to greet me, always looking like a million dollars in a red or green suit with a Christmas pin on her lapel. I called her my "Christmas Angel," and she was. She is now married to our wonderful choir director and minister of music in our church in Palm Desert, and still a lovely friend.

That first day was a blur of confusion as plane tickets were canceled for Christmas back in Nebraska, and a constant stream of medical personnel was in and out of my room. That night I fell asleep asking God for answers; I don't think I had ever been so discouraged. I knew the Lord was with me, but I could not feel His Presence. I absolutely knew this was one of those times when I was being "carried": there was only one set of footprints in the sand, and they weren't mine! About three o'clock in the morning, I woke up to find a hematology technician standing on my right, very lightly holding my arm. Oh no, more needles! As I watched her, I became aware she was praying over me. Her eyes were closed, and her lips were silently moving. She was a beautiful African American woman, maybe in her twenties or early thirties. She wore the blue slacks and smock of her profession, and had a plain silver cross around her neck; she wore no other jewelry. I could see her plainly, because there was a constant light on behind my bed. Finally, I said to her, "Thank you for praying for me. I can feel it." She was so sweet! She told me she prayed for all her patients. She had such a quiet, peaceful countenance about her.

She wasn't in a hurry and seemed to enjoy our quiet conversation as much as I did. I told her she couldn't get blood out of the arm she was holding—it had been poked unsuccessfully all day long—but she just smiled and said, "No problem." And it wasn't. I watched the needle enter my vein and hardly felt it. She talked to me the whole time as I watched my dark rich blood fill up the little vial. When she finally left my room, I felt a peace that was beyond my understanding, and the only thing I could say was, "Thank You, Lord, I know I am going to be all right now." I had turned the corner on this journey.

When I was dismissed several days later, I asked the volunteer who was wheeling my chair to stop by the nurses' station so I could thank them. (They had stopped yelling at me after the first day.) I asked them for the name of the hematology technician who worked nights and described her perfectly. They looked utterly perplexed as they told me no one by that description worked at Eisenhower Hospital. I grinned all the way to the car. I knew an angel had visited me that night! I hope I will meet her again someday. I liked her so much, and I never got a chance to properly thank her.

Now, let's continue.

## *Chapter 2*

As we continue to read, you will note this gospel is written around eight miracles John calls signs, and there is not a parable in sight! In chapter 2, we have a sign that is only told in the book of John about a wedding that took place in the village of Cana of Galilee, a place yet to be located by archaeologists. I remember hearing or reading many years ago that this might even have been John's own wedding, because his mother and Jesus' mother were related, and it was apparent Mary was helping with the details of this very important wedding fest, like a close relative would. When Jesus responded to His mother, it was with tenderness and respect, but it was also apparent He had moved beyond His mother and was now listening to His Father. If the apostle John was directly involved, possibly even the groom, he would surely remember this sign with great admiration and gratefulness. (The groom was always the host of the wedding feast.) The six stone jars were the kind used for ceremonial washing, representing the Jewish law and the old covenant, now filled with new wine by the One bringing in the New Covenant of grace, mercy, and forgiveness. The wine was a vital part of the feast, as it was the only beverage of choice in the first century. To be out of wine would have been a catastrophe of the gravest kind and appallingly humiliating to the groom. That the Synoptic Gospels did not report his first miracle probably indicates those writers were unaware of it. However, the results of this story and miraculous sign were, "He thus revealed His glory and the Disciples put their faith in Him" (Jn. 2:11).

The second story in chapter 2, which has been reported in the Synoptic Gospels, is about Jesus' wrath at the turning of His Father's house into a market. John puts this story toward the beginning of his gospel, and it probably should have been toward the end of His ministry, as it would surely have provoked the Sanhedrin, chief priests, and scribes to an uncontrollable fury, and they may have used this incident for a final confrontation before Jesus' teaching was accomplished. The only thing John's gospel does that the other three do not is to describe three Passovers, telling us His ministry was nearly three years in length. The first Passover is noted in John 2:13. "Now the Passover of the Jews was at hand, and Jesus went up to Jerusalem." It was one of these occasions when Jesus proclaimed to the merchants desecrating the temple, "'Destroy this temple and I will raise it again in three days'" (Jn. 2:19). I wonder how soon after this statement John realized it was His body Jesus was referring to. Hindsight can be a valuable teacher: "But the temple He had spoken of was His body" (Jn. 2:21).

We are told He did many miraculous signs at the Passover, and many believed in His name. The last sentence of chapter 2 tells us Jesus "knew all men" and would not entrust himself to them. He may have been thinking of, "The heart is deceitful above all things and beyond cure" (Jer. 17:9).

*Chapter 3*

We come now to what must certainly be the most spiritually anointed chapter in the entire Bible. If you haven't already, please stop now and read chapter 3, and then come back to me. Jesus is still in Jerusalem for the Passover feast and has already called attention to Himself by many miracles John chooses not to name. A wealthy, influential Pharisee named Nicodemus comes to see Him at night. Alone. Nicodemus is a member of the Sanhedrin, the ruling body of Jews, and has no doubt heard stories from his fellow cohorts and may even have witnessed some of the miracles performed that very week. I suspect Nicodemus was a spiritually alive, searching-for-truth man who came at night so he could have a private conversation with Jesus and get some answers. We already know Nicodemus has respect for Jesus, because he has called Him "Rabbi," a respected term for a spiritual teacher; Nicodemus was also a spiritual teacher, by the way. Half of this chapter, through verse 21, is the conversation with Nicodemus.

This story is only told to us in the gospel of John, and it is the only teaching on being born again, which can also be translated as "born from above." Notice Nicodemus hasn't even asked a question before Jesus reads his heart and gets right down to the spiritual answers he has come for: "'I tell you the truth; no one can enter the Kingdom of God unless he has been born of water and the Spirit'" (Jn. 3:5).

Whenever the Bible refers to water, it figuratively refers to cleansing . . . purification, and being born again gives us the idea of a new, fresh, and clean start. Jesus has recently been baptized, and in this chapter, He goes again into the Judean countryside for the purpose of baptizing, washing away the old and getting ready for the new—in this case, the Spirit, referring to the Holy Spirit, the third part of the Trinity. Nicodemus is, of course, clueless. Can't you just see him scratching his head, trying to figure out Jesus' teaching in terms he can understand?

When Jesus continues His teaching and uses plural terms as to His testimony in the eleventh verse, He is talking in terms of those apostles around Him, who have seen and can testify to His miracles and signs that can come from no one but God. In the fourteenth verse, Jesus refers back to an incident that happened during the Exodus, when people started to grumble against Moses, against the food, against the water, against everything they could think of. The Lord sent venomous snakes to kill them, before they realized their grumbling was a sin and came to Moses asking for redemption and to God asking for forgiveness. Moses made a bronze snake and lifted it up on a pole, and whenever the Jews looked at the snake, they were saved and redeemed. It wasn't the snake that redeemed them; it was their confession and faith that God told them to believe that saved them. Jesus tells this story knowing Nicodemus, a teacher of the Jews, would understand.

> "Just as Moses lifted up the snake in the desert, so the Son of man must be lifted up that everyone who believes in Him may have Eternal life. "For God so loved the world that He gave His one and only Son, that whoever believes in Him shall not perish, but have eternal life." (Jn. 3:14-16)

> "For God did not send His son into the world to condemn the world, but to save the world through Him. Whoever believes in Him is not condemned, but whoever does not believe stands condemned already, because he did not believe in the name of God's one and only Son." (Jn. 3:17-18)

I think Jesus must have loved Nicodemus very much to have given him such thorough teaching, and I also think it is somewhat of a miracle that we have these words written down for all eternity to know, believe, and study. I think most people, at least in Christian circles, could quote John 3:16 by memory, but I have included the sentences both before and directly afterward, because to me, they are just as important. They both give a reason and a consequence!

Nicodemus obviously wanted this to be a private discussion by coming alone and at night. Here is my theory. I believe without a doubt Nicodemus became a Jewish believer shortly after this evening. (I will point this out later in the book.) It is also my belief that Nicodemus probably related it word for word to John and maybe to all the apostles after the crucifixion and resurrection, when everyone was saying, "Don't you remember when He said . . . ?" We even do that now after our loved ones die. How many times have you been to a funeral or talking about a loved one who has died and remember a precious story about him or her? You recount the experience with joy to all those around you. "Yes, I remember . . . wasn't it wonderful?" Think about it. We'll meet Nicodemus in heaven. You mark my words!

The remainder of the chapter points out there was definitely a time when Jesus' ministry and John the Baptist's very much coincided, before John was imprisoned and beheaded, and John goes to his fate, telling everyone who would listen he was the "best man," and not the "groom." The finishing paragraph to this great chapter is an "altar call" if I ever heard one! John the Baptist's witness:

> "The Father loves the Son and has placed everything in His hands Whoever believes in the Son has eternal life, but whoever rejects the Son will not see life, for God's wrath remains on him" (Jn. 3:35-36)

### *Chapter 4*

Chapter 4 gives us yet another story unique to the book of John. This one is about the Samaritan woman by the well. Let's see now . . . Jesus sits by the well, hot, tired, and dusty, while his apostles have gone for food. He has an encounter with a Samaritan woman. It was noon, and the well was well known throughout the area as "Jacob's Well"—one hundred feet deep and holding clear, cold water. But Jesus has no container or means to retrieve water, so He speaks with a Samaritan woman, something not condoned in the first century, first of all because she was a woman in a public place, and second of all, because she was a Samaritan, only half Jewish. These people were descendants of those deported or killed in the fall of the Northern Kingdom in 722 BC (2 Kings 17:23-40), who intermarried with heathen colonists brought in from Babylon by Assyrian conquerors. They were regarded as unclean traitors to Jewish blood, and they only believe in the first five books of the Old Testament (the Talmud) as their scriptures. When Jesus asks this woman for a drink of water, it was a very unusual request, and she is flabbergasted. Especially when He tells her He will give her a gift of living water. As a part-Jew, she may have been familiar with the term "living water" from the wells of salvation in Isaiah 12:13 and "thirsty" for the Living God in Psalm 42:1, and the River of Life in Ezekiel 47:1-12. But come to think of it, if she only believed in the first five books, it was remarkable she knew the Messiah was coming and would explain everything to her. Little did she know this was happening right that minute! The teaching Jesus puts forth to her is transforming:

> "You Samaritans worship what you do not know, for salvation is from the Jews. Yet a time is coming and has now come when the true worshipers will worship in spirit and truth, for they are the kind of worshipers the Father seeks. God is spirit, and his worshipers must worship in Spirit and truth." (Jn. 4:22b-24)

That He told her all about herself is also amazing and got her attention in a hurry! The fact that Jesus identifies Himself to her is also wonderful after she says Messiah is coming and will explain everything to them. Jesus' answer comes directly from Exodus 3:14. This is one of the books she would know: "'I, who speak to you, am He.'"

When the apostles returned, hopefully with sandwiches and chips, salad, and hummus, or the first-century rendition thereof, they were surprised He was talking to a woman, because it was against tradition to speak to a woman in a public place, as pointed out previously. That she was at the public place at noon was also unusual and must have told Jesus a lot, because women did not go to the well at noon, in the heat of the day, and definitely not alone. She might have been shunned by the village women because of her marital lifestyle or lack thereof. But it didn't keep her from spreading the word about Jesus, and they ended up staying for two days, presumably teaching and praying for the Samaritans that they, too, might believe and spread the word about the Son of God.

The remainder of chapter 4 is an account of the healing in Cana of an official's son, who was close to death. The official speaks to Jesus with beautiful respect so that Jesus can see his belief and grant his request long distance. The official realizes from his servant's message that the healing took place at the exact same time he had talked with Jesus. This is such a beautiful example of what happens when the head of a household comes to Christ. The chapter ends by telling us that he and all his household believed. Hallelujah! This was the second sign John tells us about.

> Thank you, Lord, for our reading today of Your Word. Bless all who read it and also believe. Amen.

## CHAPTER 31

# JOHN FIVE - SEVEN

My morning meditation comes from Psalm 37. The direction and promises have blessed me and I hope they will you also.

> "Trust in the Lord and do good; Dwell in the land and feed on His faithfulness. Delight yourself also in the Lord, and He shall give you the desires of your heart. Commit your way to the Lord. Trust also in Him, and he shall bring it to pass. He shall bring forth your righteousness as the light, and your justice as the noonday." (Ps. 37:3-6)

> "The steps of a good man are ordered by the Lord, and He delights in his way. Though he fall, he shall not be utterly cast down; For the Lord upholds him with His hand" (Ps. 37:23)

> "Depart from evil and do good; And dwell forevermore, for the Lord loves justice and does not forsake His saints; they are preserved forever, but the descendants of the wicked shall be cut off. The righteous shall inherit the land and dwell in it forever" (Ps. 37:27-29)

> "But the salvation of the righteous is from the Lord; He is their strength in time of trouble. And the Lord shall help them deliver them from the wicked and save them because they trust in Him." (Ps. 37:39-40)

Good morning, Lord, and thank You for Your word through the Psalms this beautiful Colorado morning! The snow is a thing of the past, and summer has arrived in the high country. Our front yard is a field of daisies, which we could not see several days ago because of the snow. Yesterday afternoon I was in the den, where our computer and desk are located. Overlooking our backyard is a pine forest between our nearest neighbor and us, which always reminds me to pray for them and to be sad this year that they will not be spending much time in the mountains because of health issues.

As I was looking out the window, I was quite surprised to see a lone deer grazing on the greenery very near our house. She very plainly saw me watching her but went right on grazing instead of running off. I called Bob to see her, because she was so pretty, and even though they are quite prolific here in the mountains, we really don't see as many of them as we would like to. We love our mountain critters in whatever form, and Bob has already filled our hummingbird feeders, and the mountain jays are feasting on the goodies Bob puts out for them, just as if we had been here all along. It's nice to be back in our summer routine. We even played tennis this morning and were delighted to see many of our friends returning also.

I spent several hours on the computer and finally left late afternoon to go to the kitchen to begin our dinner preparations. There is a window above my gas burners that allows me to see our entire back forest while I am cooking. As I glanced outside, I was surprised to see the deer had moved back into the pines though still quite visible from my vantage point. I called attention to her so Bob could see that she was still there, and as I was talking to Bob, the deer "dropped" something. As she bent over to lick it, I realized she had just given birth to a little "Bambi." Bob and I watched in silent fascination as the little fawn got shakily to its legs and found her first meal. We could easily see its brown and beige spots and noticed how well the baby blended into the forest. They stayed within our sight for about fifteen minutes, but before they left, Mama Deer led Bambi over to our window so we could have a closer look. Then they both went east toward the creek. We felt like new grandparents! And of course, we worried about that precious little creature, especially since we had seen the coyote in the same area. What a miracle!

About a week later, Bob called me to the front window, where a grown deer was feasting on our daisy greens. As we watched, she left and came back a few minutes later with twin Bambis. Of course we wondered if it was "our" deer, who had later produced a second offspring. We'll never know, but what a treat for us!

Now back to John!

## *Chapters 5-7*

We will follow the order given to us in the Bible, but I must tell you that most New Testament scholars believe chapter 6 should have come before chapter 5 as a more natural order of events. The changes between Jerusalem and Galilee become very difficult to follow, but as we have discussed previously, the chronology of events was not very important to any of the gospel authors. The points they were making did not depend on any whens. Chapters 5 through 12 cover basic ministry, so let's not be concerned about the when and where details.

Chapter 5 gives us the third miracle in this gospel, with the healing of a man who had been an invalid for thirty-eight years. He was lying by the Sheep Gate pool and unable to get to the water when it "stirred." The strange belief here is that an angel stirred the water from time to time, apparently giving it healing properties, and whoever got to the water first would be healed of their illness. This seems a little off the wall to me, and I expect it did to Jesus as well, because He asks a very important question of the man, "'Do you want to get well?'" (Jn. 5-6b).

The question isn't as strange as it seems because, there are many people who manufacture illnesses of all kinds to cope with their lives. They might not want to be well, because they would then be accountable for themselves and possibly for others. That could prove to be too difficult for them. Sometimes it's easier to stay sick. Jesus had a way of looking right into a person's heart and "nailing them."

Of course Jesus and the healed man got in trouble with the local clergy because this happened on a Sabbath. Jesus had told the man to pick up his bed and walk to prove his healing, and this constituted "working" on the Sabbath. Sheesh! But Jesus isn't done with this man just yet. He finds him again and has another word with him. "'See, you are well again. Stop sinning or something worse will happen to you" (Jn. 5:14).

I had to smile at how Jesus had this man in the crosshairs! He read him exactly, and friends, that's exactly how the Lord reads us too. With thoroughness and compassion. There is nothing He doesn't know about us . . . even our dirtiest little secrets . . . and remarkably, He loves us anyway! A profound mystery! Takes me to my knees, and I'll tell you that it makes a very strong believer in confession out of me. Often. The story ends with the formerly sick man going away and telling the Jews it was Jesus who made him well. Been there, done that! Don't want to have to do it again, but will if called on.

The Jews were really, really angry now, not only because Jesus was healing on the Sabbath, but he is calling Himself the Son of God, giving Him priorities over the accusers. Jesus further identifies Himself, and starts the following discourse: "'The Son can do nothing by himself; He can only do what He sees His Father doing, because whatever the Father does, the Son also does'" (Jn. 5:19).

The discourse is such a good description of Jesus, who He is and His function as the Son of God. Please do read this discourse in your favorite translation. They are the words of Jesus right through to the end of the chapter. They are words of affirmation as to His identity and condemnation about lack of belief.

Chapter 6 contains the fourth recounting of the feeding of the five thousand. John the Baptist had probably died during the lapse of time that begins this chapter. This tells us the Jewish Passover was near. Jesus would be starting His second year of ministry. He gets some help in this rendition with Andrew finding a boy with food. Hey, every little bit helps! We are told the boy had five small barley loaves and two small fish. Hardly enough to feed the swelling, hungry crowd, but any help at all is sufficient for Jesus, and he multiplied the bread and fish to feed everyone, with baskets left over. The people were really worked up after this. They had seen multiple miracles of healing the sick and had been fed a lovely meal by the side of the lake. They were ready to take

Jesus by force and make Him their king. He needed to get out of there fast—and He did. He went up a mountain to pray, while His apostles set off across the lake for Capernaum. Only John knew the details about rowing three and a half miles before seeing Jesus walking on water toward them. After they heard Him say, "'It is I; don't be afraid'" (Jn. 6:20), they get Him into the boat. And don't miss the next miracle: "Then they were willing to take Him into the boat and immediately the boat reached the shore where they were heading" (Jn. 6:21).

This is an easy miracle to miss, unless you are like me and detest the idea of being on a rough lake with high winds and waves, and a long way from shore! This was incredible to me, and John was the one who reported it. I'm sure these salty fishermen were just as comfortable as I would have been miserable. I guess Jesus must have figured they had been terrified enough for one evening, and got them where they wanted to go pronto!

Of course the crowd later followed them and asked a very important question: "What must we do to do the works God requires?" (Jn. 6:28). If each of us hasn't asked this question for ourselves, we certainly should have!

And here is Jesus' answer: "The work of God is to believe in the One He sent" (Jn. 6:29). They wanted a sign. Will these people never learn? Sheesh! They have seen many signs and had eaten their fill the day before, and they still want a sign? They reminded Jesus of the manna their forefathers ate that Moses gave them, which sets up Jesus' answer:

> "It was not Moses who gave the bread from heaven, but it is my Father who gives you the true bread from heaven. For the bread of God is He who comes down from heaven and gives life to the world." (Jn. 6:32-33)

Here is where Jesus affirms one of His beautiful "I am" statements: "'I am the bread of life. He who comes to me will never go hungry and he who believes in Me will never thirst'" (Jn. 6:35).

Another quote before we move on: "'For my Father's will is that everyone who looks to the Son, and believes in Him shall have eternal life, and I will raise him up at the last day'" (Jn. 6:40). Add this to your verses on your prayer cards for nonbelievers or backsliders as you lift them up to the Lord. I know it is sometimes tedious and boring, and I could be doing something more fun, worthwhile, or educational, but believe me, nothing is more important than praying for your loved ones who do not know Jesus! Nothing! If you can't be a witness yourself, pray that God will send someone who can be. Someone's very life in eternity may depend on it. Think about the Old Testament verse: "As for me, far be it from me that I should sin against the Lord by failing to pray for you" (1 Sam. 12:23).

One more eye-opening quote from Jesus to ponder: "'No one can come to Me unless the Father who sent Me draws him, and I will raise him up at the last day'" (Jn. 6:44).

Jesus' further teaching about partaking of the Bread of Life is a reference to the Last Supper, our communion celebration, which He had not taught in this gospel yet. It was enough to frighten away many of His followers at the time and also caused Peter to exclaim, "'Lord to whom should we go? You have the words of eternal life. We believe and know you are the Holy One of God'" (Jn. 6:68). Oh that we could all say those words with conviction!

Chapter 7 opens with the curious story of Jesus' brothers (James, Joseph, Judas, and Simon; Mk. 6:3), urging Him to go to Judea for the Feast of Tabernacles, so "His disciples could see His miracles." I understand why Jesus needed to go in secret until He was in a teaching situation that was conducive to His Word, but what I didn't get was the sentence, "For even His own brothers did not believe in Him" (Jn. 7:5). It seems to me if the brothers had seen His miracles, which clearly they had, and were urging Him to go to Judea, they must have been on the very cusp of belief. We know His half-brother James became the very strong leader of the Jerusalem church after the resurrection and wrote the wonderful epistle of James in the New Testament We also know his half brother Judas wrote the very short epistle of Jude. Wouldn't you love to know what happened to Joseph, Simon, and the sisters? Someday we will know. For now, we ponder.

Jesus' ministry continues, and the people keep questioning Him throughout chapter 7. Some thought he was a prophet; some thought He was Christ (Messiah). Some brought up the point that He was from Nazareth and not Bethlehem, as the prophecy foretold in Micah 5:12. This was because they did not know He had been born in Bethlehem and spent several years there before fleeing to Egypt. The temple guards sent to get Him could not accomplish their task because of the powerful nature of His speech. During the heated discussion, Nicodemus spoke up in Jesus' defense and, trying to get the truth, asks, "Does our law condemn anyone without first hearing him to find out what he is doing?" (Jn. 7:51).

Yep . . . . if Nicodemis isn't in full belief now, he is well on his way, in my opinion. The other Pharisees responded to the effect that prophets do not come out of Galilee. Actually, they were wrong. Jonah did. And so did Nahom.

Lord, bless our reading this day and expand our understanding. Amen.

# CHAPTER 32

# JOHN EIGHT - TEN

My devotion for this day:

> "My heart is overflowing with a good theme." (Ps. 45:1-3; I would call the gospel of John a good theme, wouldn't you?)
>
> "I recite my composition concerning the King; my tongue is the pen of a ready writer." (Ps. 45:1)
>
> "Your throne, O God, is forever and ever; a scepter of Your Kingdom. You love righteousness and hate wickedness, therefore God, your God, has anointed you with the oil of gladness more than your companions." (Ps. 45:6-7)

Lord God, you are my Mentor, my God, my Guidance now and forever. If you love righteousness and hate wickedness, teach me to do the same with every choice I make, whether it be in the novels I love to read, the choice of a movie or TV program, or the choice of friends who also love You. It is so fulfilling to be with Sister Chicks in Bible study and to discuss biblical truths, concepts, and ideas based on Your teachings from the Word that pertain to our lives. It is even more exciting and encouraging to be part of our family discussions when we are fortunate enough to all be together. Surely during these times of spiritual encouragement with each other, You are showing us a little bit of what heaven will be like, and it is so awesome to experience this within relationship groups. While sitting here with an open Bible on my lap, the opposite page is pulling me toward another passage before I move on: "If we had forgotten the name of our God, or stretched out our hands to a foreign god, would not You, God, search this out? For You know the secrets of the heart" (Ps. 44:20-21).

Thank You, Father God, for this reminder. A "foreign god" in my own life might be worldliness, pride, or just a deep longing in a direction You don't have in mind for me. I am so thankful You know the secrets of my heart before I am even aware of them myself—and that you gently and firmly lead me back to the path meant for me, often giving me a glimpse of an open door I am meant to walk through at Your bidding and beyond my limited expectation or experience. You alone, O God, give us both roots and wings. Maybe it's true that life is not always fair to our way of thinking, but with Your Holy Presence, it is always an interesting, growing, and stretching adventure. Thank You for knowing any secrets within my heart and gently correcting them when necessary.

It is a beautiful summer day in the mountains, with full sunshine, blue sky, and a gentle breeze to stir the aspen leaves. Bob's daisy garden in front is so lovely this year and seems to be in full bloom already. They will last all summer long, with our cool nights and mild temperatures, unlike Nebraska, where they wither in the harsh sun within just a few weeks. As I turn the page of my Bible, I come to one of my favorite passages. How fortunate we are in the gospel that excels in giving us so many "I am" phrases, and here, now, is yet another example: "Be still and know that I am God; I will be exalted among the nations, I will be exalted in the earth" (Ps. 46:10).

To "be still" means to be quiet, to be silent, to tune out the world and all its interruptions, and to realize how special it is to know God . . . to feel His Presence . . . to know His healing touch and that he hears us when we call. How difficult that is until we can find the silence within and without our environment! This is something I have to be very intentional about, because I am, by nature, such an extrovert that I crave the energy and excitement of being around other people. As much as I love relationships, fellowship, and corporate worship, that is not where I find God. I find Him within the pages of the Bible, while sitting in my quiet time chair with the radio and other distractions off. Then realizations come to me, and I know. That kind of spiritual knowledge bubbles up from deep within and often spills forth in tears running down my face. A box of tissues by my chair is as crucial to me as pen and notebook. Bob can easily find Him in nature—by the side of a lake or walking up the path. Maybe this is not possible for me, because I seldom go into nature alone. Oh I love the mountains, and the walking paths through the forests around our home are prolific and beautiful, but there is something within me that keeps looking for the occasional bear, moose, or whatever else might be out there. Lord, thank You for making us all so different. You are so good!

Let's get back into our reading for this day.

### *Chapters 8-10*

The interesting story of a woman caught in adultery (Jn. 8:1-11) is probably not John's writing and was only included in one of the early Greek texts of the New Testament. In fact, it was included in one of the less-important texts. What could this mean? It's hard for me to contemplate an original early text of the New Testament being less important. Than what? Other minds will have to grapple with this. Mine cannot. I will have to remember to ask Andy next time I talk to him.

Jesus is in the temple teaching "all the people when the scribes and Pharisees brought Him a woman caught in adultery" (Jn. 8:1-11). When I first read this story many years ago, my first thought was *Where was the man who was equally guilty?* This sin was clearly punishable by stoning to death as found in the Law of Moses (Lev. 20:10; Deut. 22:20-24). Of course, the accusers were trying to set up Jesus . . . yet again. If Jesus did not accuse her, he would be guilty of ignoring the Law of Moses, and if He did accuse her, permitting a stoning death to occur, He would be breaking the Roman law, because only Romans could legally carry out a death sentence. His accusers thought they had Him between a rock and a hard place, but Jesus dumbfounded them all by stooping down to write on the ground and ignored the question. Oh, the question was "What do you say?" (Jn. 8:5).

This section of the story has me a little confused, because we are clearly told Jesus was teaching within the confines of the temple, which had been under construction for forty-six years, and in my mind, the temple was a magnificent building with finished floors of marble or at least polished stones. So when the text tells me Jesus "wrote on the ground" (Jn. 8:6), my mind had to shift to a dirt or sand floor somewhere within the boundaries of the temple itself. This could possibly be an outer court, where it would have been permissible to bring an accused adulteress. Oh the many questions that do come up in the Bible!

As Jesus silently wrote, and the crowd pressed Him for an answer, He said, "'He who is without sin among you, let him throw the first stone'" (Jn. 8:7). Oh my, that throws a monkey wrench into the whole dirty plan, doesn't it? And He stooped to continue writing on the ground. Interesting how one simple sentence from Jesus has brought about silence and interspection for every person present. I bet you could have heard a pin drop . . . even on a dirt floor! What Jesus wrote was not as important as what his accusers *thought* He was writing. One by one, from the oldest (presumably the ones with the most wisdom to know all people are sinners) to the youngest, they left the area. When Jesus finally looked up and saw no one but the accused woman, He healed her and forgave her with the words, "'Neither do I condemn you: Go and sin no more'" (Jn. 8:11).

Great story, isn't it? A story of healing, forgiveness, and restitution. I'm very glad the early church fathers decided to include it in the Bible—no matter where they inserted it. Because the original language is translated into English for us from the original Greek, I would not have known this was not part of the original teaching from John. As far as I'm concerned, the Holy Spirit found a perfect place to insert this story, as John's gospel is so unique as it stands.

The next paragraph gives us another wonderful "I am" statement, always worthy of a memory verse: "'I am the light of the world. He who follows me shall not walk in darkness but have the light of life'" (Jn. 8:12).

The rest of the chapter pretty much challenges the veracity of Jesus' identity with lots of "no you aren't" statements. The chapter ends with Jesus telling the Jews, "'Your father Abraham rejoiced at the thought of seeing my day; he saw it and was glad'" (Jn. 8:56). Jews exclaimed,

"You aren't old enough to have seen Abraham" (Jn. 8:57), to which Jesus exclaimed, "I tell you the truth, before Abraham was born, I am" (Jn. 8:58). Jesus had to slip away amid angry stones.

Chapter 9 is the most wonderful story about a man who was born blind. The disciples wanted to know who had sinned—the man or his parents—since he had been born blind. This seems like a silly question to us, but in the first century, almost all Jews believed that if you suffered from an illness or hardship, it must have been because of sin in your life (the case of Job, for example). This was not only a belief taught by rabbis, but Jesus may have contributed to this theory when He healed the paralytic back in chapter 6, finds him again, and tells him in no uncertain terms to stop sinning or something worse may happen! We know that all sin has debilitating consequences that often affect many people in a ripple-down pattern. But that sin causes blindness from birth is still up for debate. Jesus assures His disciples this has happened so the works of God could be revealed to them. Translation: another sign. A miracle. This is where we have another perfect "I Am" statement: "'As long as I AM in the world, I AM the light of the world'" (Jn. 9:5).

He proceeds to heal the blind man using mud made with saliva and clay. Oh my. I don't even want to think what the medical establishment would have to say about this method for several reasons, germs being among the first. But just as everything else Jesus did worked, so did this special "ointment." And without a prescription. The only "fly in this ointment" was that it happened on a Sabbath. Oh no! We know what that means! The legalists were furious all over again. The story continues like a comedic skit:

> "Who healed you?"
> "A man named Jesus."
> "Where is He?"
> "I don't know."
> "How did this happen?"
> "Clay and washing."
> "Where is He?"
> "I don't know."

Finally, in frustration, anger, and jealousy, they called in the man's parents to get their story, and the plot gets even funnier. The parents were frightened and wisely told the Jews to ask their son. After all, he was of age. And this started the redundant dialogue all over again. The parents knew anyone accepting Jesus as Messiah and Lord would be put out of the synagogue, which was, to say the least, a humiliating ostracism. I need to say at this point that not much has changed since the first century.

A prominent Jewish couple I had met several times socially in Omaha had an experience with the lady-half of the couple. While she was sitting in a hospital on deathwatch with her elderly grandmother, who had lived with the family while my acquaintance was growing up, her grandmother started to hallucinate. She had been a survivor of the death camps in Germany and had been very close to her granddaughter since coming to America to live with her family. Her granddaughter, not wanting her dear grandmother to be alone during her final hours, was sitting with her and listening to a dialogue that went something like this. "Oh no, why did they put Him on a cross? Please, God, forgive us. How could we not have known?" Clearly, the Lord was reveling things to this grandmother in her final hours, and her granddaughter, who was in her forties at the time, heard every word.

After the grandmother died peacefully, this woman called a good friend of mine in Lincoln and told her this story and asked, "Please tell me about Yeshua." This was the name her grandmother had called out. "What did that conversation mean?" My friend, a lifelong Christian, laid out the gospel to her on the telephone, explained the significance of a blood sacrifice on a cross and what it means for us. Also, what it had meant to the early Hebrew community, how the temple functioned before its final destruction, and the culmination of prophecy from all the books of the Old Testament. She also told the granddaughter how we would never have been able to understand the sacrifice on the cross if it had not been for the Old Testament and God's teaching therein. A long silence on the phone revealed this Jewish woman could do nothing about the spiritual truth that had landed in her lap, because her husband, an important businessman on his way up the corporate ladder in a basically Jewish firm, would be severely limited in his career.

Their two children were both in Hebrew school, studying for their bat and bar mitzvahs, and her mother-in-law was currently the president of their local synagogue. The social, business, cultural, and religious standing of this family in Omaha were all enmeshed in Judaism. She sadly hung up the phone, and the subject was not broached again. Nevertheless, she had heard the truth in a supernatural way that could not be denied, and one day, this family may accept the truth as presented to them. When I think about this family, which, forgive me Lord, is not often, I do lift them up in prayer.

Back to our story of the formerly blind man. When the healed man was called again to repeat his story, he was very clever when he finally asked, and I'm sure in exasperation, "Do you want to be His disciples too?" After more castigation, the healed man had a marvelous testimony:

> "Now we know God does not hear sinners, but if anyone is a worshiper of God and does His will, He hears him. Since the world began it has been unheard of that anyone opened the eyes of one born blind. If this man were not from God, He could do nothing." (Jn. 9:31-33)

It was a powerful testimony, and the Jews cast him out. The story ends with the formerly blind man absolutely believing in Jesus with these words: "Lord, I believe" (Jn. 9:38). Oh Lord, that we may all say these words from our hearts, "Lord, I believe."

Our last chapter today is chapter 10 and contains the reassuring story of Jesus calling Himself the Good Shepherd. This story contains two "I AM" statements. The first one is,

> "I AM the door [or the gate]. If anyone enters by Me, he will be saved, and will go in and out and find pasture. The thief does not come except to steal and to kill and to destroy. I have come that they might have life, and that they may have it abundantly." (Jn. 10:9-10)

This is certainly a passage to carry in our hearts and to memorize, so we may always remember Who and how we are saved!

The second I AM passage in this same chapter is:

> "I AM the Good Shepherd and I know my sheep and am known by My own." (Jn. 10:14)
>
> And other sheep I have which are not of this fold [that's us, Gentiles] them also I must bring, and they will hear my voice and there will be one flock, and one Shepherd." (Jn. 10:16)

Unfortunately, most of the Jews didn't believe Him after the first century, and most still do not. But precious ones reading this, one day we will be one body of believers, worshipping our Lord and Savior Yeshua together, Gentiles and Jews, all God's chosen people.

I cannot leave the tenth chapter of John without this passage from Jesus:

> "My sheep hear My voice and I know them and they follow Me. I give them eternal life and they shall never perish; neither shall anyone snatch them out of my hand. My Father, who has given them to Me, is greater than all; and no one is able to snatch them out of my Father's hand. I and My Father are one." (Jn. 10:27-30)
>
> Lord God, thank You for our reading today. Thank You for Your affirmations and promises, that we have knowledge and hope in our eternal future. Touch each heart reading these words and lead them gently and directly into Your hands, because You alone are able to direct all our hearts, minds, and souls. Amen.

CHAPTER 33

# JOHN ELEVEN - THIRTEEN

Good morning, Lord, and thank You for the gentle rain in the night and this morning. There is almost nothing that smells better than a pine forest after the rain! The sun is just now peeking out from behind broken clouds, which means we will probably be able to play tennis midmorning.

I got totally bogged down in Psalm 51 this morning. No wonder I am having such trouble getting through my "new" Bible! There is so much to ponder, tuck away, and underline. This Psalm, which I have used as my devotional this morning, was written by David after he committed adultery with Bathsheba and managed to have her husband, Uriah, killed. It is awesome in its depth of confession and emotion.

> "Have mercy upon me, O God, according to Your loving kindness. According to the multitude of Your tender mercies, Blot out my transgressions, wash me thoroughly from my iniquity, and cleanse me from my sin" (Ps. 51:1-2)

I hope and pray none of us will have a need to confess to either adultery or murder, but I know full well we all have other sins that equally need to be brought to the Lord, and these words cannot be improved on in their sincerity and depth of feeling: "Behold, You desire truth in the inward parts, and in the hidden part you will make me know wisdom" (Ps. 51:6).

Lord God, truth in the "inward part" means I cannot hide anything of myself from You. Being in denial about anything just won't cut it.

You will bubble it right to the surface of my consciousness, because You want me healed and whole. Maybe this is why the paralytic stayed sick for thirty-eight years. Thank You, Lord, that You *want* us to know wisdom. What a wonderful revelation! And now, one of my favorite passages. Yes, we've read it previously, but many passages bear repeating, and this is one of them:

> "Create in me a clean heart, O God, and renew a steadfast spirit within me. Do not cast me away from Your presence, and do not take Your Holy Spirit from me." (Ps. 51:10-12) and amen

This is undoubtedly a prayer I would want to pray for myself every single day before my feet hit the bedroom floor running! How I wish I were that disciplined! Is there anything in the world that feels better than a clean heart? To be confessed up, prayed up, and praised up is when a depth of peace comes to me. The frosting on the cake is when it is followed by a really anointed message from the pulpit!

I was one of those people who got real excited about my salvation and the reality of the Lord I had never known before. At a Bible study thirty-four years ago, I remember a woman a little older than me, saying about me, "Don't worry, she won't always be this on fire. She's a 'baby' Christian." I remember saying a silent prayer at that moment, asking the Lord to please not let me lose this joy . . . this knowledge of Him. That was a long time ago, and I thank God every day He honored that prayer. (I forgave that woman in my heart long ago.)

Late yesterday afternoon, the rains returned and I found "gold" in our basement. While delving through some storage boxes always meant for "someday," I found old photos from both sides of the family. More exciting to me was a ziplock bag full of four or five miniature tablets that turned out to be travel journals from my Grammie Mansfield. I had forgotten I even possessed them. She liked to write as much as I do, but apparently only when she traveled. One journal was from an automobile trip she had taken with Aunt Ora and my mom in the summer of 1929 from Boone County in Nebraska to Portland, Oregon. The three women camped along the way, unless they found the campground was "not desirable," in which case a hotel was found. The thing that really interested me about this trip was it was the summer before my mom was married to my dad in October of 1929. Yet Grammie didn't mention anything about the upcoming wedding or anything really personal. I know the wedding took place in Mom's childhood home in Albion, I know the Methodist minister officiated, and I know my mom's cousin sang at the wedding. I don't even know who gave her away at the ceremony. So many times I wish Mom was still here so I could ask her questions. I was not ready for her to die. Strange, Mom and Dad have been gone so many years, but they are so often in my thoughts and consciousness.

The small journals reminded me of why I decided to write this particular book. So many times I wanted to ask Grammie how and when she found her faith in God. I wanted to know why my aunts always talked about everything around the kitchen table, but they never talked about Jesus or their faith. I now know I had a Baptist (I don't know how many greats) grandfather who married an Indian princess from Illinois. Because she was a "heathen," they had to get on a train and go to New York City to find a minister willing to marry them. Incredible! But that may have started my family's reluctance to discuss faith or biblical concepts. And I certainly didn't know there was a Baptist in my background until long after my folks were dead—or an Indian princess, either! Thanks to a cousin's research, those tidbits came forth. I don't want that same unknowing to ever happen in my immediate family. I always want my grandchildren and great grands to know their spiritual heritage. To me, that is more important than our national roots . . . where our forefathers came from and what our ancestry is. Oh what I wouldn't give for one last session around that enamel kitchen table in Albion!

In every Bible study class I have ever taught, I have always urged my Sister Chicks to do two things: use and carry 3 × 5 index cards with favorite Bible verses and to write down their spiritual story for all their family to know. Now I am asking you to do the same. You may not think you or your story is very important, but I'm here to tell you that is not true. One day, if they don't know already, your children will want to. At least let's pray they are all spiritually inquisitive enough to want to know.

I finally got tired of sitting almost under the Ping-Pong table in the basement—yes, we have furniture down there—but the box was large, and it was easier to sit on the floor next to it as I dug for family gold. It was time to go upstairs and start our dinner. First thing tomorrow morning, I will continue with our precious John.

## *Chapters 11-13*

In Chapter 11, we have the seventh of the eight signs, or miracles, around which the book of John is written. Just as reminder of the first six, they are: water turned into wine at the wedding in Cana (Jn. 2:1-11), healing a noblman's son (Jn. 4:46-54), healing a lame man by the pool of Bethesda (Jn. 5:1-7), feeding the five thousand (Jn. 6:1-14), healing a blind man (Jn. 9:1-41). Lest I forget to tell you, the eighth sign was the catching of fish (Jn. 21:6), in a post resurrection appearance.

The story of Lazarus is only told in John, which really amazes me because all the apostles were with Jesus, and this certainly is a miracle that would be difficult to forget. We've already met this family in Luke. Martha, Mary, and Lazarus lived together in Bethany, a small village just two miles from Jerusalem. Jesus got word, presumably from a messenger, that Lazarus was sick. Jesus seemed unconcerned and told His disciples, in essence, "Don't worry, he won't die. This is something that will give God glory and the Son of God glory also" (Jn. 11:4). Jesus lingered two more days wherever He was and then said to His Disciples, "Let's go to Judea again." That's where Jerusalem and Bethany were. The disciples had good memories and immediately said, in essence, "Are you crazy? Don't you remember? The last time you were there the Jews tried to stone You" (Jn. 11:8). The disciples tried everything they could to discourage this trip, until Jesus finally told them plainly, "'Lazarus is dead. And I am glad for your sakes I was not there, that you may believe. Nevertheless, let us go to him'" (Jn. 11:14-15).

Notice, not go to grieve, mourn, or wail, but to go *to him*. Don't miss Thomas's attitude. It is priceless: "'Let us also go, that we may die with Him'" (Jn. 11:16).

Can't you just hear the sigh of resignation? These apostles were frightened, and with good cause. They could read the temperature of the scribes and Pharisees and saw stones flying as they left Jerusalem the last time. They might even have been hit by a few, and they didn't have the spiritual knowledge they would receive at Pentecost. But they were faithful and resilient at this point, and stuck with Jesus in spite of their fear. When they arrived on the outskirts of Bethany, they learned Lazarus had already been dead and in the tomb for four days. This is important. Let me tell you why. "The Jews had a belief that after death the spirit hung around the body for three days, hoping to return, and finally left on the 4$^{th}$ day when the body had started to decompose" (Fredrikson, p. 195).

We know this isn't true because Jesus said, "'Today you will be with me in Paradise'" (Lk. 23:43). What precious words! And once you died, why would you want to return? Remember Bob's grandpa?

So here's the story. They arrived to have Lazarus' death confirmed. (Of course Jesus already knew and had told them. He knows everything.) Martha, one of the grieving sisters, heard Jesus was coming and hurried out to greet Him. Notice how different these two sisters are. Martha can't sit still and is on the move, whereas Mary is so consumed with her grief, she is unaware of anything. When Martha meets Jesus and His companions, she babbles, "'Lord, if You had been here, my brother would not have died. But even now, I know whatever you ask of God, He will give you'" (Jn. 11:20-22).

I don't think Martha is accusing Jesus. I believe she is showing how much faith she has in Him. And for sure, I don't believe healing at this point was ever within her grasp. Jesus assures her, "'Your brother will rise again'" (Jn. 11:23).

Martha's reply is what all the rabbis taught, "'I know he will rise again in the resurrection at the last day" (Jn. 11:24). She meant the general resurrection; she didn't have a clue this was forthcoming for Jesus. There are just some things our minds can't immediately wrap around.

Jesus' reply is our fourth major I AM statement: "'I AM the Resurrection and the Life, He who believes in Me. Though he may die, he shall live. And whoever lives and believes in Me shall never die;" (Jn. 11:25-26). Do you believe this?

Martha's confession shows her faith as far as she could go. "'Yes, Lord, I believe that You are the Christ, the Son of God, who is to come into the Word'" (Jn. 11:27). Oh, that we might all say those words with the same faith Martha had, even in the midst of grief and pain. And remember, He still is to come.

When Martha summoned Mary, she quickly rose and went out to also meet with Jesus. She was followed by all the Jews who had come to comfort the sisters and help them mourn during the first week of grieving for their brother. Interesting that Mary said the same thing to Jesus when she fell at His feet. "'Lord, if You had been here my brother would not have died'" (Jn. 11:32). Again, I don't think this was an accusation, rather a sign of loyalty to Him and faith in His healing ability and authority.

Jesus saw her weeping, and all the Jews with her who were also weeping. He "Groaned in His Spirit and was troubled" (Jn. 11:33). Was He troubled to see His dear friends so deeply in grief, or was He troubled to see their lack of belief in an afterlife . . . an eternity? I don't know the answer, but I do know their tears brought on His tears also. As they started to show Him where the tomb was, the story tells us, "Jesus wept" (Jn. 11:35).

The Greek word used here indicates silent tears running down His cheeks rather than loud lamenting. I can relate. When Jesus sees our pain and suffering, He relates to whatever it is causing us pain, and when we are able to release that pain to Him, He will take it from us.I'll never forget one Sunday morning in church many years ago, when I got word passed down the pew that a good friend had died in the night. We had been on a "healing team" for several years, and I knew she was very ill with breast cancer. But when I heard the news, I burst into kind of silent tears during the service. My tears had nothing to do with faith; I was crying for me. I wasn't ready to let Carol go, and I had a deep need to grieve. I knew Jesus was crying with me, even as He had His arms around my friend in heaven at the time. I knew exactly where she was and that I would see her again. I just wasn't ready to let her go. I think that's how Martha and Mary felt. They just weren't ready to let go . . . especially knowing if Jesus had been there, He could have healed their brother. After all, they had seen Him heal many times in the past.

The whole group departed for the tomb. We know the apostles were there, and there might have been others also, like some of their wives and the friends who had come from Jerusalem and the neighborhood to sit Shiva with the sisters. When Jesus said, "Take the stone away" (Jn. 11:39), Martha, always the grounded, detail-oriented, taskmaster, was horrified, reminding Jesus the smell would be awful, because he had been dead four days. (Remember, the Jews do not embalm: thus, a quick burial.) Jesus said, "'Did I not say to you that if you would believe, you would see the glory of God?'" (Jn. 11:40).

Jesus lifted His eyes and said, "'Father, I thank You that You have heard Me. And I know that You always hear Me, but because of the people who are standing by, I said this that they may believe that you sent Me'" (Jn. 11:42). Then He cried out in a loud voice, "Lazarus, come forth!"

And he did . . . stumbling and wrapped up from head to toe. Jesus ordered the people to loose the wrappings he had been buried in and to let him go. I would love to talk to Lazarus and ask him what it felt like in the tomb while he was dead and waiting. I think he would say it was like he was sleeping, until his skin began to tingle with the healing, and he awoke to Jesus' voice. That would be my guess, but I'm still going to ask him. When I meet him.

Naturally, word got back to Jerusalem pronto, and the chief priests and scribes gathered the Sanhedrin, who decided this was the last straw! If they didn't do something, "Everyone will believe Him and the Romans will come and take away both our place and our nation" (Jn. 11:48). Caiphas, the high priest, was the one who suggested it might be better for one man to die than have the entire nation perish. The wheels of destruction were plotted and put into motion that very day. Sadly the plot thickens. They didn't know their intent of destruction would turn out to be glorious deliverance!

Chapter 12 opens with the week before the third Passover mentioned in John. For those who forgot to mark them, the first two Passovers were John 2:13 and John 6:4. Because Judas Iscariot was present during a supper again in Bethany, and critical of Mary anointing Jesus feet with a costly perfume, we are told Lazarus, her brother, was also present at the table. It is nice to know Lazarus is up and functioning after his experience in the tomb. I think we can safely assume all the apostles and possibly others were also present. This chapter marks the triumphal entry into Jerusalem and all its details, which are also noted in the three Synoptic Gospels and discussed in previous chapters. The witnesses who had watched Lazarus rise from the dead were telling the story all over the city, so people were anxious to see and meet this miracle man. The entire chapter is again full of, "Yes, of course He is the Messiah," and, "No, of course He could not be. We need to get rid of Him before the whole world believes in Him." And in the midst of the chaos and busy preparations for the Passover, Jesus is still teaching, still trying to make people understand His function on earth. Jesus tells the people,

> "If anyone serves Me, let him follow Me, and where I am, there My servant will be also. If anyone serves Me, him my Father will honor. Now My soul is troubled, and what shall I say? Father, save Me from this hour? But for this purpose I have come to this hour. Father, glorify Your name." (Jn. 12:26-27)

A voice came out of heaven, saying, "I have both glorified it and will glorify it again" (Jn. 12:28).

Jesus said to the crowd:

> "This voice did not come because of Me, but for your sake, now is the judgment of this world; now the ruler of this world will be cast out. And I, if I am lifted up from the earth, will draw all people to Myself." (Jn. 12:30-33)

This is a promise we, as believes, can't wait to see happen. Oh how exciting it would be to be here on earth to see the belief, praise, and worship come flying out of all corners of the earth! I will leave this chapter with the following quote from Jesus:

> "He who believes in Me, believes not in Me, but in Him who sent me. And he who sees Me, sees Him who sent Me." (Jn. 12:43-45)

> "and if anyone hears my words and does not believe, I do not judge him, for I did not come to judge the world, but to save the world." (Jn. 12:47)

> "for I have not spoken on my own authority, but the Father who sent Me gave me a command, what I should say and what I should speak. And I know that His command is everlasting life. Therefore, whatever I speak, just as the Father has told Me, so I speak." (Jn. 12:49-50)

Chapters 13 through 17 are specific teachings for Jesus' believers. His public ministry is over, and as He starts the final hours of His life on earth, we have some of the most beautiful teaching in the entire Bible. What a privilege we have to actually get in on this teaching and to take advantage of His words and tuck them into our hearts, just as the apostles did.

Chapter 13 gives yet another teaching totally unique to the book of John. The scene is the upper room, where Jesus and His apostles had just eaten a meal. The apostles were squabbling over who was the greatest among them. Really now! These grown men had all spent the last three years with Jesus, and they were arguing over which one of them was the greatest. Check it out also in Luke 22:24. (I can't make up anything this outlandish!) Jesus, knowing His time was very limited before His sacrifice on the cross, still has some bottom-line teaching to do that had to do with humility, servant hood, and spiritual cleansing. He silently got up from the meal, and one by one, began to wash the feet of His apostles. Can't you just imagine the silence of the shocked apostles? In our modern culture, we can hardly appreciate the magnitude of this gesture, because most of us wear shoes most of the time, unless you are my grandson, Joshua. And even when we do wear sandals, which is our favorite choice of footwear in the desert, we usually walk on clean floors, clean sidewalks, and sculptured laws. Not so in first-century Israel. The footwear was always sandals, and feet were always filthy from direct contact with roads and sanitary conditions that were far less than ideal. The lowest in caste of household servants usually had the unfortunate job of removing dirty sandals from one's feet, and I don't know if this involved washing feet or not . . . probably not. It was despicable! What Jesus was doing for the apostles was almost unthinkable. Only Simon Peter could find his tongue to protest, to which Jesus replied:

> "What I am doing you do not understand now, but you will know after this." (Jn. 13:7)

> "If I do not wash you, you have no part with me." (Jn. 13:8)

This is again one of those situations where Simon Peter can't keep his mouth shut and just learn. He still complains, "'Lord, not my feet, but my hands and head as well'" (Jn. 13:9).

Jesus went on to teach,

> "Do you know what I have done for you? You call Me Teacher and Lord and say well, for I AM. If then, your Teacher and Lord have washed your feet, you ought to wash one another's feet. For I have given you an example that you should do as I have done for you." (Jn. 13:12-15)

> "If you know these things, blessed are you if you do them." (Jn. 13:17)

Jesus goes on to identify, at least quietly to John (who is the apostle leaning on Him), who His betrayer will be. When Judas Iscariot leaves the room, I believe the apostles are clueless as to what is unfolding.

In this gospel, we are not told the teaching of communion. Remember, this book was written long after the other three gospels, and presumably everyone John knows has already celebrated communion for many years, so it was a teaching that need not be repeated. It does seem a little strange that John was the only one who wrote about the foot washing, which seems so symbolic of spiritual cleansing to me.

But then, John had a long time to think about these teachings and to internalize their meanings. He knew what needed to be repeated and what didn't.

Jesus announces His departure to the apostles and gives one more teaching:

> "A new commandment I give to you, that you love one another. As I have loved you, you also love one another. By this all men will know you are My Disciples, if you love one another." (Jn. 13:34-35)

This chapter ends with Jesus telling Peter he will deny Him three times before the cock crows. Funny how everyone seems to remember that one! Human nature, I guess.

> Thank You, Father, that You alone can bypass our all-too-common human nature and forgive us anyway. Amen.

# CHAPTER 34

# JOHN FOURTEEN

Oh Lord, what a perfect devotion before we even start back with John:

> "He who dwells in the secret place of the Most High shall abide under the shadow of the Almighty. I will say of the Lord, "He is my refuge and my Fortress,"
>
> My God, in Him I trust.
>
> Surely He shall deliver you from the snare of the Fowler, and from pestilence, and under His wings you shall take refuse, His truth shall be your shield and buckler.
>
> You shall not be afraid of the terror by night, Nor of the arrow that flies by day, Nor of the pestilence that walks in darkness, Nor the destruction that lays waste at noonday. A thousand may fall at your side, but it shall not come near you. Only with your eyes shall you look and see the reward of the wicked." (Ps. 91:1-8)
>
> Because you have made the Lord, who is my Refuge, even the Most High, your dwelling place, no evil shall come before you, nor any plague come near your dwelling: For He shall give His angels charge over you, to keep you in all your ways. In their hands they shall bear you up, lest you dash your foot against a stone.

> He shall call upon Me, and I will answer him; I will be with him in trouble; I will deliver him and honor him, With long life I will satisfy him And show him my salvation" (Ps. 91:15-16)

Lord God, Your word is so incredible through this Psalm. I drink it in like I have thirsted for a long time. Years ago, our pastor in Frisco gave a sermon on this Psalm by drawing a large cloud or umbrella (easier than drawing a wing), with us sitting under it, safe under God's wing of protection, with fiery darts of pestilence falling down all around us. I've never forgotten that message and even drew an umbrella in the margin of my Bible over this Psalm to help me remember. For me, pestilence represents fear, cancer, strokes, evil authority, temptations for worldly things, materialism, need to control, and loss of time. The Bible lists pestilence as adultery, fornication, uncleanness, lewdness, idolatry, and six more disgusting sins in Galatians 5:19. Lord God, I do pray against all these, and one by one, I tuck all my loved ones under the shadow of Your wings, for You promised protection to those who belong to You. Yes, we see these evils; who can live in this world and not be aware of them? But Your protection and promises with Your rod and Your staff remind me of the safety I have in You. I have often wondered how many times traffic has delayed me to keep me safe from harm, or a phone call changes plans that would not have been conducive to the lifestyle of righteousness You want for me. Do you suppose we will ever know about these things? Perhaps not; we believe by faith.

Our senior pastor here in Colorado is very ill with a degenerative auto-immune disease and is now a candidate for a liver transplant to save his life. It is devastating news to us. He was able to preach yesterday and blessed our little church that was packed to the seams, but he ended up in the hospital again last night. Dear God, he is only in his fifties, and You know how greatly he has impacted the lives of so many here in Summit County and brought peace and understanding to every person who has sat under his teaching. Please heal him, Lord, and give both Bruce and Donna, his wife, Your peace and patience until a miracle healing or donor liver can be found.

I have almost avoided this next chapter, in fact the next several, because they are so very special. I'm afraid I can never express how much they have meant to me in the past thirty-five years. But we'll never receive the blessing unless we get to them, so let's start with the opening phrase from Chapter 14, and continue on.

## *Chapter 14*

From the words of Jesus:

> "Let not your heart be troubled, you believe in God, believe also in Me. In My Father's house are many mansions; if it were not so, I would have told you. I go to prepare a place for you. And if I go and prepare a place for you, I will come again and receive you to Myself, that where I am, there you may be also. And where I go, you know, and the way, you know." (Jn. 14:1-4)

Thomas asked Him, "'Lord, we don't know where You are going and how can we know the way?'" (Jn. 14:5). Thomas is really growing on me! I love his openness and the questions he asks.

Jesus answered him, "'I am the way, the truth and the life. No one comes to the Father except through Me'" (Jn. 14:6). I love that verse so much, I incorporated it into my e-mail address, so I would see it often and remember. These verses are so comforting to me. I love thinking of my parents in a "mansion" in heaven. Their earthly home was a very modest trailer park in Florida, and the home I grew up in was a comfortable two-story home in a very middle-class neighborhood in Omaha. We assumed one bathroom for the four of us was perfectly adequate. My parents didn't have much in the way of material goods. Nor did we need them or seem to want them. The opening verses of chapter 14 go right to my heart, because I almost always believed in God. Before I knew Him as a concept or theology, as a small child I talked regularly to my much-loved teddy bear. As I grew to believe in the Father-God, I put teddy aside and talked to God regularly. I don't know how this initial belief came to be, but when I first read the words, "'You believe in God, believe also in Me,'" it was as if Jesus had reached through the page of the Bible to say, "I'm talking to you." And by then I did get it. Him. An astounding revelation to my limited mind! And the opening words, "'Let not your heart be troubled,'" oh my. My heart has been troubled so many times, and it is soothed every time I go back to these words. I don't have to be troubled, because God is in control and has it all figured out. I only need to believe and to trust in Him. That word "trust" means so much to me.

The same year I was saved was perhaps the hardest year of my life; certainly the first six months after I regained my health were the hardest. I had been in bed for twenty-one days, with Bob bearing the responsibility of the entire household. And when I did emerge from my bedroom, I was not the same person who went into it. Everything about me had changed—my beliefs, my outlook, my interests, and especially my interests in anything spiritual. Bob was uninterested, and at one point told me if I mentioned the name of Jesus one more time, he would be out the door. Through a series of misunderstandings that summer, an incident happened that brought us to the brink of separation, which was unthinkable to me. One night when we went to bed, Bob told me he would be leaving in the morning. And he went to sleep! I had only been a Christian for a few months and was absolutely frantic with being troubled. I prayed. I cried. I talked to Jesus as if He were right next to me. About three o'clock in the morning, I heard a voice inside my head—that's the only way I can explain it—and the Voice said, "Trust in the Lord with all your heart, and lean not on your own understanding. Follow Me in all your ways, and I will direct your path."

I sat straight up in bed, grabbed a pencil and an envelope from my bedside lamp table, went into the bathroom, and asked, "Lord, would you give me those words again?" He did, and I wrote them down, word for word. In the morning, Bob decided to stay in our marriage and try to work out our differences in whatever way we could. What a relief! Our long talks in the following weeks turned out to be some of the best times of communication in our entire marriage.

But back to the verse I was given that night. I knew it must have come from the Bible, but I did not have a clue where or how to find it. So back I went to my friend Judy, who taught me about a concordance and how to use one. I had not read the book of Proverbs yet, but sure enough, there was "my" verse in Proverbs 3:5-6. When I realized the

Lord was communicating with Bible verses, it strengthened my resolve to learn the Bible as quickly and thoroughly as possible!

Now back to the opening phrase of John 14.

Many years ago, when we first had a winter home in Rancho Mirage, we joined a country club in our neighborhood that had a beautiful tennis facility, as well as golf, which wasn't our interest. But the tennis director arranged a mixed-doubles game for us with another couple, and we began the process of making friends with like-minded people. We liked the couple very much, and because of their surname, we assumed (rightly) that they were Jewish. Jean asked me what had brought us to the desert from our home in Nebraska, and I explained that our son was currently a student at Pepperdine University, and we were attracted to the mild winters where we could enjoy outdoor activities. Jean picked up on the "Pepperdine" and immediately and abruptly asked, "Isn't that a Christian college?

*Oh no,* I thought, *we are new members of this club and a possible problem? Lord, you're going to have to help me here,* I prayed. "Yes, as a matter of fact, it is." I answered.

She shot back very quickly. "Are you Christians?"

*Lord, you are in charge here. Help.* "Yes, we are Christians." I breathed.

"Are you *born-again* Christians?" she asked.

*Oh Lord, I don't know what is going on here, but please be in this conversation.* "Yes, Jean, we are born-again Christians." I almost felt like adding, "take it or leave it, that's what we are."

Then she blurted, "Praise the Lord, so are we!" I almost fell over the water fountain! I explained that I had assumed at least her husband to be Jewish, to which she replied of course they both were and were "completed Jews." (Jewish believers who put their faith in Jesus as Messiah and Lord.) Those were our first friends at Mission Hills.

The reason I remember them just now is that many years later, Jean had an aggressive case of breast cancer, years after my own bout. When we left the desert one early spring, she was almost bedridden and bald. She'd had multiple surgeries and was undergoing chemo and radiation. I wasn't sure we would ever see her again. The only thing we could do was pray. When we returned in the fall, Jean returned to the tennis courts. She told me these beginning verses in John 14 kept her going through the worst of her battles, and she memorized them and repeated them daily. Wow! Yes, that's how powerful biblical phrases are. Sadly, these friends left the desert to be closer to children who were not believers, and we lost touch. But I have no doubt I will see them again soon. (Time is relative.)

In answer to Philip's request, "Lord, show us the Father and it is sufficient for us" (Jn. 14:8), Jesus makes it very clear that He is in the Father and that the Father is in Him, and if they couldn't believe that on its own merit, then to believe Him for all the miracles they had seen Him perform. No one could do those works or say those words without being God, who has done all the works through Jesus.

Jesus says if we believe in Him, we also will do even greater works, because He is going to the Father in just a matter of hours., as the resurrection is very near. And here we have a remarkable teaching on prayer: "'And whatever you ask in My name, that I will do, that the Father may be glorified in the Son. If you ask anything in My name, I will do it'" (Jn. 14:13-14). Certainly a verse to tuck into our hearts and minds, to believe and to do often. It reminds me of a time one winter when we were in the desert and our phone rang one morning at about 5:30. We are normally early risers, but this call woke us up. It was my Jewish girlfriend in Denver, calling from a hospital to tell me her husband had just suffered a burst aneurysm and was in surgery. His chances of living were slim to none. Her anxiety made my heart race, and I told her I would pray right then on the phone with her, but she should know that I pray to the Father in Jesus' name. Gwen replied, "I don't care who you pray to . . . just please do it!" And I did. And she listened. And her Christian husband survived and continues to be a loving husband to my friend today. And we give God the glory. And praise and thanks! A reprieve!

The section starting at verse 15 is such an important teaching on the coming of the Holy Spirit. It fills in the gaps from Jesus' teaching to Nicodemus on being born again. Read with me:

> "And if you love me, keep My commandments, and I will pray to the Father, and He will give you Another Helper, that He may abide

> with you forever . . . the Spirit of truth, whom the world cannot receive because it neither sees Him nor knows Him, but you know Him for He dwells in you, and will be in you. I will not leave you as orphans, I will come to you." (Jn. 14:15-18)

Go with me back to two words in this verse. The word "Another"; I have capped it so you can find it easily. The word another is *allos* in the original Greek and means "one of equal quality." The second word I want you to find is "Helper," and it is translated from *parakletes,* which means "one who comforts, aids, brings encouragement." Jesus is teaching His apostles the entire concept of the Trinity, who, how, and when. Even the results:

> "He who has My commandments and keeps them, it is he who loves Me. And he who loves Me will be loved by My Father, and I will love him and manifest Myself to him." (Jn. 14:21)

What a bold statement verse 21 is! We have an expression in evangelical circles that we have "invited Jesus to come into our hearts," which is our declaration of belief in Him, who He is, and how we turn our lives over to Him for His control. Now we know that Jesus is not literally in our hearts, because we know He has ascended back into heaven after the resurrection and His teaching for forty additional days (Acts 1:3). And we know that Jesus now sits at the right hand of God the Father Almighty, waiting for future events to happen on earth. This is a truth we affirm each time we repeat the Apostle's Creed or check out Matthew 16:64 and Luke 22:29. But what Jesus means by He will "manifest Himself in us" is the indwelling Presence of the Holy Spirit after we have believed and surrendered our lives to Jesus as Messiah, Savior, and Lord. If anyone reading this has not experienced the indwelling of the Spirit personally, you can appreciate how confused the apostles must have been at this teaching when it was originally taught. Of course by the time this book of John was written, the apostles had all died or been martyred.

Further questions by one of the apostles brought about more information on the Holy Spirit:

"If anyone loves Me, he will keep my word, and My Father will love him, and We will come to him and make our home with him." (Jn. 14:23)

"These things I have spoken to you while being present with you. But the Helper, the Holy Spirit, whom the Father will send in My name, He will teach you all things and bring to your remembrance all things I have said to you." (Jn. 14:25-26)

"My peace I leave with you. My peace I give to you, not as the world gives do I give to you. Let not your hearts be troubled, neither let it be afraid." (Jn. 14:27)

## CHAPTER 35

# JOHN FIFTEEN - SEVENTEEN

Good morning, Lord, and thank You for a lovely sunny day in the mountains. I have come to Psalm 119 this morning, which is the longest Psalm in the Bible, and will choose some of my favorites as our devotional this day. Oh what a teaching tool for me!

> "You have commanded us to keep Your precepts diligently. Oh that my ways were directed to keep Your statutes. "(Ps. 119:4-5)

> "Your word I have hidden in my heart, that I might not sin against You." (Ps. 119:11)

> "I will meditate on Your precepts, and contemplate Your ways. I will delight myself in Your statutes; I will not forget Your word." (Ps. 119:15-16)

> "Teach me, O Lord, the way of your statutes, and I shall keep them to the end. Give me understanding and I shall keep Your law; indeed, I shall observe it with my whole heart." (Ps. 119:33)

> "Your word is a lamp unto my feet a light unto my path." (Ps. 119:105)

Oh Lord, yesterday afternoon I was on the phone in the den, watching out the back window, when around the corner of our cabin lumbered a gorgeous black bear. She must have been several hundred pounds; she was so huge! And she doesn't actually "walk," she "lumbers," with her front paws turned in. She was followed by two adorable black bear cubs. I literally hung up the phone with a quick apology to my friend and called Bob to the rear windows to watch her progress. By the time we both reached the door to our back deck, Mama Bear was trying to climb up the side of our cabin to reach the deck, probably in pursuit of our hummingbird feeder. Bob impulsively opened the back door, not four feet away from her, raised his arms above his head, and told her very nicely she could not come up, and to take her babies and leave. And she did! But not before Bob shot a photo of her. My heart was racing wildly at the sight of this enormous animal, and I couldn't believe Bob thought to grab the camera. We knew she was in the 'hood, because our neighbors down the street, Tom and Bobbi, had sent us photos via the Internet of this bear family playing on their hammock and deck chairs. We had been warned that this bear was so smart she had learned to get into cars, and if we had guests who needed to leave their car in the driveway, to make sure it was locked with no food inside. What fun! Mike and Kim were here for a biking weekend and just missed our wildlife visitors. We occasionally see a squirrel and a skunk in our yard in Lincoln, and in the fall, we have a deer family visit us to dine on the wild pears in our backyard. They are always welcome, unlike these recent visitors.

Now, dear ones, on with the gospel of John.

## *Chapters 15-17*

The metaphor that begins chapter 15 is a lovely word picture of our relationship to God. It is specifically spelled out that Jesus (the speaker) is the true Vine. He says "true" Vine, because Israel has been called "the vine" in many Old Testament verses, and now Jesus is saying, in effect, "Pay attention. I am the true Vine!" Father God is the "vinedresser," or head gardener, and you and I are the branches, who are attached to the vine. The entire job of the branches is to grow fruit . . . to be productive. And if we are not firmly attached to the vine, we will not receive the nutrients we need to be successful. Nor will we fulfill our destiny as Christians who are following the commandments of the Lord. Did I mention there are twenty-three I AM statements in the book of John? Seven of the metaphors are major statements, this being the final one: "'I am the Vine. You are the branches. He who abides in Me, and I in him, bears much fruit, for without Me, you can do nothing'" (Jn. 15:5).

The story itself tells us if a branch does not bear fruit, it is taken away, and every branch that does bear fruit He (God) prunes so more fruit will grow. As I mentioned before, I am convinced I was being "pruned" when I had the strokes. I have a very quick mouth that could often be sarcastic and misunderstood, unless you had a sense of humor similar to mine. The trouble was, not everyone knew me well enough to know when I was joking or just being sarcastic. I think the Lord needed to "prune" my mouth, which He definitely did. After the strokes, I could no longer get the quips out fast enough to be relevant to the conversation, as I was forced to slow my thinking so the words could be understood. I am grateful for the pruning. It made me realize I needed to be kinder, especially with new people I really wanted to get to know better. It made me think first and speak second. God gave us two ears and only one mouth. He wants us to be quick to listen and slow to speak. I have had to learn that the hard way. I have an acquaintance in the desert whom I occasionally need to be on the same tennis court with. Every word that comes out of her mouth is either negative or sarcastic. I used to think she must really dislike me but have decided it probably had nothing to do with me. It's as if God were saying, "This is what you sounded like. How do you like it?" Ouch! Forgive me, Lord. I had no idea! Hindsight is such a wonderful, if not sometimes painful, teacher. The Lord has assured us in this chapter that if His words abide in us, we may ask whatever we desire, and it will be done, which means we will bear much fruit and be disciples of Christ. It's true! Read it in your own translation in John 15:7-8.

Jesus gives one last commandment before He goes to the cross, and it is repeated twice in this chapter; don't miss it.

> "This is my commandment that you love one another, as I have loved you." (Jn. 15:12)

> "You did not choose Me, but I chose you, and appointed you that you should go and bear fruit, and that your fruit should remain, that whatever you ask the Father in My name He may give you, that you love one another." (Jn. 15:16-17)

A tall order for a sinful world, but all things are possible through Christ, who strengthens us (Phil. 4:13). Even loving the unlovable. Maybe especially loving the unlovable! Try it, and see what incredible relationships evolve when the Lord directs your actions, words, and emotions.

Jesus ends the chapter by repeating the promise of sending the Holy Spirit from the Father who will testify of Him. Chapter 15 melds almost flawlessly into chapter 16, continuing His final teaching to His beloved apostles.

Jesus warns His followers in chapter 16 that they will be put out of the synagogues, which they were, and warns them that "whoever kills you will think he offers God a service" (Jn. 16:2b).

Isn't that exactly what Caiaphas was thinking back in chapter 11, when the plot thickened to eliminate Jesus "before the whole world believes Him"? Of course, he was also thinking about his own position and what he would lose. It seems to me in the past decade we can also apply this principle to the terrorists who brought down the World Trade Centers. Jesus goes on to say these things happened (and presumably will continue to happen), because the ones involved do not know either our Father God or the Messiah, Jesus. The Lord is warning His apostles about what will take place that very night. But I think we can heed warnings like this whenever we find them, as long as we do not misinterpret the Bible or God's command to love each other. What a reason for evangelism! The Lord goes on to tell his followers plainly that He is going away:

> "Nevertheless I tell you the truth, it is to your advantage that I go away, for if I do not go away, the Helper will not come to you. And when He has come, He will convict the world of sin, and of righteousness and of judgment." (Jn. 16:7-8)

Jesus' teaches further on the Holy Spirit:

> "However, when He, the Spirit of truth has come, He will guide you into all truth, for He will not speak on His own authority, but whatever He hears, He will speak, and He will tell you things to come." (Jn. 16:13)

The remainder of chapter 16 is the difficult telling of Christ's death and resurrection, and, of course, they didn't understand the part about "You will see Me again" because of the initial sorrow of His death on the cross. But Jesus assures them that even though they could not understand just then, when they see Him again after the resurrection, their sorrow will be replaced by incredible joy that no one can take from them. I particularly loved the analogy of the pain of labor—been there, done that—and how true is it that no matter how bad it was, the pain is forgotten at the miracle of counting tiny fingers and toes and experiencing the miracle of birth. Again, Jesus repeats His former teaching:

> "In that day you will ask in My name, and I do not say to you I shall pray to the Father for you, for the Father Himself loves you because you have loved Me and have believed that I came from God. I came forth from the Father and have come into the world. Again, I leave the world and go to the Father." (Jn. 16:26-28)

He is not only preparing His apostles, He is also preparing us to function in a world gone astray. He has warned us continually in all four gospels of the difficult signs of the coming tribulation. John ends this chapter with these words of comfort from Jesus:

> "These things I have spoken to you that in Me you will have peace. In the world you will have tribulation, but be of good cheer, I have overcome the world." (Jn. 16:33)

When I consider all the heartaches and difficulties that represent my prayer cards for friends who are believers and hope their husbands, sons, daughters, loved ones, will one day come to know the Lord, it makes my heart ache for them and strengthens my resolve to pray even for those loved ones I don't know, because I see the hurt their choices are causing. The Lord has a perfect plan for this, too, and my responsibility is simply to pray. I don't even have to know the outcome. I just know my prayers are collected in a bowl sitting in front of the throne, and I am comforted knowing this.

Chapter 17 contains three of the most beautiful prayers I have ever read . . . all by Jesus. In the first one, He is praying for Himself, knowing His suffering is imminent and that He has completed the task He was sent to earth to do. Oh that we could say the same one day! I have no idea what task I was born for; maybe it was just to know Christ and through Him to know the Father God, and to know the reality of the Holy Spirit within. Just knowing is certainly not enough. We need to carry through the knowing, follow the commandments, and believe the hundreds of promises . . . and to live our lives like we do believe. Oh Lord, I fall so short of Your expectations for me! Please do not give up on me. As long as I am alive and still functioning, I am still trying to follow You in all my ways. I am still a work in progress!

The second prayer in Chapter 17 is for His disciples, the followers He is temporarily leaving behind who will spread the words of Jesus to a hungry world, along with the indwelling of the Holy Spirit, to begin what we know of as the "church age." Those early disciples and apostles were incredible. One day we will meet them. Can you just imagine how awesome that will be?

The third prayer of Chapter 17 is the most remarkable to me, because He is praying for us! For those of us who believe the words we are reading in the Bible. It is unbelievable that Jesus thought to pray for us, who wouldn't be born for hundreds of years! It is awesome beyond words.

> "I do not pray for those alone [the disciples], but also for those who will believe in Me through their words; that they may be one as You, Father, are in Me and I in You, that they also may be one in Us, that the world may believe that You sent me . . ." (Jn. 17:20-21)

> "Father, I desire that they also, whom You gave me will be with Me where I am, that they may behold My glory which You have given Me. For You loved Me before the foundation of the world. Oh righteous Father, the world has not known You, but I have known You, and these [believers] have known that You sent Me. And I have declared to them Your Name, and I will declare it, that the love with which You loved Me may be in them, and I in them." (Jn. 17:24-26)

Please, please get out your favorite translation and read chapter 17. The love of Christ just pours forth from the page, and I can only thank God over and over for preserving these precious words over the years to bless us and encourage us in our daily walk.

> Lord God, You are so good! I stand amazed at Your glory . . . Your wisdom and love for us . . . such undeserving people we are. Please God, don't give up on us! Amen.

# CHAPTER 36

# JOHN EIGHTEEN - NINETEEN

*Chapters 18-19*

Dear Lord, what a wonderful summer we have had here in Breckenridge. We have had several visitors over the past few weeks and have been blessed by their visits. Our "Senior's Tennis at the Rec Center continues to change drastically, which means we are happy to make new friends and sad to discover some real favorites cannot return, either because of the altitude or health constraints. It reminds me that all things change, and so must we. Some of the changes brought on by older age are difficult, such as losing friends, losing health, and being restricted in our activities by anxiety or health. I look at Bob's beautiful white hair, even though it is now thinner, and I am amazed at the number of years that have passed. I'm sure he looks at me the same way. We are returning to Nebraska a little early this summer because of our fifty-fifth high school reunion, which coincides with my twenty-fourth annual girlfriends' reunion in Omaha. Funny how, after just a short time together, we no longer see each other as others do. We see younger versions; the spark and energy of who we once were are still visible with the right eyes. Even though we have all grown wiser, I hope, and changed both physically and in many other ways, the wrinkles, extra pounds, and double chins are invisible to us lifelong friends from all over the United States, though we only have our high school years and our youth in the wonderful 1950s in common. It is a strong bond that has held our friendships and our love for one another all these years, especially my girlfriends' group of twelve special friends. It is a gift from You, Lord, and I am grateful. You have gifted me with special friends in Nebraska, the desert, and here in Colorado. And even if they may be "newer" friends in comparison, they are still lifelong friends for however long that may be. What a wonderful gift to have loving friends who know so much about my failures and weaknesses and love me anyway. I can't ask for anything better!

As we pack and close up the house until a possible trip this winter, I can't help but reflect on our summer—the pleasure of still being able to play and enjoy the competition of tennis several times a week, and the fun of having two new duplicate bridge partners this summer, who both enjoy the thrill of success and the agony of defeat as selflessly as I, always with an expectation and hope of doing better next time. Oh Lord, please help me to always keep that attitude. Maybe next time, whatever it is, I'll do better . . . I'll comprehend a little quicker . . . I'll be a better partner . . . to my husband . . . to my family . . . to my friends . . . to whatever and wherever You lead me. Lord, I am very aware the end of this journal is coming very soon, and I have doubts. Is it going to be good enough to pass on to future generations? Have I answered questions they might have about me? Is it selfish to want them to know their spiritual heritage? Is it worth stripping myself bare at times? Have I been honest and thorough enough with my thoughts about the four gospels? I hope so. I pray so. Lord, as my devotion this morning, I want to reread Psalm 121 before getting back to John. I pray this for myself, for our special pastor here in Summit County, and for his wife; they have suffered so much this summer.

> "I will lift up my eyes to the hills . . . from whence comes my help? My help comes from the Lord, Who made heaven and earth. He will not allow your foot to be moved, He who keeps Israel shall neither slumber no sleep."

> "The Lord is your keeper, The Lord is your shade at your right hand, the sun will not strike you by day, nor the moon by night."

> "The Lord will preserve you from all evil, He shall preserve your going out and your coming in, from this time forth and even forevermore." (Psalm 121)

> Oh Lord, You know how many times I have come to You with this Psalm with a great big call for help! It seems like the times I have needed help the most have been in the desert, either going through radiation or looking at the mountains through a window from the hospital, and this Psalm has always comforted and encouraged me. Thank You. May the precious ones reading this also find comfort in these words, no matter what the circumstances. Amen.

John, chapters 18 and 19 I am grouping together, because in my mind, they belong together. We have read these stories three times in the other gospels, and I am sure you have noticed, as I have, each gospel has a little different slant on the same tragedy of the arrest of Jesus and the trials He suffers. I will remind you that the previous chapter was entirely prayers by Jesus. The first was for Himself, with the full realization and knowledge of what He was about to endure. I had a friend once who told me in all seriousness she never prayed for herself. She considered it a selfish act. I couldn't get out of bed in the morning without praying for myself! I definitely need all the help I can get . . . spiritually, mentally, and physically. Especially with my words. Last winter, our women's Bible study in Palm Desert studied the words women use, and it was an incredible study that brought about illumination and resolve.

While my Bible was still open to Psalm 121, the opposite page had this phrase highlighted in yellow, which always means "Pay attention!" I took time to pray these words for me. Let me share.

> "Set a guard O Lord, over my mouth, keep watch over the door of my lips, Do not incline my heart to any evil thing, to practice wicked works with men who work iniquity, and do not let me eat of their delicacies." (Psalm 141:3-4)

Isn't it a comfort to ask for this kind of guidance before you go out the door? I'm thinking I should type it and tape it to my back door to read every time I leave the house. Jesus is our Mentor and our Guide. Of course we pray for ourselves!

His second prayer is for His disciples, His followers. I don't remember John ever using the word "apostle" in his book, so remember this includes many others who followed Him, like the seventy-two He sent forth in two of the gospels, or the young boy Mark and his mother, or the family of Martha, Mary, and Lazarus.

The third prayer in chapter 17 is for *us*. For all of us who now follow and believe in Him. Oh my. Blows my mind!

Directly after these prayers, He went with His disciples into a garden (Jn. 18:1). We know it was on the slopes of the Mount of Olives and was called Gethsemane (Mt. 26:36; Mk. 14:32), which means "oil press." John doesn't tell us about Jesus going a stone's throw away to pray alone or the apostles not being able to stay awake. He gets right to the fact Judas Iscariot is leading a detachment of troops, officers from the chief priests and Pharisees, coming with lanterns, torches, and weapons. Jesus does not wait for their first offense; He takes command of the situation from the beginning, asking before anyone can open their mouth, "'Whom are you seeking?'" (Jn. 18:4).

They answered, "'Jesus of Nazareth'" (Jn. 18:5).

Jesus replied, "'I am He'" (Jn. 18:5b). The troops and presumably all the people with them, "Drew back and fell to the ground" (Jn. 18:6).

John is the only gospel writer to give us this information. The power and authority in Jesus' voice literally compelled this crowd to the ground. I believe Jesus was establishing they were only seeking Him so He could intervene for the safety of the eleven apostles who had come with Him into the garden, as the next sentence confirms. And, bless his heart, Simon Peter, both afraid and brave, struck the servant of the high priest and cut off his ear, for which he was gently but firmly reprimanded by Jesus, who reminded Peter this was exactly the path His Father had given Him. Luke, the physician, is the only writer who lets us know Jesus heals the ear of the servant, whose name was Malchus, before allowing Himself to be led off to the first of several trials. The first one was the Jewish trial before Annas, who no longer held office but had influence as the father-in-law of the high priest Caiaphas. We are told in this gospel that both Simon Peter and John followed Jesus and the crowd. We are specifically told in the other gospels that the remaining apostles were scattered. I'm sure they were very frightened and confused, and did not know what else to do but go hang out somewhere and pray.

It is interesting that John was immediately admitted into the courtyard of the high priest because he was "known to them," and he was the one who spoke to the gatekeeper to allow Peter entrance. Many years ago, I either read or heard that John's father, Zebedee, was a successful fish merchant who probably kept a second home in Jerusalem because of many business trips there. That was probably how the high priest and his servants knew John. This family was from Galilee, but they were not the fishing "country bumpkins" you might imagine. They were successful merchants with servants. I can imagine that Zebedee, being a Jewish father, was disappointed to lose both his sons to Jesus and His ministry, but the business of fishing and life went on without them. It is also interesting that in this gospel, John never refers to himself by name. Here he is called "another Disciple" and the "one known to the High Priest" (Jn. 18:15).

This is where we read the story of Peter's denial of knowing Jesus. And it is also where Peter disappears from the story for a while. Matthew tells us when the rooster crowed, Peter remembered Jesus' prediction and went out and "wept bitterly" (Mt. 26:74). In Luke's gospel, we are told when the rooster crowed, Jesus, who must have been in the courtyard at the time, "turned and looked at Peter" (Lk. 22:61). Oh the pain Peter must have felt! Remorse, guilt, fear. It's very difficult to imagine. I suspect at this point Peter left and found his family or the other apostles, who may have been together. Misery loves company. But maybe not. Maybe Peter just needed to be alone and process what had just happened during the long, confusing night. You'll remember Simon Peter was pretty much the lead apostle; his name was always mentioned first, and he was part of the inner circle with James and John. If this could happen to him, don't kid yourselves: it could happen to us. We don't know what life has in store for any of us, but I do pray that we as a family can always stay strong in our faith and our witness.

John's account of Peter's denial happened after Jesus was sent to Caiaphas. He had been despicably treated by Annas and sent bound for the second Jewish trial by the high priest, the details for which are not related by John. The first Roman trial happened in the Praetorium, but the Jews could not enter because the Passover meal was that very day; they didn't want to be "defiled" by entering a Gentile building. Oh my, I cannot explain the difference in timing here, because in all the gospels, Jesus had eaten the Passover meal with His apostles the night before, which was His last teaching with them, and in this gospel, the Jews were in preparation day for Passover. It is a marvelous question to take to our pastors, priests, or rabbis, and may have something to do with a two night Seder.

The first Roman trial took place before Pilate, who initially wanted no part of this "Jewish problem," and said to the Jewish accusers, "'You take Him and judge Him according to Your own law'" (Jn 18:31). That didn't work, you may recall, because the Jews didn't have the authority to sentence anyone to death, and they would settle for nothing less! Pilate questions Jesus carefully and concludes he can, "'find no fault in Him at all'" (Jn. 18:38).

At the second Roman trial before Pilate, which goes into chapter 19, he tried to have Jesus released as a Passover "gift." That didn't work; the crowd insisted Barabbas, a known robber, be released. Pilate tried to satisfy the Jewish crowd by having Jesus scourged. That was when a twisted crown of thorns was put on His head and a purple robe on His shoulders. (I know, I know, Matthew says the robe was "scarlet" [Mt. 27:28]. Lots of men are color blind, and I'll remind you, John was there; Matthew was "scattered.") Let's not nitpick this minor point. Again Pilate says, "'Behold, I am bringing Him out to you, that you may know that I find no fault in Him'" (Jn. 19:4).

When Jesus appeared, scourged, bloody, and beaten, the ugly crowd could do nothing but cry out for His crucifixion. One again Pilate said, "'You take Him and crucify Him, for I find no fault in Him'" (Jn. 19:6b).

The Jews replied they had a law that said He should die, because He claimed to be the Son of God. This probably refers back to Leviticus 24:16: "Whoever blasphemes the name of the Lord will surely be put to death."

I think the hackles were rising on Pilate's head with all he was hearing. Afraid, he went back to Jesus for some answers he didn't get. He was incredulous, and asked Jesus, "'Don't you know I have power to crucify You and power to release you?'" (Jn. 19:10).

Jesus answered, "'You could have no power at all against Me unless it had been given from above. Therefore the one who delivered Me to you has the greater sin'" (Jn. 19:11).

It seems to me the one who delivered Him must have been the chief priest. Oh my. I would not want to be in his sandals at the judgment seat! Pilate, convinced Jesus was innocent, tried again to release Him, but nothing was working. This plan had been worked out from the beginning of time, and events were happening exactly as the Father planned. When the Jews accused Pilate of not being Caesar's friend, he caved! He had his priorities, and they were all about keeping his job, his authority, and the peace—not to make waves. As Pilate took his judgment seat, Matthew tells us Pilate's wife sent him a note: "'Have nothing to do with this just man, for I have suffered many things today in a dream because of Him'" (Mt. 27:19).

Jesus was sent to Golgotha, meaning "the skull." (The word "Calvary," which we hear in church songs all the time, is not mentioned in my translations, but it means the same in Latin.) Pilate wrote the title to put on the cross: "Jesus of Nazareth, the King of the Jews" (Jn. 19:19). Written in Hebrew, Greek, and Latin, it was meant as mockery, but it is interesting that Pilate would not change it to appease the Jews. What he meant as mockery will prove to be absolutely true! Don't you just love it when things happen like that?

The crucifixion took place as we read in the other gospels, with this added difference. The gospel of John is the only one that mentions the Roman guards who divided up Jesus' clothes into four piles, which gives us the number of executioners. The piles were probably an outer garment, belt, sandals, and head covering. The "tunic was worn next to the skin and because it was seamless, they thought not to divide it, but to cast lots for it." (John MacArthur Study Bible, commentary, page 1624. ) Wouldn't you love to know where it went and its history? I always assumed this to be the "shroud," but now I'm thinking the shroud may have been a garment brought in by Nicodemus or Joseph to cover the unclothed body. Oh so many questions! Since the Shroud of Turin had an imprint of a man's facial bones as well, I think it had to have been something put on Him at the tomb. Such unknown details! I will leave that one for you—and me—to ponder.

We are told in John who believers were who watched the crucifixion: "His mother [Mary], His mother's sister [some think that was Salome], Mary the wife of Clopas, and Mary Magdalene" (Jn. 19:25). And of course John, the only apostle to be at the foot of the cross. When Jesus looked down and saw His mother, He very tenderly gave her to John, and we are told from that moment, John took her into his home (Jn. 19:28). Remember, she was John's aunt, so this is a natural arrangement. His brothers had not yet declared their belief in Him.

The last words of Jesus recorded in John are, "I thirst" (Jn. 19:28).

There are several things of interest here. First of all, the hyssop reed was the same object used to put blood on the doorposts at the original Passover back in Egypt. Second, it doesn't say Jesus "died"; it says, "He gave up His Spirit." Willingly. Not fighting God's plan. Willingly. For each of us. A sacrificial lamb shedding its blood and giving up His life for every sin you and I ever committed, or ever will commit! Is it enough to just say "Thank you, Jesus"? I don't think so! How could it *ever* be enough? How can we, with such limited understanding, ever take this in and process the meaning? I am sitting in my quiet time chair, with tears dripping down my face and balled up Kleenex all over the floor, and no, I will never be able to comprehend the complexity of this holy moment at the cross. I can only again offer myself to Him, and it is *never* enough. I can never be good enough or deserving of what Jesus did for me on that cross . . . or what he does every day of my life! It is beyond my human comprehension. It is Grace. Plain and simple . . . Grace.

None of the supernatural events told in the other gospels are reported in John. (The sun didn't shine, dead people didn't come out of their tombs, and so on.) I think he did not want us to take our minds off the cross. It was more than enough. John was totally focused on Jesus. It was as if it was dark, and it was, and an earthquake happened, and it did, but they were of no consequence to John. He had instructions to take care of Jesus' mother, and that's what he would do. Did you know that Mary's name is not mentioned anywhere in this gospel? Not once. Interesting.

John's timing of the crucifixion is also different from the other three gospels. In Matthew, Mark, and Luke, we are told specifically the apostles celebrated Passover the night before in an upper room, where crucial teaching took place, including the communion celebration, which is not mentioned in John. Instead, only John told us about the foot washing, which took place "after supper" (Jn.13:2), extensive teaching on the Holy Spirit, teaching about His "departure," wonderful words of comfort to His disciples, which we gladly "soak" in, memorize, and relish. But there is no mention of the Passover supper itself. Instead, John intimates this was "Preparation Day," the day before the feast, and at the hour of Jesus' death, in the dark at three o'clock in the afternoon, it was the exact time the priest in the temple would slit the throat of the paschal lamb with the words, "It is finished," which is one word in Greek—*tetelestai.* The other gospels tell us it was shouted in triumph.

I cannot explain the difference in timing between John's gospel and the other three. I remember reading long ago that every so many years there was something in the Hebrew calendar called a "special Sabbath," which may have thrown someone askew or changed the timing of the Passover supper, but it's very unlikely the other three writers would not have known that, so let's throw out that theory. I simply don't know. It's another question for minds brighter than mine. But does it matter? Would it change anything? I think not. Sometimes it's good to have mysteries in our lives. It surely does keep me from being bored!

The burial of Jesus is a complete wonder to me! Not one or two of His own disciples or apostles, but two Jewish men, both prominent and wealthy members of the Sanhedrin—the ruling body of the Jews led by the high priest—came to claim and bury the body of Jesus. That Joseph of Arimathea risked this reputation and possibly even his life to ask for the body is almost unbelievable! And bless his heart, here comes Nicodemus, who met with Jesus by night, joining Joseph in the burial process. It was probably significant that Joseph possessed a newly hewn tomb in which to place the body of Jesus. Normally these tombs had shelves that could hold several bodies, and when complete decomposition occurred, the bones were placed in a box called an ossuary. We talked about this before. The fact is, thanks to Joseph and Nicodemus, Jesus was buried as a king, alone and in a brand new tomb, and with Nicodemus bringing a mixture of myrrh and aloes, definitely indicating royalty. Bless these two Jewish men! They did for Him in death what they dared not to do while He was alive. They believed in Him. I can't wait to meet both of them. They fulfilled their life purpose and did for Jesus what even His own apostles could not.

At this point, the story comes to a lovely crescendo, and the next two chapters are possibly the most significant in the entire Bible. I'm glad to take a break and sleep on all we've read today.

> Thank You, Lord, for Your death on a cross that we might live with you forever. Help all of us incorporate the meaning of what we have just read into our minds and hearts. Amen.

# CHAPTER 37

# JOHN TWENTY - TWENTY-ONE

*Chapters 20-21*

Have you ever saved the best for last? Maybe eaten everything on your plate except for the one special bite of roast chicken, or had your eye on a wrapped package under the tree with your name on it and saved it to open last? I think that's what I have done with using my favorite Psalms as devotionals this month. And now we are starting on the last chapter of the gospel, and I am happy to share the thoughts of the wonderful Psalm 139. Allow it to sink into your soul. I promise you will be blessed by it.

> "Lord, You have searched me and know me, You know my sitting down and my rising up, You understand my thoughts afar off. You comprehend my path and my lying down. You are acquainted with all my ways, for there is not a word on my tongue, but behold Lord. You know it altogether.
>
> You have hedged me behind and before, and laid Your hand upon me. Such knowledge is too wonderful for me; it is high. I cannot attain it.
>
> Where can I go from Your Spirit? Or where can I flee from Your Presence? If I ascend into heaven, You are there; If I make my bed in hell, behold, You are there. If I take the wings of the morning,

and dwell in the uttermost parts of the sea, even there Your hand shall lead me, and Your right hand shall hold me, even the night shall be light about me; Indeed, the darkness shall not hide from You, but the night shines as the day; the darkness and light are both alike to You.

For You have formed my inward parts; You covered me in my mother's womb. I will praise You, for I am fearfully and wonderfully made; marvelous are Your works, and that my soul knows very well. My frame was not hidden from You when I was made in secret, and skillfully wrought in the lowest part of the earth. Your eyes saw my substance, being yet unformed. And in Your book they were all written, the days fashioned for me, when as yet there were none of them.

How precious are Your thoughts to me, O God! How great the sum of them! If I should count them, they would be more in number than the sand. When I awake, I am still with You." (Ps. 139:1-18)

"Search me, O God, and know my heart; try me and know my anxieties; and see if there is any wicked way in me, and lead me in the way everlasting." (Ps. 139:33-34)

Are these not the most beautiful words you have ever read? Anyone who does not think God loves him or her should just read this over and over until it sinks in. It is a love letter to each of us from God Almighty. Amazing. Awesome. Uplifting. Life-changing. Open your heart and believe these words, precious ones, and live like the very special person God made you to be.

Now let's return to the gospel of John.

The final two chapters of John are the crown jewel of the entire gospel—what the entire book has been pointing toward. John starts by telling us this good news story starting on the first day of the week (Sunday). And because of that, our Sabbath was forever changed from the Jewish Saturday to a Christian Sabbath of Sundays. I really should not call it a Christian Sabbath, because I know some very fine believers who are just as saved as I am and are members of the Seventh Day Adventists. They continue to worship on Saturdays, with the belief that if the Lord wanted to change our day of worship, He would have told us. But then again, does it really matter? I can worship just as well on any day of the week or whenever my particular church doors are open. It's a matter of wanting to be with people who believe as we do, and it's a lot more meaningful to sing songs of praise with other people, rather than sit by myself in my quiet time chair. And who would want to take communion alone? The significance of taking communion as a community of believers is one of the most spiritually uplifting acts of belief we can do. In my church in Lincoln, my friend Brenda is one of the ushers who serve communion elements to the section Bob and I usually occupy. I always look forward to seeing her serve our section. It is a blessing. When I was serving as an elder in a former church, the privilege of serving communion was perhaps the most rewarding service I have ever been part of. Maybe when we get to heaven, every day will be a Sabbath day, or we might honor the second coming or some other day. We just don't know. Oh so much to look forward to! Sometimes I can hardly wait!

John reports that Mary Magdalene went to the tomb early on Sunday morning. Now I'm sure she did, but I'm equally sure she did not go alone. She was coming to finish the task of preparing Jesus' body with more spices and herbs, and I'm pretty sure she would have asked for help with this act of service. She probably didn't know that Joseph and Nicodemus had done a good job with this service on Friday afternoon, before the beginning of the special Jewish Sabbath and the celebration of Passover. The other gospels tell us Mary Magdalene was accompanied by Mary, the mother of James the Less, son of Alphaeus (Mt. 28:1; Lk. 24:10; Mk. 16:1); Joanna, the wife of Herod's steward (Lk. 24:10); and Salome, the mother of James and John. In this particular case, John, the author/apostle, was not there . . . yet.

When the women discovered the stone had been rolled away and the tomb was empty, Mary "Mag" ran to Peter and John with the devastating news: Jesus' body was gone. Remember, this was before dawn, so John must have been staying with Peter and his wife. The two men ran to the tomb. John reported he was the fastest, and he would have remembered that fact. He was there. They both went into the tomb and what they saw was astounding. Nothing was in disarray. The linen clothes must have been lying on the slab as if Jesus had just passed right through them, which He had. If grave robbers had wanted to steal the body, they certainly would not have taken time to unwrap it and leave the linen cloths in such a neat arrangement. Think about it. But the most interesting and goose-bumping words to me were the handkerchief (or napkin) that had been around Jesus' head, was, "not with the linen clothes, but folded together in a place by itself" (Jn. 20:7).

I can't tell you how many times I have read that phrase over the past thirty-five years and thought nothing of it. Please get your own Bible, and read that phrase while I tell you *why* it is so significant. In the first century, whenever a Jewish man was done eating, he would rumple up the napkin and throw it back on the table, meaning, "I am finished." If the napkin was neatly folded on the table, it meant, "I am coming back." Is that a goose-bumper or what? Oh, sorry, Barbara, "God-bumper!" Now who would know that unless you were a student of Hebrew culture from the first century? I just learned this last year, and I am still excited about this hidden treasure from the tomb. I hope you are too.

Scripture says: "Then the other Disciple, who came to the tomb first [that would be John, who won the race], went in also, and he saw and believed" (Jn. 20:8). Saw and believed what? Had to be he believed Jesus was resurrected and lived. John tells us he was the "first to believe."

Not knowing what to do with that knowledge, they went home. Scripture says "to their own homes." Okay, they had pertinent information but didn't know yet what it meant or what to do about it. Most of the apostles lived in lake country (as fishermen), so I assume they really went back to where they were staying . . . and most probably to the upper room in Jerusalem.

The scene shifts back to Mary Magdalene, who apparently returned to the tomb, and this is where she encounters Jesus. She thinks He is the gardener until He says "Mary." Remember, the sheep know their

Shepherd's voice, and as soon as she heard His voice and the way He said her name, she knew. What a moment! What an incredible privilege for her to be the first to see the resurrected Messiah . . . Christ. Jesus said, "Do not cling to Me, for I have not yet ascended to My Father, but go to my brethren and say to them, 'I am ascending to My Father and your Father, and to My God and your God'" (Jn. 20:17).

She did as she was told. Interesting that before this, the apostles/ disciples had been called servants or friends, but now a new relationship of "brothers" was declared. That same night, Sunday, when the disciples were together behind locked doors, Jesus came to them and twice said, "Peace to you" (Jn. 20:19, 21). There was a reason for these words. You absolutely cannot be fearful or anxious when you are surrounded by peace. It is an impossibility . . . an oxymoron. Jesus knew what they needed, and He provided it.

After His initial greeting, "He breathed on them and said to them, 'Receive the Holy Spirit.' If you forgive the sins of any, they are forgiven them. If you retain the sins of any, they are retained" (Jn. 20:22). He breathed His own breath into them as a way of sharing Himself with them and as symbolic of God's own breath being poured into Adam when he was formed. It was also a promise of the Holy Spirit, which would come permanently after the next forty days. I believe that whole room was filled with joy and praise and celebration with a taste of what was to come.

Thomas had not been present with them, but you better believe he heard in detail what he had missed. And he didn't believe because he wasn't there. Some things you just have to experience for yourself before you can wrap your mind around it. I would say in that week, at that time in history, resurrection was right up there at the top of the list. This is where we get the expression, "Are you a doubting Thomas?" My maternal grandfather, whom I never knew, was named Edward Thomas, but I know he was a strong Christian believer. After all, he was married to my precious Grammie! Eight days later, Thomas was with the disciples when Jesus came again to them and especially proved Himself to Thomas, whose reaction was, "My Lord and my God!" (Jn. 21:28). He doubted no longer.

The very best part of this story was Jesus' reply: "'Thomas, because you have seen Me, You have believed. Blessed are those who have not seen and yet believed'" (Jn. 20:29).

Oh my! You know He is referring to us, don't you? And because we believe, we are blessed. I absolutely believe that, and thank God every day for those blessings! And now we have the key sentence of this gospel . . . the reason it was written:

> But these [words] are written that you may believe that Jesus is the Christ, the Son of God, and that believing you may have life in His Name." (Jn. 20:31)

The last chapter of John begins with a fishing trip to Galilee while the disciples waited for the Lord. The Sea of Tiberias is the same as the Sea of Galilee. Probably the reason they went is told in another gospel: "Then Jesus said to them [the two Marys], 'Do not be afraid. Go and tell my brethren to go to Galilee and there they will see Me'" (Mt. 28:10).

In this chapter, we are told only seven of the disciples went, and, of course, I wonder why all of them didn't go? I'm betting Matthew, who had been a tax collector, was one of those not too interested in an outdoor fishing trip, but I can't guess about the others. The scene is a lovely lake, and the disciples had been fishing at night with no success. As the sun rose, they saw the figure of a man on the beach, calling to them and telling them to cast their nets on the right side of the boat. Picture this—the sun is rising behind a solitary figure on the beach, features completely obliterated by shadows. But after the voice was heard, John recognized Jesus and told Peter, "It is the Lord" (Jn. 21:7). Peter got so excited he grabbed his pants (or whatever his "outer garment" was) and jumped right into the lake to hurry to Jesus. This dedicated fisherman forgot all about his huge catch of fish in his haste to get to the Lord. He may have denied Him in extreme circumstances, but Peter's love and dedication to Jesus simply never wavered after that. He is definitely very excited to realize Who is waiting on the shore.

Have you ever been cold and hungry and wished for warmth and food? On a girlfriends' reunion several years ago, nine of us rented a cabin in the Black Hills of South Dakota. On the second day after our arrival, six of us decided to pile into Peggy's Suburban and sightsee around the presidential monuments. It was a beautiful, sunny, fall day when we started out. But after several hours, the weather started to deteriorate badly. We were caught in a downpour on an observation deck and got thoroughly soaked running back to the vehicle. By the time we returned to our rental cabin, it was after 6 p.m., still raining cats and dogs, and nearly dark. Not a good time to get lost.(that too!) By the time we returned, we were all still soaked, tired, and hungry. We dragged ourselves into the cabin to the most delightful welcome! Sharon, from Los Angeles, had made her special macaroni and three-cheese casserole, hand carrying the cheeses on the plane. Susie had found a linen cloth, set the table with wildflowers gathered before the rain began, and made a wonderful fire in the fireplace. Marlene had tossed a salad and opened the wine. Although the cabin itself was kind of old and crummy—it had seen much better years—I don't think I had ever seen a more welcome sight! I think that's how the disciples must have felt, except more so, discouraged after a long night of fishing without a catch, until Jesus helped them. Cold and hungry (after all, it was still spring), and coming to the beach with a nice fire to warm them, fish on the coals, and warm bread. And best of all, another appearance by Jesus. It can't get much better than that, now can it? No wonder Peter jumped right into the lake.

The remainder of the chapter really places Peter on center stage with Jesus, and we get in on all the details. After they had eaten breakfast, Jesus asked Peter, "'Simon, son of Jonah, do you love Me more than these?'" (Jn. 21:16).

I believe He waved His hand at the fishing boats, nets, gear, and the huge catch of fish waiting to be salted and processed. This represented Peter's lifestyle, his income, and his expertise. That would be hard to give up for many men. So many individuals are a product of what they do, not who they are. Take away their careers, and they wouldn't know what do with themselves. Case in point: there was a well-known and successful football coach, by the name of Paul "Bear" Bryant, who coached into his senior years at the University of Alabama. When he finally did retire, he joked at his retirement banquet that he would probably just "croak" from boredom. He died within a month of his retirement. I think this is what Jesus was asking Peter. Peter's reply was, "'Yes, Lord, You know I love You'" (Jn. 21:16). The answer came again, "'Yes Lord, You know that I love You.'"

Jesus said, "'Tend my sheep.'" Jesus asked a third time, "'Simon, son of Jonah, do you love Me?'"

Peter was grieved to hear this a third time. His answer was, "'Lord, you know all things. You know that I love You.'"

Jesus replied, "'Feed my sheep.'"

Jesus may have asked three times to eliminate and wipe clean the slate from Peter's denial on the night of His arrest. The next words of Jesus, also directed to Peter, told him to expect death by other hands. Thus, a warning, followed by "'Follow Me'" (Jn. 21:19). What a great example we have that Jesus can and will forgive anything you or I could ever do when we return to Him. He will not only forgive, He will use us and allow us the privilege of ministering for Him and in His name—no matter how unworthy or unprepared we think we are.

Jesus had just given Peter his assignment for life: to be a shepherd to the flock. "Feeding" carries the implication to teach as well as to protect and shelter. Peter would be a shepherd. Just then, John walked by, causing Peter to ask, "'What about that man?" (Jn. 21:121).

Jesus' reply, although sounding abrupt, said in effect, "That is not for you to worry about. If I want him to live until I return, that is not your concern. You, follow Me." That started the rumor that John would not die, which, of course, was not true. But it did give John reason to live a very long life, full of testimonies about what he had seen and heard and experienced firsthand. He did this beautifully with a productive life of ministry. John not only wrote this gospel but three epistles and the book of Revelation.

So Peter's assignment was to be a shepherd, which he did until he was martyred by Nero around AD 67-68, reportedly by crucifixion upside-down, because he felt unworthy to die in the same manner as the Lord.

We have come to the end of a walk through all four gospels and the end of a season for me also, as we head back to Lincoln in anticipation of whatever is next.

> Lord God, I would ask You to bless the person reading this and to open doors of His or Her spiritual journey so it becomes richer, deeper and more fulfilling than ever before, and to encourage a closer walk with You in all your ways. I thank You and praise You that I was able to fulfill an idea my friend Victoria put into my consciousness last spring. Lord, You are my Savior, my Guide, my Inspiration, my Teacher, and my Healer, physically, emotionally, and spiritually. Help all of us to know our own life assignment from You. Amen.

CPSIA information can be obtained at www.ICGtesting.com
Printed in the USA
BVOW03s1200230215

388915BV00002B/4/P

9 781449 752972